THE
LABOR OF
FAITH

THE LABOR OF FAITH

GENDER

AND POWER

IN BLACK

APOSTOLIC

PENTECOSTALISM

Judith Casselberry

Duke University Press · Durham and London · 2017

© 2017 DUKE UNIVERSITY PRESS. All rights reserved
Printed in the United States of America on acid-free paper ∞
Interior design by Courtney Leigh Baker; cover design by Matthew Tauch.
Typeset in Trade Gothic and Minion Pro by Westchester Publishing Services

Library of Congress Cataloging-in-Publication Data
Names: Casselberry, Judith, [date] author.
Title: The labor of faith : gender and power in Black Apostolic
Pentecostalism / Judith Casselberry.
Description: Durham : Duke University Press, 2017. |
Includes bibliographical references and index.
Identifiers: LCCN 2016048392 (print)
LCCN 2016050622 (ebook)
ISBN 9780822363835 (hardcover : alk. paper)
ISBN 9780822369035 (pbk. : alk. paper)
ISBN 9780822372974 (ebook)
Subjects: LCSH: African American Pentecostals. | African American women
in church work. | African American women—Religious life. |
Church of Our Lord Jesus Christ of the Apostolic Faith. | African American
churches—New York (State)—New York. |
Harlem (New York, N.Y.)—Religious life and customs.
Classification: LCC BR1644.3 .C37 2017 (print) |
LCC BR1644.3 (ebook) | DDC 289.9/40820973—dc23
LC record available at https://lccn.loc.gov/2016048392

Cover art: Photograph by Marquise Rose.

Dedicated to the
memory of my mother, father, and sister,
who are on the other side—
Bettye Groomer Casselberry Vance,
William C. Casselberry Jr.,
and Stephanie Renee Casselberry

CONTENTS

PROLOGUE

"Well, Judith, you certainly have stepped into a world." Sitting at breakfast in a Brooklyn restaurant, one of my mentors succinctly summed up my circumstances. I laughed—such an accurate and economical response to my opening fifteen minutes of stories about beginning research in the church.

I entered the world of Apostolic Pentecostalism without having had any long-term, ongoing relationship with a church community. My dad was career military, which kept us on the move. Our inconsistent church life shuttled between generic army Protestant (when we lived on a base), local community churches (when we lived off-base), and sometimes no church. But we always prayed our "thank you for this food" and "now I lay me down to sleep." My most memorable church time took place in Denver during my junior high school years. We lived just southeast of Five Points on 23rd and Downing Street in my grandmother's house and attended a nearby Presbyterian church. Because my mom had been born and raised in Denver, we knew folks in the church beyond Sunday. That, however, didn't keep me there, and I asked permission to join the Methodist church down our street—this was not based on theological reasoning, but rather I happened to see the upcoming calendar of events for the Methodist youth group. The trips looked exciting. Thus, my early investment in church life had nothing to do with sin, salvation, the Bible, Black religious life, or thoughts of the hereafter. I wanted to go camping in the Rockies. My knowledge of and interest in Black women's church work came later in life from friends relating experiences of growing up in church communities. My interest in the world of the spirit grew later in life, as well, but my interest in Black Holiness-Pentecostal women developed in grad school.

The winding route to researching women in Apostolic Pentecostalism began before my doctoral work in African American studies and anthropology. I had discovered that a number of my favorite vocalists/performers had come up in Pentecostal churches—Sister Rosetta Tharpe, Sam Cooke, Marvin Gaye, and Deniece Williams. I wondered in what ways, if at all, the common religious denominator translated into approaches to music making. To my mind, the specifics of the denomination were important—moving away from "*the* Black Church" as a unit of analysis in gospel and popular music production. My undergraduate and master's work in music and ethnomusicology provided a strong foundation, but I needed to learn a great deal more about Holiness-Pentecostalism before I could make any claims about these artists' approach to sound and performance. At the start of my doctoral work, I threw myself into the literature on Black American Christianity, with particular attention to Holiness Pentecostals. The dearth of scholarship on women's experiences and expression was astounding, given that they make up the majority of participants. It became clear to me that I needed to better understand the role of women in the life of Holiness-Pentecostal churches and address the gap in scholarship.

A perfect combination of deliberative action, questionable (at the time) moves, and good fortune—some would say divine intervention—brought me into the world of Black Apostolic Pentecostalism and specifically of the women of Church of Our Lord Jesus Christ of the Apostolic Faith, Inc. (COOLJC), the subject of this book. In the spring of my first year of grad school, I was advised to spend the coming summer in library research—continuing to review the literature on Black American religious history and social science studies of Holiness-Pentecostalism. Soon after I received that advice, Toshi Reagon asked if I could join the summer European tour of a Black sacred sound opera, *The Temptation of Saint Anthony,* for which she was the musical director. Inspired by the nineteenth-century text by Gustave Flaubert, the piece is a collaboration between award-winning composer Dr. Bernice Johnson Reagon and world-renowned theater director Robert Wilson. I had a long history with the Reagons. Dr. Reagon's work as a civil rights activist, historian, and founder of Sweet Honey in the Rock helped shape my understanding of Black political, academic, and cultural work, while Toshi and I had been working together in a variety of musical configurations for nearly twenty years. I genuinely wrestled with the decision—advance my new research or work with the Reagons and Wilson. The music won. At the time, I know some on my committee thought it a bad decision. And, honestly, if I only considered my academic path, I was not sure it was the smartest move either.

As it turned out, I connected with a cast member on the tour who would bring me into COOLJC. On a flight between engagements, I was talking to two cast members about my budding research into Holiness-Pentecostalism. I happened to mention a recent text I had read about Pearl and Aaron Holmes, African American Pentecostal missionaries in Liberia in the early twentieth century. "Excuse me, what did you just say?" asked a third cast member. I repeated myself, and she looked at me with both disbelief and delight. "Pearl and Aaron Holmes are my grandparents. My mother's parents." Mind-blowing. We moved into deep conversation about my interest and her family and church. She was Apostolic Pentecostal and belonged to COOLJC, a historically Black oneness denomination. "When we get back to New York," she beamed, "you have to come to my church!" Upon returning to school in the fall, I moved into research on denominational distinctions within Holiness-Pentecostalism. By the end of the semester, I felt ready to accept the invitation to visit my new friend's church, True Deliverance Church of the Apostolic Faith, Inc., in Queens; it took my research in directions I could never have imagined.

Fieldwork is all about adjustments. I entered the church with training in music, ethnomusicology, African American studies, and anthropology. Soon after entering the church community, I realized that studying Holiness-Pentecostalism through social science and humanities texts did not give me an understanding of the significance of scriptural interpretation and theology for members. My lack of Bible training would be a problem. These were Bible people. In addition to structured learning in Sunday school, weeknight Bible study, and sermons, scriptural references laced every aspect of church life—songs, testimonies, casual conversations, and even joking around. I had already intended to immerse myself in COOLJC activities, but I needed to do to serious catch-up Bible study to understand my surroundings.

Another key adjustment I had to make involved my sense of time. Attending all-day religious activities required that I "settle in." Initially, I found the temporal world of church overwhelming and disorienting. My first Sunday, I arrived around nine thirty in the morning for Sunday school, which was followed by worship services, dinner in the social hall, one hour of corporate prayer, and evening service. I left close to four in the afternoon, as dinner was winding down (before prayer and evening service)—completely exhausted. Sacred time operated at macro- and microlevels. The long Sunday was infused with smaller events, extended by worshippers, singers, or preachers "as the Spirit moved." For example, a singer could hold on to a lyric or phrase, cycling over and over, responding to and pushing the spiritual energy in the sanctuary. Each section of the service nonetheless started on time. Sunday school started at nine thirty, and at exactly eleven o'clock a young man walked through the sanctuary ringing a bell to signal the end of the lessons. By eleven thirty each class (arranged by age group) had reported attendance, monies collected, and presented on the day's lesson. The Praise and Worship Team prepared the sanctuary for worship with song, and at a quarter to twelve, the choir processional began. Corporate prayer after dinner began promptly at four o'clock and the evening service at five thirty. Bishop Cook, the pastor of True Deliverance Church, was a stickler when it came to punctuality. "If you say you're going to do something at a certain time, and you don't," he explained, "you're a liar." At the same time, services ran with the understanding that the Holy Ghost would "have His way," creating a relationship with time that was both fixed and fluid. Church folks were always open to the possibility of temporal shifts between the natural and supernatural.

Surprisingly, one issue I anticipated having to deal with did not arise—the push of church members to bring me to Jesus. (They do not use the term *convert*.) As we will see in the chapter on altar workers, to be saved "you have to have your mind made up." One conversation I had with a member proved enlightening in this regard. She had two children, one saved and one not, and mentioned that the unsaved child would go to the movies with her cousins (who were not in the church). I was surprised because I understood the movies to be one of a number of prohibited social activities. "We teach them what we want them to know, but she's not saved, and when she is, she'll listen to the Holy Ghost and us." Initially, members saw me as a visitor and treated me as such—welcoming me and making no assumptions about how long I would be in attendance. Most knew I was not saved, and after the pastor announced that I was an anthropologist working on my doctorate, they knew I was conducting fieldwork. After a number of months, folks would sometimes joke that I was at church more consistently than some members, always on time or early and present throughout the week—of course, this was my "full-time job." I believe they felt God would deal with me, in "His own time," in helping me to make up my mind. Overall, I experienced a "tell, don't ask" culture. Members made personal issues public through testimony. I was very rarely asked personal questions, including about my relationship with God. This may not be the case with all Holiness-Pentecostal communities or all Apostolic Pentecostal churches, but my experience proved instructive. Members' attitudes toward the unsaved dispelled a misconception I brought in with me about overly zealous church members pushing newcomers toward Jesus.

I say all this to give the reader a sense of who is writing and some sense of my experience. These brief points just scratch the surface of my story in COOLJC. I found this work extremely challenging and rewarding—learning how to pray (for hours at a time, including all-night prayer), learning a new level of patience, and learning about a warm, kind, generous, and amazing religious community. In what follows, I appear sporadically when my presence puts the narrative in context because this is a book about the women of COOLJC. The stories that follow may not map directly onto other Holiness-Pentecostal denominations, but they help us understand women in a denomination that has never received any sustained scholarly attention. And there is still so much more to know.

ACKNOWLEDGMENTS

I extend my deepest gratitude to members of the Church of Our Lord Jesus Christ of the Apostolic Faith, Inc., and specifically the family of True Deliverance Church; this project would not have been feasible without their openness and warmth. In particular, I want to thank the late Bishop Crosley J. Cook for giving me entrée and wholeheartedly supporting my scholarly aspirations. I am grateful to Mother Harrington, Mother Powell, Mother Thomas, Mother Jackson, Mother Bettis, Mother Sockwell, and the late Mothers Bligen, Holland, and Pea, who gave prayers, love, and encouragement. The kindness and generosity of Donna Holland, Melanie Martin, Deirdre Moore, Marie Lashley, Maizie Rice, Kamiko Rice-Barker, Dolores Griffith, Joyce Brown, Karen Fields, Georgia Williams, and Dr. Celeste Ashe Johnson are without measure. Thank you to Minister Lashley, Minister Cobb, and Deacon Moore, and especially Minister Harrington for keeping me rolling with car repairs I could afford! And to my family in and out of True Deliverance Church—Steven, Etienne, Stephon, and Jhetti Lashley, thank you for allowing me to become a part of your lives and for becoming part of mine. I am especially indebted to Marcelle Davies-Lashley for introducing me to her church family and being a loyal advocate and a true, true, for-sure, unwavering, 24-7 teacher, sister, and friend.

My research into Holiness-Pentecostalism began during my graduate years at Yale University. The intellectual inspiration and guidance of my advisor, John F. Szwed, and committee members Paul Gilroy and Kathryn M. Dudley helped me formulate foundational questions, which persisted throughout all subsequent revisions of this work. I thank Kamari Maxine Clark, Jennifer Baszile, Kellie Jones, and Hazel Carby for invaluable contributions to the development of my critical thinking. I am grateful to Helena

Hansen, Ping-Ann Addo, and Lyneise Williams for their camaraderie and assistance in the formative years of this study.

For funding my research in its early and final stages, I would like to thank the Ford Foundation for the Dissertation Diversity Fellowship and Postdoctoral Fellowship, and the Louisville Institute for awarding me the Dissertation Fellowship and First Book Grant for Minority Scholars. I, too, appreciate the intellectual community each institution opened to me, through annual Ford Foundation conferences and Louisville Winter Seminars. My time as an inaugural postdoctoral fellow at the Center for African American Studies at Princeton University brought me into a vibrant intellectual community, which allowed me to deepen my analysis of African American religions and cultures. Judith Weisenfeld, Valerie Smith, R. Marie Griffith, Daphne Brooks, and Alexandra Vasquez provided intellectual insight across a range of disciplinary perspectives and, importantly, friendship. Thank you to Eddie Glaude and Cornell West for valuable counsel. To my dear friend, cohort, neighbor, and brother Jose Emmanuel Raymundo, I cannot imagine my time at Princeton without your razor-sharp mind, kind heart, and hysterical biting wit. I'm sure the innumerable times you reduced me to tears of laughter extended my days on this planet!

My time at the Women's Studies in Religion Program at Harvard Divinity School, in 2012–2013, helped me bring a deeper theological analysis into conversation with my anthropological approach to race, gender, and religion. In addition to director Ann Braude, I am grateful for a brilliant and generous cohort who engaged my work with great care—Kristen Bloomer, Lori Pearson, Hauwa Ibrahim, Zilka Spahić Šiljak, and Gemma Betros. I am thankful for the warmth and encouragement of other members of the Harvard Divinity School community—David and Louanne Hempton, Jacob Olupona, Davíd Carrasco, Leilah Ahmed, Amy Hollywood, and, especially, Aisha Beliso-De Jesús.

I am appreciative of Marla F. Frederick, Cheryl Townsend Gilkes, Sue Houchins, and Elizabeth McAlister, colleagues and friends who have contributed significantly to my growth as a scholar. I am thankful for wonderful friends and colleagues at Bowdoin College—Brian Purnell, Jennifer Scanlon, Olufemi Vaughn, Tess Chakalakal, Elizabeth Pritchard, and Krista VanVleet—who provide unconditional support, keen insight, and critical feedback. And my maroon sister, Jessica Marie Johnson, and others in the No Slackers Writing Group kept me on task during hard times.

I am blessed with family and friends who love and support me in all my endeavors. My sister, Dr. Cheryl Casselberry Munday, and brother-in-law, Reuben A. Munday, are always ready with the perfect combination of encouragement, practical advice, and humor. Arline Hernandez has had my back for many years and helped me organize life when all I could concentrate on was this undertaking. Maureen Mahon and J. Bob Alotta, thank you for being solid go-to friends in all things. Before, during, and after my course work, fieldwork, and writing, my sister, Toshi Reagon, and Dr. Bernice Johnson Reagon involved me in inspirational artistic projects, which have kept me musically, mentally, and spiritually nourished and balanced. Barbara Nabors-Glass; Nikol Nabors Jackson; my stepfather, Richard Vance; and my brother, John Casselberry, remain staunch supporters. Most of all, Juanita Colón, who is without equal in her benevolence, unwavering care, and dependability, made it possible for me to complete this work. In all these relationships and opportunities I am indeed grateful, and I praise God from whom all blessings flow.

An earlier version of chapters 2 and 4, in a different form, appeared in *Transforming Anthropology: Journal of the Association of Black Anthropologists* 21, no. 1 (April 2013), pp. 72–86. An earlier version of chapter 5, in a different form, appeared in *Harvard Divinity Bulletin* 42, nos. 1/2 (Winter/Spring 2014), pp. 33–43.

INTRODUCTION

I will show thee my faith by my works.

James 2:18

"If the women had been in charge, those columns would be clean—*white-white*." Mother Dorothy Shaw's tone was dry, matter-of-fact.[1] She rolled her eyes, shook her head, and chuckled slightly. "The men wanted to handle it, so they did." We had just walked up to the newly constructed open mausoleum at the gravesite of Bishop Robert C. Lawson and Carrie F. Lawson, his wife. Black smudges dotted the twelve narrow Victorian columns of the modest structure. A cement floor, sixteen feet by twelve feet, was framed on three sides by cinder blocks—three rows high. The not-quite-white columns sat atop the cinder-block wall and rose eight feet to the trusses of an A-frame roof. The back wall was adorned with gray granite tiles from the floor to near the ceiling. A few feet in front of the back wall, a double-wide tombstone marked the couple's resting place. As they did every year, church folks had gathered at the Hudson Valley, New York, site for the Annual Founder's Day Celebration. Each year, mostly senior members of the Harlem-based denomination made the 1½-hour drive from the mother church to Shrub Oak, New York, to honor Bishop Lawson, who in 1919 had established the religious organization.

On its face, Mother Shaw's comment could seem as though it was about the surface, but she was talking about more than a sponge and a little Formula 409. In general, the church's women think they work harder than most men and are more responsive to the day-in and day-out needs of the church. One could attribute this to sheer numbers. There are so many more women than men in the church that the women, of course, handle the bulk of the work. However, women like Mother Shaw talk about a disparity in work ethics. Mother Lorraine Threadgill had served on the Kitchen Committee for eighteen years. She and others on the committee rotated to prepare free dinners in the social hall, each Sunday after service. She recalled the short-lived oversight of the fifth-Sunday dinner by the Brotherhood. She said fifth Sunday happened only four times a year, and the Brotherhood's charge of meals lasted only three years because "they never made enough food, and . . . most of them got their wives to cook it anyway." She acknowledged, "Minister Houston is a good cook, so he was doing it mostly all himself." Finally, the men decided to handle the task by buying chicken from a fast-food place. Laughing, Mother Threadgill continued, "They would bring about ten pieces of chicken. How are you going to bring some ten pieces of chicken with all these people? But you know how men are, so now Sister Lancer does the fifth Sunday."

Women in the church often used "small" examples to make larger points. As a member of the Founder's Day planning committee, Mother Shaw had been involved in preparations that led up to that day, in addition to her other church responsibilities. Mother Threadgill, along with the Kitchen Committee, served on the Usher Board and in the senior choir, and she administered regular blood pressure checks to seniors. Women tended not to make distinctions between different tasks as far as the appropriate religious work ethic they should bring to bear. Whether they were teaching Sunday school, teaching Bible class, ushering, heading an auxiliary, sponsoring services, organizing prayer breakfasts, producing religious tracts, setting up after-school programs, embroidering communion linen, running the kitchen, singing with or directing a choir, playing instruments, preparing gift baskets, taking up the offering, raising funds, praying for souls at the altar, or ministering to the sick, imprisoned, or homeless, work should be done "heartily, as to the Lord, and not unto men" (Col. 3:23).[2]

This book is about the religious labor of these women.

FAITH

The women in this study belong to the Church of Our Lord Jesus Christ of the Apostolic Faith, Inc. (COOLJC, pronounced "cool JC"). Sitting under the umbrella of Holiness-Pentecostalism, COOLJC receives its core theological underpinning from the second book of Acts, which tells the story of the day of Pentecost. Fifty days after the crucifixion of Jesus, the Holy Ghost descended on the apostles and others gathered in the "upper room," fulfilling God's promise. The event is described as "a sound from heaven as of a rushing mighty wind," and each one present was "filled with the Holy Ghost, and began to speak with other tongues, as the Spirit gave them utterance" (Acts 2:2, 4). Thus, in keeping with the larger body of spirit-centered Pentecostal worshippers, COOLJC members merge theology, spiritual experience, and demonstrative worship. Members live out theology in experience and embodied practices of praise and testimony—verbally through speech, shouts, and singing and nonverbally through hand clapping, foot stomping, running, and the "Holy Dance."[3] Similar to many other Pentecostal groups, the church also anticipates the Rapture in "the end times," when the saints will be "caught up in the air" and saved from the ensuing apocalypse.[4] In spiritual and mundane activities alike, church members operate under the overarching frame of the imminent Second Coming of Jesus Christ, "like a thief in the night" (1 Thess. 5:2).[5] The return of Jesus has been at the heart of COOLJC doctrine since the church's inception.

Distinct from the majority of Pentecostal groups, COOLJC is a classical oneness or Jesus-only denomination, asserting "the absolute deity of Jesus" and one person in the Godhead.[6] The church bases oneness theology on John 10:30, 12:44–45, and Acts 2:38; the Acts verse calls for the repentant to "be baptized every one of you in the name of Jesus Christ for the remission of sins, and ye shall receive the gift of the Holy Ghost."[7] Conversion therefore requires immersion baptism in the name of Jesus (instead of the Father, Son, and Holy Ghost) and Spirit baptism, evidenced by speaking in tongues. Other gifts of the Spirit may be bestowed on "saints" (as they refer to themselves) as well, such as prophecy, visions, dreams, and divine healing. The church identifies as Apostolic Pentecostal because they follow the Spirit-infilling example of the apostles on the day of Pentecost and the ensuing mission of spreading the gospel. In every worship service, members work to bring down the Holy Ghost, thus generating recurrent Bible time.

Scholarly approaches to the complexities of Black American women of faith initially focused on political resistance with minimal attention to the role of religion.[8] While making vital contributions to our understanding of Black women's political and social power relations, these scholars of the post-Reconstruction and civil rights eras shied away from providing an in-depth exploration of religious faith as defined and experienced by the women and communities in question.[9] "The religious lives of African-American women," Judith Weisenfeld asserts, "loom large as a substantial and yet largely undiscovered terrain in the study of religion in America."[10] Critical studies in African American women's religious history unearth the details of women's lives and advance our understanding of the ways in which the intersections of gender, race, and class shape and are shaped by the religious worlds of women. Evelyn Brooks Higginbotham's study of turn-of-the-century Black Baptist women demonstrates the ways in which they "linked social regeneration . . . to spiritual regeneration" in developing and implementing strategies to ameliorate the social conditions of Black people.[11] Similarly, as Weisenfeld makes known, Black YWCA women in New York during the first half of the twentieth century merged Christian ethics and social activism to address social, educational, and cultural issues.[12] Bettye Collier-Thomas, in *Jesus, Jobs, and Justice: African American Women and Religion,* provides a sweeping study that reveals an inseparable connection between Black women's Christian mission and social activism across time and denominations. With these women we see faith and the institution of the church used as springboards to social, civic, and political associations, sometimes under the auspices of the church, sometimes in distinct faith-inspired organizations for Black advancement.[13]

Pushing inquiry into spirituality further, anthropologist Marla F. Frederick, in her ethnography of southern Black Baptist women, offers an astute analysis of "the profound influence of faith" on everyday actions, including civic activism, care ethics, and decisions about intimate relationships. Frederick utilizes the distinction between religion and spirituality given by the women in her study. Spirituality "evoked the idea of maturation over time," which would manifest in "how one follows 'the direction of the Holy Spirit.' "[14] The Holy Spirit also catalyzes action in Anthea D. Butler's historical study of women's sanctified world in the Church of God in Christ, although with important differences. For Holiness-Pentecostals, the manifestation of the Holy Spirit is more demonstrative than in Baptist practices. In fact, some in Frederick's study view highly expressive worship as "merely performances" and "question the motive of those *receiving* the Holy Spirit."[15] Butler's attention to the impact of sanctification through Spirit infilling takes on the ways in which embodied spiritual authority empowered women as church organizers, educators, and fund-raisers as they built the largest African American Holiness-Pentecostal denomination. Sanctification then becomes a distinct interpretive lens in the civic and economic realms as the women of the Church of God in Christ move out to sanctify the world. Deidre Helen Crumbley makes a meaningful contribution to the study of gender, race, and migration in a sanctified community in her ethnography of a storefront church in Philadelphia, founded and pastored by "Mother Brown."[16] Combining historical and ethnographic methods, Crumbley provides vital insight into female-driven, grassroots religious institution building. These works by Higginbotham, Weisenfeld, Collier-Thomas, Frederick, Butler, and Crumbley have contributed significantly to our understandings of Black women of faith and "the actual work that their faith produced" in the world.[17]

Distinct from the historical studies, I look at the religious worlds of twenty-first-century Black women. Whereas Frederick's ethnography exploring the faith practices of twentieth-century Black women offers insight into a rural southern Baptist community, this work focuses on a New York–based Pentecostal denomination. While much of the language and spiritual practice of the saints in Crumbley's study resonate with COOLJC, the church folks in her Philadelphia church do not self-identify as Pentecostal, nor are they part of a larger network of churches. This study is also set apart from earlier works because my interest lies more in the circumstances of producing a holy Black female personhood within faith communities and less in the connection of the religious worlds of Black women to social, civic, and political activism. When church work is analyzed under the rubric of civic and political work, the contours of spiritual labor can remain understudied. Whether Black women bring spiritual authority into sociopolitical domains in a quantifiable way or not indicates neither their recognition of power nor the work entailed in developing, sustaining, and sometimes ceding authority within the church. Linking social, civic, and political activism to an analysis of women's spiritual transformations can obscure the ways in which they understand power and the labor necessary to develop and sustain it. Given that Black women have disproportionately high levels of participation in religious life relative to the general population, and given that, in keeping with the situation in other Pentecostal bodies, women compose 75–80 percent of the active adult membership in COOLJC, this work is vital in expanding our understanding of the particularities of Black women's investment in religious communities.[18]

"Unless agentive value is placed on the labor involved in personal transformation," Frederick argues, "what is often characterized as 'accommodation' does not take into consideration the work of individuals in forming productive personal lives."[19] Understanding the full extent of women's religious labor, regardless of its measurable significance outside of the church, is critical if we are to recognize the full extent of African American women's labor, past, present, and future. This book teases out the contours of "the labor involved" in spiritual transformations that have both personal and communal implications. I aim to answer Weisenfeld's call to "fully appreciate the range of approaches that African-American women have taken to participate as agents in their own religious lives and in the religious lives of their communities."[20] Although the women of COOLJC are not compelled to take part in church activities, their individual religious conviction, their desires for a strong church community, and pressure from male leadership converge to level tremendous demands on the women's time and energy. As noted above, COOLJC women serve the church community in every way, with the exception of performing water baptism and pastoring. Yet scholars have failed to analyze contemporary Black women's faith work as labor in its own right.

LABOR

As early as 1912, Maggie Lena Walker, a public intellectual, labor activist, and entrepreneur, and the first Black woman bank president, queried, "How many *occupations* have Negro Women? Let us count them: Negro women are domestic menials, teachers and church builders."[21] To my mind, in identifying the church work of Black women as an occupation, Walker places the effort and outcome of women's religious labor in its proper context. This book integrates the spiritual, material, social, and structural spheres of the work of COOLJC women, to highlight the mechanisms and complicated *meaning* of Black women's labor. Church work is as significant, labor intensive, and critical to personhood, family, and community as wage work, work within the family and home, and community service work.

So, why labor? I began this project examining relationships between informal and formal authority in COOLJC, to understand the extent to which spiritual authority creates a particular type of female power in male-headed Black Apostolic Pentecostal churches. Over time, and with invaluable feedback from colleagues, it became apparent that I needed to consider the quantity and quality of the work these women *do* to produce, navigate, claim, and sustain spiritual authority.[22] To tease out the co-constituted nature of churchwomen's spiritual worker-provider authority, within the context of gendered and raced identities, labor theories provide valuable approaches for determining the ways in which women experience and express power within the church community.

Since the 1980s, labor studies by social scientists have tracked the impact of shifting economies. Increases in service-based economies have expanded our understanding of skill away from nineteenth- and early twentieth-century models of strictly craft or manufacturing work, to include emotional, intimate, and aesthetic labor. These frameworks are useful analytical tools for examining the different registers of labor carried out by COOLJC women, so that we might understand the extent of their spiritual, material, and organizational efforts as they construct individual and communal religious identities and spaces. Exploration of religious labor in COOLJC may prove to have wide applicability as well; however, I argue that it is particularly significant for understanding those who, like the women in this study, spend a great deal of time and energy doing religious work.

First, *emotional labor* studies analyze relational aspects of work. In 1983 Arlie Russell Hochschild's groundbreaking study opened the field by examining emotional face-to-face, worker-to-client requirements that are part and parcel of the job, yet unnamed as such. She also introduced *emotion management*, which has since become an umbrella term encompassing emotional labor and emotional work. Hochschild, however, keeps the dichotomy of public and private intact, defining *emotional labor* as paid-public and *emotion work* as unpaid-private.[23] Three decades of scholarship across the social sciences have since called attention to lived overlapping experiences that upend an either-or model and include analysis of worker-to-worker and worker-to-management negotiations; the organizational benefits of employing skilled emotional workers; unremunerated, yet required labor; unseen and unacknowledged work; gendered and raced expectations; family life; and "boundary-spanning" emotion management between home and work.[24]

Next, analysis of *intimate labor* brings together the reproductive and caring labor of women within the context of commodification. Eileen Boris and Rhacel Parreñas disrupt the idea of analytically discrete types of caring work and instead place them along a spectrum. In this way, they broaden our understanding of "work that involves embodied and affective interactions" and its relation with market forces.[25] Intimate labor studies address the many ways money and intimate life converge in formal and informal economies. In 1912, when Maggie Walker identified church building as a primary occupation of Black women, she drew attention to the labor of institution building, so we might understand the ways in which intimate (reproductive and caring) labor is directly connected to church economics. Finally, *aesthetic labor* studies examine the ways in which presentation of self is integral to job performance, as the worker is required to materialize institutional values in one's appearance and behavior. To understand a wide range of work settings, Chris Warhurst and Dennis Nickson argue that aesthetic labor must be considered along with emotional labor (I would add intimate labor), because it "foregrounds embodiment, revealing how the corporeality, not just feelings of employees are organizationally appropriated and transmuted for commercial benefit."[26] Embodied theology in worship and tenets regarding dress converge in COOLJC conceptions of the "beauty of holiness," making aesthetic labor essential within the organization.

We might also examine women's religious labor within frameworks provided by analysis of feminized labor in global markets. As global manufacturing and service economies witness the feminization of labor, with corporations combing the globe for plentiful cheap labor, studies of caring labor and globalization show us the historical legacy of care work and social-political inequality. Sharon Harley calls attention to the overwhelming majorities of women of color in many labor pools, making them "powerful as global actors . . . [and] indispensable to the maintenance of a system of global capitalism."[27] Associating "worker power" with overt organized resistance has been foundational to conceptualizations of labor as an area of study.[28] Harley's approach allows us to analyze power apart from resistance, providing a more nuanced way to examine the "indispensable" role of "powerful" churchwomen in the preservation of COOLJC, a female majority, male-headed institution that adheres to tenets of submission and obedience.

POWER

As noted above, thinking about power brought me to this place. Women in COOLJC operate in complex webs of formal and informal power. Women and men alike enjoy spiritual authority through Holy Ghost anointing, yet church doctrine mandates a male-headed hierarchy that prohibits the ordination of women and excludes them from any permanent decision-making position. Tenets of submission and obedience further impact the power dynamics as women create myriad ways of carrying out their work.

On the one hand, women's official auxiliaries are formally integrated into the vertical church structure, without definitive hierarchical authority. On the other hand, women operate in primarily horizontal networks of spiritual authority that weave through the vertical church polity. Women, for example, hold term-limited offices (as president, vice president, and the like) within auxiliaries but are recognized as a "sister" or "mother" in the overarching church structure. All converted women are sisters, as men are "brothers."[29] After a sister exhibits years of sustained spiritual and communal leadership, the local church pastor may elevate her to mother. Apostolic churches rely on mothers' spiritual gifts, organizational acumen, and institutional memory for their very existence. At the same time, sisters in mentorship are the church's primary workforce, foundation, financial base, and future—especially given their numbers relative to the overall church membership.

Analyses of gender power struggles within Black churches across time and denominations have been vital in grounding my understanding of these issues in a contemporary setting. Sociologist Cheryl Townsend Gilkes and historians Anthea D. Butler and Bettye Collier-Thomas speak to the tension between women's and men's linked fates in struggles for racial equality and in gender power relations, in which women work to define and maintain a self-conscious holy Black female personhood and advance a communal agenda within male-dominated religious organizations and wider publics. To acknowledge "the social fact of gendered antagonism in religion," Gilkes argues, "means always addressing the patterns and processes that women and men construct as they go about the routine of doing sacred work."[30] The women in the pages that follow rely on "the patterns and processes" developed by previous generations of churchwomen and develop new strategies "as they go about the routine of doing sacred work" in the twenty-first century.[31]

The power of the Holy Ghost substantiates COOLJC women's understanding of sacred work. The importance of oneness theology cannot be overstated; God, Jesus, and the Holy Ghost are one. Saints seek to reveal the indwelling Jesus, folding anointed power into the power to serve. Here tenets of submission and obedience can be the site of gender power negotiations. "Black women and men share a religious life," Gilkes states, "but often disagree about how that life should be organized and the relative importance of women's roles to that life."[32] Women's sense of holy Black female personhood informs the manner in which they create strategies to navigate "on-the-job" tensions when directives from the male-headed polity and the guidance of the Holy Ghost appear to be out of alignment.

The Labor of Faith is the first sustained ethnographic study of Black American Apostolic Pentecostal women, and I hope to shed light on the particularities of the religious labor carried out by these women. What work do they do? How do they do it? What are the circumstances? What are the benefits to the self, the community, and the institution? Spiritual authority and the character of female power within a male-headed hierarchy anchor my inquiry into churchwomen's labor. Therefore, two interrelated sets of questions regarding Apostolic women's power, and the labor required to develop and exercise that power, guide my inquiry. First, what are the ways in which adherents define, understand, experience, and exhibit spiritual authority? To what extent does spiritual authority enable a particular form of Black female power in a male-headed religious community? Second, what are the ways in which the labor of women shapes and is shaped by structural male domination? What specific work do women have to do to become holy and live a holy Black womanhood in patriarchal spaces, which they are instrumental in (re-)producing?

METHODOLOGY

Day 1: I parked my car on the busy commercial street across from True Deliverance Church of the Apostolic Faith. Sitting for a moment to decompress from the long drive through upstate New York and into Queens, I stared at the face of the building. The yellow-brick façade contrasted with the windowed and gated fronts of the surrounding shops. Over the left half of the single-story edifice was a second-floor residential structure. A sign over the entryway of the building read: "The Church with the Old Time Power"—Blessings • Miracles • Healings • True Love; Pastor and Founder, Bishop Crosley J. Cook; Chief Apostle, Bishop W. Bonner; Establishmentarian, Bishop R. C. Lawson; Christian School opening September 2003—Day Care (3 months) to 7th Grade (12 years). I gathered my Bible and purse, got out of the car, and ventured across. In so many ways, this was not my world. I was not raised in a church community. At this point the only thing I knew I had in common with most of the folks here was that we were Black women. I hoped that would ease my entry and pave the way for them to accept me.

Soon after my first visit to True Deliverance Church, I presented Bishop Cook, the pastor, with a two-page formal letter of introduction, explaining my project and requesting his permission to make "his house" my home base within COOLJC. He accepted the letter, slipping it into his outer suit jacket pocket, and said nothing else to me about it. I continued attending services, taking notes, acquainting myself with the members, and generally learning my way around. I hesitated to bring it up, thinking that he would inform me when he had made a decision and that my pressing the subject would not help my cause.

After six weeks had passed, I decided to approach him. "Bishop Cook, did you get a chance to read my letter?" I asked. He looked at me, smiled slightly, and said, "You write long letters." "Well," I explained, "I wanted to be sure to let you know exactly what my intentions are and what I'm hoping to accomplish." "I see," he said. There was a moment of silence. "Well, we'll see." Walking away, he repeated, "OK, then, we'll see." I knew no more than when I had approached him. Since he didn't directly turn down my proposal, I decided to stay the course and continue as before. The worst-case scenario would be that I would have to change sites, but the information gleaned here would still hold value.

About a month later my school schedule took me away for a few weeks. When I returned, it was a Friday night service. Bishop Cook was characteristically seated in his folding chair at the side entrance to the sanctuary, giving him a view of both the entrance and the sanctuary. As I moved toward him, he gave me a warm and welcoming smile. With a slight laugh, he said, "Well, Sister, where have you been?" I explained that school demands had kept me out of town.

"Well," he said, his eyes twinkling, "you missed a lot. You could have taken a whole *lot* of notes."

"I'm glad to be back." I replied.

Permission granted.

This exchange held two lessons for me, which I did not grasp at the time. First, Bishop Cook was indoctrinating me into the ways of church work. Keep your head down and do the work; don't talk about it. An introductory letter told him very little; my attending and taking "a whole *lot* of notes" told him more. Women in COOLJC do not talk about all they do. To determine the extent and specifics of women's labor, I had to ask probing questions, witness them in action, or learn through coworkers. The second lesson was related to the ways of church work in that my time was not "God's time."

My plan was to spend the next five months conducting part-time fieldwork, as I finished course work and exams for my doctoral degree, followed by a year of full-time participant-observation fieldwork. As it turned out, a year and a half became two and a half years. Over the course of my fieldwork, from January 2004 to July 2006, I regularly attended church activities including Sunday school and morning and evening services, Monday prayer services and Bible study, Wednesday prayer and missionary services, Friday night choir rehearsals and services, and weekday six o'clock morning and noon prayer on occasion. I joined in as a general congregant in worship, group singing, scriptural readings, prayer, all-night prayer, fasting, and altar calls. I participated as a presenter in Bible study and Sunday school, as an invited speaker at Sunday and Wednesday evening services, and as a soloist at Friday and Sunday services. I attended quarterly regional and annual national organizational convocations in New York, Virginia, South Carolina, and Missouri.

I completed fifty in-depth interviews, collected six oral histories of church elders, collected conversion narratives, administered a survey to church congregants, and documented over a hundred hours of church services on video. Church tracts, bulletins, and organizational and auxiliary publications provided information on current church issues and concerns, and I gathered historical organizational data at the Schomburg Center for Research in Black Culture in New York City, in the Sherry Sherrod DuPree African-American Pentecostal and Holiness collection, 1876–1989, and the Alexander and Shirlene Stewart Pentecostal collection, 1925–1993. I returned to the church community sporadically during 2007 and 2008. In the summer and fall of 2012, I returned again, attending services, conducting numerous follow-up interviews, and traveling to the Annual International Holy Convocation in North Carolina and the International Women's Council Conference in New Jersey.

I have been able to move in and out with relative ease because of the warmth and generosity of the saints. The church members form a close-knit group owing to a common worldview and stringent doctrine, which regulate practices and behavior—everything from social activities to dress. A critical portion of my research consisted of socializing with members at church-sponsored events and, of equal significance, in their homes, at family gatherings, at baby showers, and at "homegoings" (funerals), and during mundane activities such as eating out, shopping, running errands, and picking up children from school and summer camp. While it was exhilarating, it was exhausting. (And, different from most churchwomen, I did not have another job and children to attend to. Full-time fieldwork was my primary responsibility.[33]) So many saints contributed to this project. In addition to the direct interviews and my anthropological "deep hanging" noted above, numerous kind saints welcomed me at churches and conventions. To help carry key issues and concepts addressed in this study, some saints are more present on these pages than others. For methodological and theoretical reasons, I have chosen to expend little ink on physical descriptions of individuals but to have them rise into view through particular areas of labor. The anthropological gaze (if you will) that I adopt deliberately views women through their labor. I included personal-church histories to help distinguish each woman who emerges as an individual through her labor. My approach also ties into the theological perspectives of the church, which I consider significant. "Even a child is known by his doings, whether his work *be* pure, and whether *it be* right" (Prov. 20:11), and "Wherefore by their fruits ye shall know them" (Matt. 7:20).

OVERVIEW

Chapter 1, "The Instruments of Faith," examines the tools of faith and processes of reconciliation that were brought to bear following the illness and shocking death of a beloved church sister. Church members needed to make sense of divine healing and death, of the promise of answered prayer and predestination. Saints regularly utilize physical, intellectual, and spiritual activities—including song, worship, prayer, testimony, and Bible study—in multiple weekly services and in everyday settings to interpret their experiences and grow in Christ. After the death of their sister, they relied on the same tool kit in a directed fashion, as they worked to align their inward dispositions with theology and church doctrine.

The theology, doctrine, and practices of this twenty-first-century New York–based religious organization are rooted in late nineteenth- and early twentieth-century classical Holiness-Pentecostalism. Chapter 2, "Church Building," follows the winding western and midwestern roots and routes that led to COOLJC's founding in Harlem in 1919 by Robert C. and Carrie F. Lawson. During the early years, Robert Lawson published distinctive theological expositions, which attacked racist and antimiscegenation ideologies by placing Black women at the center of the atonement. His extensive religious, social, political, economic, and civic engagement, along with Carrie Lawson's radio presence as the "Praying Mother of the Air," elevated the church community to national stature. After Robert Lawson's death in

1961 (Carrie passed in 1948), COOLJC experienced a change in leadership and structural reorganization under William L. and Ethel Mae Bonner, and those structures are still in place today. The final section of the chapter examines the establishment of a COOLJC church in Queens, New York, in the mid-1970s, True Deliverance Church, by Crosley J. and Reva E. Cook. Although the official founding and formal leadership of COOLJC and its churches are understood as the province of male ministers, "Church Building" inserts the pivotal work of the wives. The influential legacies of these women garner some attention in church documentation; however, the role of Black women as "helpmeets" in institution building receives more detailed acknowledgment in oral histories. As a result, the contributions of these women to founding sensibilities have been understated in printed church histories and undervalued in scholarship.

It is the rank-and-file female majority, however, that constitutes the workforce and economic foundation of the church. "Church Sustaining," chapter 3, explores the overlapping organizational and spiritual labor of women through the women's auxiliaries. Women began arranging horizontal networks to further the mission of the Jesus-only church in the early 1920s. Through "women's auxiliaries"—the International Missionary Department, the Women's Council, and the Ministers' and Deacons' Wives Guild—formal and informal management at microlevels (re-)produces doctrinal notions of Black religious female personhood. This, in turn, reinforces the vertically structured regional, state, and national hierarchical male leadership. The women of COOLJC promote male headship at church and at home, and chapter 4, "Women's Work," examines the emotional labor and strategies employed to produce "women-driven patriarchies" undergirded by teachings of submission and obedience. It then considers emotional labor in the workplace and positions of institutionalized power, as women confront the challenges of their existence in the worldly labor force, all the while bolstered by a religious community that demands full societal inclusion and an on-the-job meritocracy. As women carry out "boundary-spanning" emotion management, moving between supporting religiously based and resisting race-based patriarchal systems, self-identification as sanctified shapes, and is shaped by, the areas they deem oppressive or empowering in the church community, at home, and in the secular labor force. They therefore devise covert methods to circumvent structures to "get the job done," as well as overt strategies that demonstrate a "militant assertion of personhood," all according to their standards of religious righteousness.[34]

Chapter 5, "Harvesting Souls for Christ," delves into the labor of women at the altar. Altar workers attend to the needs of the saved and unsaved who come for prayer in the final segment of worship services. "Harvesting souls" names the particular work of bringing people fully into the body of the church through the conversion experience of Spirit baptism, evidenced by speaking in tongues. In efforts to deepen our understanding of individual and communal religious identity, scholars of Pentecostalism give us numerous perspectives on what motivates newcomers to convert. Two key queries drive many studies: what are the circumstances under which people convert, and what are the implications for subjectivity, community, and society?[35] This chapter departs from previous studies by asking, what are the contours of women's labor as they (re-)produce a culture of bringing newcomers fully into Pentecostalism? I look at altar work through the lens of intimate labor, an approach that joins together and expands studies of women's emotional, caring, and reproductive labor. An analysis of altar work points out the pivotal work of bringing new followers into the church, carried out by networks of women who pass along intimate practices through an apprenticeship model, cultivating new generations to take up the mantle of harvesting souls, for the benefit of the individual seeker and the institution of the church. These intimate practices tie church members to each other and bolster allegiance to the church community and doctrine, while expanding the labor force and financial base of the institution and reinforcing women's spiritual authority.

Saints in COOLJC evaluate internal and external qualities in accessing spiritual power. Chapter 6, "The Beauty of Holiness," explores the ways in which women perform aesthetic labor in material and immaterial realms to (re-)produce and (re-)interpret the meanings of living a holy life. Regulations on dress, which the church codifies most rigorously on women's bodies, demonstrate the standard of respectable appearance. Examining the aesthetics of presentation, we gain insight into the particular ways saints understand that a woman, by her appearance, exemplifies one of the "ambassadors for Christ" and the institution (2 Cor. 5:20). At the same time as she visually sets a standard, she is also a conduit for access to sacred realms. Women perform aesthetic labor in unrestrained liturgical practices—music making and worship—rendering the invisible (spirit) visible (embodied) to model the beauty and power of holiness. By way of unrestrained and restrained bodily practices, women address ideologies of power and respectability that are foundational to understandings of gender in COOLJC.

Women's spiritual and material aesthetic work reinforces communal and self-understanding of women as spiritual gatekeepers while keeping church polity intact.

In the pages that follow, I hope to do justice to the women who spent so much time with me, bringing me into the many aspects of their day-to-day lives and sharing the intimacies of worship. Complex, brilliant, amazing, hysterically funny, troubled, hardworking, and godly—women in the COOLJC community crosscut ages, occupations, and religious upbringings. They ranged in age from mid-twenties to early nineties. Their work positions outside of church included nurse, school principal, judge, social worker, bank vice president, homemaker, day care worker, college women's basketball coach, high school chemistry teacher, home health aide, hospital nutritionist, and graduate student. Some were born into COOLJC or Holiness-Pentecostalism; others came from Catholic, Lutheran, Baptist, and Methodist churches. Their perspectives are the heart of this ethnography.

1

THE
INSTRUMENTS
OF FAITH

At nine thirty in the morning, my cell phone rang. It was Sister Ruth Holmes. "Hi. I'm on my way to Louise's house." She paused. "You know why," she said softly. "She went to sleep this morning."[1] I jumped up. "I'm on my way."

Louise Franklin had passed away—forty-six years young—from a brain tumor, cancer. Six months earlier, in June, she had begun having severe headaches that prompted a series of diagnostic exams. In August X-rays revealed a growth in her brain about the size of a quarter. By October it had grown to the size of a small grapefruit. In mid-November she entered the hospital, but before surgery she slipped into a coma and never recovered. A divorced single mother, she left two teenage children.

I arrived at Louise's house around ten thirty on that cold December morning. Mother Joan Morris, broom in hand, answered the door. "Praise the Lord," she greeted me in the way of the saints (as church members refer to themselves).[2] We hugged; then she continued sweeping the carpeted hallway. At the end of the long hallway, beyond the front door, Mother Geneva

Reeves was cleaning the bathroom with the deep concentration to detail that can come with grief, as if the repeated motion of the sponge on the sink could eventually wipe away the sorrow. I went in and touched her back; she turned, and we embraced.

When I arrived at the Queens-based True Deliverance Church (TDC) about a year earlier, Mother Reeves and I connected almost immediately and had since grown close. From the beginning, she had showed an interest in my work, which opened the way for many conversations. (Sister Holmes and I had just visited her and her husband, Minister Joe Reeves, after Bible study a few nights before Louise passed away. We had talked and laughed; eaten chips, salmon, and grits; and drank coffee until four in the morning.) Mother Reeves is a complicated woman, deeply spiritual and discerning with a great sense of humor, yet a taskmaster in the ways of holiness, particularly as it pertains to women's dress and comportment. She admittedly does not trust women, while, at the same time, she expresses admiration for successful Black women.

Our hug in the bathroom was long and, I hoped, some measure of comfort for her. It was for me.

"Have you eaten?" I asked.

"No, I can't. I don't eat early," she replied.

"Do you want something to drink—tea, water?"

"No."

"If you need *anything*, just say it."

She nodded, tears welling, unable to continue speaking. We hugged again, and she returned to her cleaning.

In the kitchen Sister Anne Farmer sat at the table, mechanically eating scrambled eggs and home fries from a small Styrofoam takeout box. We hugged. "Praise Him," we said simultaneously. Her eyes filled with tears as she shook her head. Sister Susan Charles came in from the dining room, where she, too, had been cleaning.

"Praise Him, Sister Judith." We hugged. "How are you?" she asked.

"I'm OK, how about you?"

Her lips tightened across her teeth, and she gave a slight shrug—kind of like, "What can I say?"

"What needs to be done?" I asked.

"Well," Mother Morris said, entering the kitchen, "the stair and hallway carpets need to be finished." I didn't know whether she was tired of sweeping or just wanted to be in the kitchen with the other saints. I think the latter. I picked up where she had left off in the hallway, then moved on to sweep the stairs.

Numerous phone calls that morning had dispatched saints to begin the series of tasks that come with a death. This work is intense, concentrated in time, and done while juggling the rest of life's obligations. "It easily could be twenty-four hours, seven days a week," one saint later explained, "because the moment you find out that somebody passes, everything in your organized *real* life stops to go meet the need of that person." She continued, "So, literally, you can get a call that somebody passed away at one o'clock in the morning. Everybody is going to be at the house by one forty-five—gotten up out of their beds and come to the aid of that family to see what they need."

This certainly was the case with Louise's passing; a flood of questions had to be addressed. Does someone need to go to the hospital and view her before meeting with the funeral home? Who will go make arrangements with the funeral home? Do we need to shop for clothes to lay her to rest in? Someone will need to gather information from family and friends for the obituary. The order of the homegoing service needs to be planned—check with the church and set a date. Who will prepare the repast—do the grocery shopping and cooking? And the house needs to be readied to receive family and friends.

Louise's house was a mess. Her children, understandably, had given it no attention in quite some time. The saints had been coming regularly, since Louise had taken ill, to help with meals and cleaning, but now it was different. Divine healing was a central tenet of the church. No one had expected her to die, so the meals, the cleaning, the laundry, all that work, up until now, had been stopgap measures awaiting her return. Now the cleaning had to be deep, not only to receive the many folks who would be coming through in the days to come, but also to befit how much the house meant to Louise.

She was proud of this two-story, four-bedroom home, situated on a narrow one-way street in Bedford Stuyvesant, Brooklyn. She bought it on her own and had done quite a bit of the renovation work herself. "She got that house and fixed it up like she was a he-man," one of the church mothers remembered. "Taking down walls, discovering doors and windows, and all that stuff herself, she was a hardworking gal." The first time I visited here, some months earlier at a Saturday afternoon summer barbecue, Louise showed me around. We began in the long front hallway.

"I had a hard time getting this [wall] even," she recalled, "'cause the house has settled and the floor and ceiling aren't level with each other. But I think I did a pretty good job."

"I think you did a really good job," I told her.

"Yes," she replied. "God is good."

Louise continued the tour, past stairs to the right leading to the second floor and, to the left, laid out in railroad fashion, entryways to the living room, formal dining room, and large, eat-in kitchen. The kitchen had a huge walk-in pantry at the back corner, full of Costco-sized packages of paper towels and napkins, canned and dry goods, condiments, and large bags of candy. (Louise was very close to the children at church and always brought them little gift bags of treats.) On this party day, the kitchen was abuzz with women from church preparing volumes of food to take outside. Two fans ran at top speed in a vain attempt to alleviate the heat of bodies, the oven, burners on the stove, and steaming pots.

Louise started helping with the food preparation, so my tour ended in the kitchen, and I made my way out to the newly cemented backyard. The gathering was in full swing. Most folks in attendance were from TDC, along with some from other churches in the parent organization, the Church of Our Lord Jesus Christ of the Apostolic Faith, Inc., or, as they call themselves, COOLJC ("cool-jc"). As well, some non-churchgoing family and friends were on hand. Up against the house, a large canopy kept the sun off two large folding banquet tables that held plasticware, condiments, and restaurant-sized aluminum trays full of macaroni-tuna, potato, and green salads. Next to them, a young man attended a large barbecue grill crowded with hamburgers, hot dogs, and chicken. A few feet away, folks sat in folding chairs and at tables, cross-talking and laughing. One table hosted a lively card game that drew animated input from a few bystanders. At the far end of the yard, a half-dozen young men and boys were shooting hoops and talking much mess.

On the cold December morning of Louise's passing, the laughter and aromas from that summer afternoon seemed long gone. Smells of Clorox, Pledge, Ajax, and dust mingled in the air as the saints prepared the house for grieving family and loved ones. Armed with ammonia and bleach, Mother Reeves left the bathroom and came into the kitchen, to begin the process of cleaning every utensil, dish, and surface. Amid the sounds of cleaning and thick silence of grief, from the kitchen she began singing a slow, plaintive hymn, in a rich alto-tenor register:

Thank you, Lord.
Thank you, Lord.
Thank you, Lord.
I just want to thank you, Lord.

Having spent most of her sixty-two years in church, Mother Reeves had been singing "to the glory of the Lord" for a long time. (Originally from North Carolina, she migrated to New York in 1970 with her husband and four young sons. The transition brought her out of a rural Baptist upbringing and into an urban Apostolic Pentecostal community.) Her song began softly, internally, and with each repetition it swelled in volume and intensity. Pulling, stretching each word—*thaaaan-kuuuu-Laurrrrd*—her resonant overtones cradled each syllable. Her gospel vibrato carried sadness; her vocal mastery relayed conviction.

In this moment, Mother Reeves took up another level of religious labor, beyond the physical and task-oriented cleaning of the space; her spiritual and emotional labor started shoring up religious confidence and soothing the hurt of the women gathered, her own included. Louise's death flew in the face of the saints' experiences and church teachings of divine healing and answered prayer: "And whatsoever ye shall ask in my name, that will I do, that the Father may be glorified in the Son. If ye shall ask any thing in my name, I will do *it*" (John 14:13–14). What is more, Louise had confessed before the church and one-on-one with friends, "God told me I'm healed." In these initial hours, before the family and wider church community gathered, these good women needed to bolster each other because some would later be responsible for conveying, in word and deed, confidence in the wisdom of God's plan for everyone. The church community now had to grapple with the paradoxes of divine healing and death, of Jesus's promise to answer prayer and predestination.

"WORK AT LIVING A HOLY LIFE"
Baptism in the Holy Ghost is an event, while living in holiness is a process that requires religious labor. To develop and fortify a holy life, a saint expends considerable energy on individual practices and communal activities including worshipping, praying, and giving testimony; absorbing and reiterating scripture in Sunday school, Bible study, orations, and conversation; and explaining current experiences and reinterpreting past events through

the lens of church theology. If she remains steadfast, in the end, by way of the crucifixion and resurrection of Jesus Christ, she has the promise of eternal life.

The women of COOLJC face challenges to their faith all the time. Over time they hone religious skills that they then bring to bear on every aspect of living in "the beauty of holiness" (1 Chron. 16:29).[3] The manner in which they contended with Louise's initial diagnosis, and then her unexpected passing, was, in many ways, no different from how they managed less traumatic, even mundane, events. Engaging physical, emotional, spiritual, and intellectual resources, they worked to align their dispositions with their religious convictions and church doctrine. Sister Addie Thomas highlighted the task at hand when, during Monday night Bible study, she said, "Walking with Christ means you decide about how you gonna act all the time. You don't follow your natural mind. You follow your spiritual mind. You let the Holy Ghost lead and guide you." She explained that wanting to live "in the world" was "natural." In fact, she contended, "Holiness is not natural. It's unnatural. You have to work against the world. You have to work at living a holy life." She described faith in terms of physical, emotional, mental, and spiritual exertion needed to bring one's internal state into harmony with one's religious commitment and doctrine.

Thomas J. Csordas uses the concept of disposition, in the context of Catholic charismatic healing, to look at the "expectancy or 'faith to be healed.'" In addition to a follower's internal state or "expectancy," he also calls attention to "the disposition of persons within the healing process vis-à-vis social networks and symbolic resources," in other words, the ways in which people place themselves within religious settings.[4] For our purposes, thinking about disposition in this way allows a doubling that can account for both a saint's inner mind or will and also her placement and level of engagement within the religious environment. Her positioning within sacred spaces and her interior state fold back into and reinforce each other as a result of specific strategies.

Sister Thomas pointed out the two registers of disposition. "To work against the world [and] . . . to work at living a holy life," she "decides" (engaging inner will) "how [to] act" (determining her placement within the religious environment). This requires developing skills, and, as with any skill set, the amount of exertion, effort, and practice determines the level of expertise attained. Both the context and content of Sister Thomas's comments speak to the training saints undertake. First, her comments took place at Monday's

Bible class, one of three weeknight services—Wednesday's missionary service and Friday's Joy Night service being the other two. Through immersion (literal positioning) in multiple weekly services, she received training in COOLJC theology, doctrine, and practices so that she could develop and learn how to "follow [her] spiritual mind."

Second, her observations show that practices shape disposition; repeated action ("work," not "natural" desire) kept her "living a holy life." Sister Thomas's declaration also resonates with Saba Mahmood's analysis of Egyptian Islamic women. Mahmood calls attention to the idea of "ethical pedagogy" (applicable to both Islam and Pentecostalism), in which the virtuous interior of a devout woman develops by way of specific practices. She argues, "Action does not issue forth from natural feelings but *creates* them. . . . [R]epeated *bodily act[s]* . . . train one's memory, desire, and intellect to behave according to established standards of conduct."[5] Yet, distinct from Islamic women, Sister Thomas pointed out that, along with work, the Holy Ghost "leads and guides" her in making the right choices to live holy, "according to established standards of conduct."[6] In the daily work of living holy, the borders between individual will and the "move of the Holy Ghost" are fluid and constantly being negotiated. Saints "decide about how [they] . . . act all the time," while letting the "Holy Ghost lead and guide [them]."

Mother Reeves intoning, "Thank you, Lord," on that solemn morning operated in the fluid space of deciding and letting the Holy Ghost lead. But why did she sing? We can think about her unction to sing as a means of production that demonstrated an "exercise in the strategy of choice," in which she was "exercising her sense of economy of signification."[7] She knew from learning and practice which particular instrument within the Apostolic tool kit would help her come closest to achieving the desired results. She exhibited what Catherine Bell names "a sense of ritual" and "ritual mastery." Mother Reeves's sense and mastery developed over time and "indicate[d] something of the 'work' of ritualization."[8] Her specialized knowledge was "an embodied knowing," the means through which she demonstrated her sense of which customary practices may prove effective in a given situation.[9] In this case, it was song, and she sang to minister to those present, herself included. What work did this song do? How did this action navigate the paradox of divine healing and death? How might her actions have aligned her disposition with her religious conviction and church teachings? To answer these questions, we need to understand more about the saints' confidence in divine healing, the promise of prayer, predestination, and eternal life, and, specifically, the practices that shape and are shaped by convictions—the work of faith.

TOOLS FOR FAITH WORK

Members of COOLJC use specific tools to carry out the work of faith. In what follows, I first examine selected elements of church services and their directed purpose in light of Louise's illness. I then move to the mechanism used by saints to navigate the final trauma of losing her. Each instrument of faith has physical (embodied), intellectual (theological), and psychic (supernatural) components that members engaged. Looking at the devices and strategies members employed shows how each produced and strengthened personal and corporate religious conviction. Understanding the means by which saints fashion the religious environment will allow us to further appreciate Mother Reeves's move to song work.

During the four months of Louise's illness, worship services were geared toward healing. Every service begins with song, as the Praise and Worship Team ignites congregational singing and prepares the sanctuary for worship. From the time of Louise's initial diagnosis, songs like "What a Mighty God We Serve" and "When the Praises Go Up the Blessings Come Down" bolstered everyone's confidence in the power of praise to summon "mighty God" and restore the health of their sister. Songs are general, leaving interpretive space for individuals, and for the church as a whole, when faced with community crisis. So, no matter how difficult the circumstances, "if you praise him, he'll make it alright" and "I can depend on God" to heal. In COOLJC, as with Pentecostalism generally, members regularly convey the theological underpinnings of religious conviction through music.[10] The congregation's confidence in God's healing power reverberated from the choir stands and pews, even as ministers reinforced it from the pulpit.

One Sunday sermon, soon after Louise's first symptoms, Minister Edwin Lee chose the topic "I Know He's Able" and drew on Matthew 9:27–30, which recounts the story of Jesus restoring sight for two blind men. Highlighting verses 28 and 29, he read, "And Jesus saith unto them, Believe ye that I am able to do this? They said unto him, Yea, Lord. Then touched he their eyes, saying, According to your faith be it unto you." Minister Lee performed his "preacherly" role as "a witness who searches scriptures on behalf of the community to speak what he . . . has found."[11] Moving from scripture, he told the church, "This is about faith and praise." Sister Adele Lee, his wife, stood early on during the sermon, praying aloud and encouraging him. "Thank you, Jesus. Preach the Word!" she exclaimed, bearing him up.[12] Other women joined her physical witness; they stood, urged the preacher on, clapped, and sent up praises to God. Physically joining the sermon, women signaled that Minister Lee was delivering a "successful" message. Thomas Hoyt Jr., writing on the significance of testimony within African American religion, places preaching within that tradition "because preaching is such a shared practice, it demands a response."[13]

Gerald L. Davis, in a study of African American sermonic composition, identifies a "circularity principle" driving the organizing structure within the sermon itself. An ideal sermonic form is set in motion, and, by way of a series of preacher-congregation interactions, participants push the "performance event" to its realized form.[14] Saints recognize the preacher as "the man of God" anointed to deliver a "Word from God." When members activate call-and-response with the preacher, all involved help elevate the message. Buoyed by the give-and-take, Minister Lee passionately brought his sermon to a close, "I know that I know that I know, He is able!" "Not think," he bellowed, "but know!" Bishop Crosley J. Cook, the octogenarian founder and pastor of TDC, restated the message in his closing remarks. "God is able to do anything but fail," he confirmed. "We're so glad to see Sister Louise. God is able. . . . [She] made her way to church on Friday and today. She's to have a biopsy on Wednesday. 'Walk by faith and not by sight' [2 Cor. 5:7]."

WE BELIEVE IN DIVINE HEALING

From the pulpit, preachers gave members the biblical foundation to walk by faith and not by sight, while the opening statement on the sign above the front door announces spiritual confidence to passersby and parishioners alike: "*The Church with the Old Time Power*"—Blessings • Miracles • Healings • True Love. Novices attending the New Converts Sunday school class learn core principles of the church as part of their initial training:

What We Believe: The Apostolic Doctrine

1 Repentance by Faith—Acts 2:38
2 Water baptism in the name of Jesus for the remission of sins— John 3:5, Acts 2:38
3 The infilling of the Holy Spirit with initial evidence of speaking in tongues—Acts 2:4
4 The infallibility of the Bible, the word of God—Isaiah 40:8, Colossians 3:16, Hebrews 4:12

5   The absolute deity of Jesus Christ—Colossians 2:9, Acts 4:12

6   Living Holy, praying, fasting, and paying tithes—1 Peter 1:16, Hebrews 12:14

7   The Rapture of the Church, the second coming of Christ—1 Thessalonians 4:13–18

8   Miracles—Matthew 8:1–5, Genesis 1:27

9   Divine Healing—Acts 9:32–34, Matthew 8:6

10   Communion as memorial—1 Corinthians 11:26

11   Fruit of the Spirit—Galatians 5:22–23, Hebrews 11:1

Church doctrine—reinforced in songs, sermons, and scripture—assured followers that they could experience miraculous healings. Over the months between her diagnosis and her passing, Louise's medical treatment (and scheduled surgery) did not undermine the church's certainty that divine healing was on the horizon. Healing can be instantaneous, or, in the case of a slower process, the earthly physician comes under the province of God, who uses the physician to reveal the source of illness, guides the doctor to accurate and effective treatment, and strengthens the body in recovery.[15] "We believe in divine healing," Bishop Cook told the congregation. "But we don't tell you not to go to the doctor. . . . Go to the doctor and get verification of your healing." Most COOLJC saints also visited doctors for regular preventive and emergency care, and some members were active or retired health-care professionals.[16] Mother Lorraine Threadgill, a retired registered nurse, provided regular blood pressure checks for older members, both at church and also through home visits. Saints saw Mother Jessie England's ability to diagnose ailments (later confirmed by doctor's visits) as the combined result of her years as a registered nurse and her spiritual gift of discernment.

Tensions between medical science and "God's wonder-working power," in a Western context, seem to trouble scholars more than church members. Allan Anderson maintains that the miracle-working power of the New Testament "is particularly effective in those parts of the world least affected by modernization, secularization and scientific rationalism." He goes on to suggest, "The central role given to healing is probably no longer a prominent feature for Western Pentecostalism."[17] The presence of divine healing in American Protestantism has a long history, however, and continues today. The biblical foundations of faith-healing communities during the latter half of the nineteenth century resonated with early twentieth-century Pentecostal theological perspectives.[18] In her study of divine healing in the latter half of the nineteenth century, Beth Curtis reveals that the historical record "calls into question a long-standing and extremely influential tendency to segregate 'mainstream' from 'unorthodox' . . . and 'evangelical' from 'liberal' forms of American religion."[19] As a result, scholars have discounted the continued place of faith healing in American religious life. More than signaling a diminished prominence of divine healing, the saints' engagement with science demonstrates complex negotiations of the religious and scientific domains of knowledge. Members use medical diagnoses not only "to get verification of . . . healing" but also to determine a course of action. Regardless of the extent of medical intervention in the healing process—extensive or none at all—saints use medical diagnosis to direct their prayer. After each of Louise's doctor appointments, with each new bit of information, saints would come together to "touch and agree" and target prayers to effect her healing. And they did so because they had seen it work before in the community.

TESTIMONY AND PRAYER

On weeknights, the church service opens with song and testimony, so anyone can speak or lead a song about "trials and tribulations" and "the goodness of Jesus." Deacon Bill Charles testified quite often about his healing from lung cancer. "I had blood clots on my right lung, and then that lung collapsed," he recalled. "Then they discovered blood clots on my left lung. Bishop was so precise with his prayers, 'take the blood clots,' and he asked the body to create no more." The deacon testified to doctors' bafflement when the cancer disappeared. Healing testimonies confirm the Bible's lived reality. Narratives of divine intervention substantiate biblical stories of healing and allow saints to transcend the temporal divide between then and now. Stories of divine healing serve as evidence of God's promise to answer prayer. Healing testimonies cover a spectrum of illnesses and injuries, from minor aches and pains to the life-threatening. Deacon Charles's testimony, like most, avoids specifics about medical procedures, treatments, or medications but instead highlights the spiritual work involved—primarily "staying at the altar" (praying) and "staying in the Word" (studying the Bible).

As entrée into her own healing testimony, during the time of Louise's illness, Mother Esther Pea recited Psalms 34:1 ("I will bless the LORD at all times: his praise shall continually be in my mouth") and 46:1 and 5 ("God is our refuge and strength, a very present help in trouble. . . . God is in the midst of her; she shall not be moved: God shall help her, and that right early"). "The more we praise Him, the more we are blessed. Keep praise continually in your mouth," Mother Pea advised. "He has blessed my eyes," she told the saints. "If you ask Him to do it, He will. And if you lay out on this floor at the altar, He will do it. I prayed for two years for Him to take away my cataracts. I prayed to keep my sight, and He took those cataracts away." Her next statement drew laughter and many a hearty "Amen!" With a slight chuckle, she added, "I can't hear so good, but as long as I can see I'm OK."

As the testimonies of Deacon Charles and Mother Pea show, saints utilized prayer as a primary tool to build relationships with God and tap into the "Old Time Power" promoted on the sign crowning the church entranceway. Mother Pea came to TDC in 1975, the same year Bishop and Mother Cook first opened the doors. At the time of Louise's illness, she was ninety-two and the senior matriarch—the Mother of the Church. Recognized as a "prayer warrior," she attended noonday prayer Monday through Friday. Her testimony about cataracts followed a "Back to the Altar" prayer service, which was under her charge. On the third Wednesday of each month, she and other saints prayed from nine in the morning until nine at night. She often prayed prostrate, thus her advice to "lay out on this floor at the altar."

In addition to prayer during worship services, the church offered numerous services dedicated to prayer: Sunday consecrated prayer, 4:00–5:00 p.m.; Monday night prayer, 7:30–9:00 p.m.; Wednesday Mother's Prayer, 9:00 a.m.– 1:00 p.m.; Saturday Youth Prayer, 7:30–9:00 p.m.; each weekday, 6 a.m. and noonday prayers; the twelve-hour "Back to the Altar" prayer Mother Pea led once a month; as well as occasional all-night prayer services from dusk to dawn. Recalling part of her prayer regimen before her retirement in 1989, Mother Pea said, "Friday night we had shut-in prayer, . . . all-night prayer. I [would] come straight from work. . . . I was working on Saturday then. I [would] stay [for] all-night prayer, get up, go home and take a shower, and go to work. Come back home, get my things together for Sunday morning, and didn't feel tired. God will do a lot of things for you if you get sensitive with Him. . . . He'll take all your tiredness." Even without knowing specifics about the focus of her petitions, we see the ways in which prayer generated mental and physical transformations for Mother Pea. Her recollection, though, did not convey the intense effort and training called for in prayer work.

Saints talked about the energy required to avoid distractions—from outside or of their own making, distractions ultimately identified as "the enemy" (Satan) attempting to separate a saint from Jesus, which motivated her to push harder toward Jesus. And the push, for most, is forceful, calling for mental, spiritual, and physical exertion. Moaning, singing short melodic motifs, chanting, rapidly repeating words or phrases, weeping, wailing, clapping, speaking in tongues, and stomping make up the sound of prayer. Prayer services last at least an hour, although saints come and go at will. Working to "get a prayer through" and "go to the throne of grace" demands focus and stamina. Unless physically incapable, saints pray on their knees, facing a pew. They also go to the altar to kneel, stand, or sometimes lay face down, and it is not uncommon for a saint to walk around the perimeter of the sanctuary "crying out to the Lord." (One of the more striking moments I witnessed was a saint circling the room, singing in tongues.)

In her study of contemporary American (neo-Pentecostal) evangelicals, Tanya Luhrmann notes the relational goal and cognitive demands of prayer as well.[20] "Through hard work . . . you develop that relationship [with] God."[21] Important differences, however, exist between the neo-Pentecostal Vineyard churches in her study and the classical Pentecostal COOLJC. The Vineyard churches arose when White mainstream Christian leaders collaborated with the "Jesus people" of the 1970s, a Christian hippie movement, to serve a predominantly White middle-class population. The lineage of COOLJC, the mother church of TDC, weaves from the Azusa Street Revival to the midwestern Pentecostal Assemblies of the World and into Harlem, where, in 1919, Robert C. and Carrie F. Lawson established COOLJC, a historically Black denomination (see chapter 2). Genealogy and race and gender histories matter when we examine the ways in which Pentecostals understand and perform religious work.

Church genealogy, and the specific American race and gender histories out of which Pentecostal groups emerged, can account for different perceptions of who listens to prayers. Vineyard members refer to God as a "friend," while COOLJC saints most often see God-Jesus as protector, provider, and comforter. "What is striking," Luhrmann notes, "is how hard people work to feel confident that the God who speaks to them in their mind is also the real external God who led the Jews out from slavery and died upon the cross."[22] The neo-Pentecostal evangelicals in her study may have needed to do more cognitive work to bridge a divide that Black Christians bridged through historical experience. Their God did deliver them from slavery, and "the loveliest lynchee was our Lord."[23]

There are important differences between the two groups in their corporate prayer routines as well. The Vineyard provides fewer prayer services in church; apart from prayer during Sunday worship, smaller groups gather weekly for prayer and discussion, often in the homes of congregants. Coming to church for prayer means that COOLJC women have to be "dressed according to the standard" (skirts that fall below the knee, stockings, closed-toe shoes, sleeved tops, and head coverings), adhering to rules of attire not present in Vineyard "come-as-you-are" churches. The multiple weekly prayer services within COOLJC churches increase the expectation of church leadership regarding women's participation. At the same time, multiple services heighten members' self-imposed pressures to grow personally and to grow the church. Women also bring children, so prayer services, like all services, comprised up to 80 percent women and children. Bringing children means that to be present on weeknights, mothers hustle between work, home, dinner preparation, and children's homework.

Regardless of the extra effort, COOLJC members view the numerous opportunities to pray together as highly beneficial. In addition to their own edification, these offer opportunities to encourage unsaved children to "seek the Lord" by praying with peers, without mothers directly evangelizing their own children. Children and new members learn how to pray from corporate prayer services; reproducing the specific manner of prayer reinforces individual and group distinctiveness as COOLJC. "Seekers," who are not fully converted, use prayer time to "tarry" for the Holy Ghost—to receive Spirit baptism and speak in tongues. Each conversion saves a soul, building the church and the Kingdom (see chapter 5). Saints, moreover, consider corporate prayer especially potent. So, while individual prayer speaks to specific petitions, group prayer powerfully addresses any challenges facing the church as a whole—like Louise's brain tumor.

Saints pray because "God answers prayer," "prayer changes things," and prayer changes the petitioner. It offers the most effective means of developing an intimate relationship with God, to which all saints aspire. Prayer opens lines of communication, enabling saints to come more fully into an understanding of what God expects. For the saints, direct communication addresses the ontological and epistemological foundations of COOLJC members—what the nature of their being is and how they know what they know—the indwelling Holy Ghost. Minister James Thomas, the youngest of TDC's five ministers, explained, "The gap between the highest in us and the lowest in God is filled by prayer and the Holy Ghost."

Sister Jeanette Allen recounted an experience that illustrated the ways in which prayer filled the gap between her own and God's knowledge. A seasoned saint with a South Carolina Pentecostal upbringing, she migrated to New York in the early 1960s, at eighteen years of age, and remained immersed in Pentecostalism.[24] Just like every Sunday at TDC, after dinner in the church's downstairs social hall at three o'clock in the afternoon, she climbed the stairs to the sanctuary for four o'clock prayer. At the top of the stairs, she turned right into the sanctuary anteroom, where churchgoers deposit coats and other items they don't need during services. Reaching into a tote bag below her coat, she pulled out high-heeled shoes to change into after wearing slippers during dinner. She moved to the shelves past the coats and grabbed a kneeling pillow off a pile next to stacked Bibles. She went into the darkened sanctuary and, a few rows from the front, placed her Bible and purse on the pew, the pillow on the floor, and knelt facing the bench, arms and elbows resting next to her Bible. At some point during the hour, she saw a "picture" of her son, his girlfriend, and their three children in a car accident. In that moment, she asked herself, "Is this a vision I'm having?" After church that night, "I knelt down to pray just before I went to bed, and my cell phone rang," she said. "It was my son, screaming, 'Mommy, Mommy, you gotta come!'" He and his family had been in a car accident. While traveling seventy miles per hour on a major highway, the hood flew off and smashed his windshield. "It was only God," she insisted, that prevented her from "going to a funeral today."

Throughout the week she had been praying for protection, "asking God to keep us covered under His blood." After the vision during Sunday prayer she kept praying. "I saw it before it happened, and I said, *Lord, I thank you. I* . . . said, *Lord, just take me through.* And I believe that that's [the work of] praying mothers, you know. . . . I'm not patting myself on the back for nothing—God did it. God did it." Through prayer Sister Allen petitioned God to protect her family ("Keep us covered under His blood."). At the same time, she received information that prepared her for future events and further directed her petition ("When I saw it, I kept on praying."). And God answered her specific prayer, to protect her family in the car accident.

The experiences and narratives of Deacon Charles, Mother Pea, and Sister Allen demonstrate how the church knows itself, each member a part of one body in Christ, and each individual experience a communal experience.

Each testimony of healing, blessings, and protection verified "the move of God" in the church. That's why they had every confidence that God would heal Louise.

LOUISE FRANKLIN

Louise Franklin was born and raised in Brooklyn, attending Beulah Church of Christ in Coney Island. Spirit filled as a teenager, she was an active church member working with the Missionary, Helping Hands, and Sunday School Departments. For two decades TDC benefited from her industriousness. In addition to being an altar worker—tarrying with seekers—she served through the Usher Board, Praise and Worship Team, Armor Bearers Young People Union, Mini-Church (for children), Fourth Sunday Kitchen Committee, and Voices of True Deliverance Choir, as well as assisting the Financial Committee with data entry. She joined TDC in 1984, after marrying the son of one of the church's ministers. They separated after a few years, but she remained at the church, while her husband left. She eventually divorced, which is unusual within COOLJC. Unless a spouse is deceased, remarriage is prohibited, so saints go to great lengths to reconcile problematic unions or else remain permanently separated when reconciliation is unlikely. Staying at TDC enabled Louise's young children to maintain close ties to their grandparents and aunts on their father's side, who were active members. This was important because her parents were deceased, and none of her five siblings belonged to COOLJC.

The children of TDC loved Louise because she gave them special attention. She worked hard, organizing field trips to amusement parks, sleepovers at her house, and children's church services—complete with goody gift bags for everyone. Her seemingly endless provisions for the children brought her and Mother Reeves close. Several months after Louise's death, Mother Reeves reminisced, "We became good friends after my husband took her to that bulk shopping. She loved to shop." (Minister Joe Reeves loved "that bulk shopping" too—the Reeves were always prepared to feed whoever walked through the door, and to send them home with leftovers.)

Laughing, Mother Reeves continued, "She used to always get Joe by his necktie, pull him by his necktie. She had a few inches [in height] on him, you know. And I would say, 'Louise, you know you can't be doing that. He's a preacher. You can't be just yoking him up like that. It doesn't look nice.

You can't just yoke the preacher up like that.' And she'd say, [holding him by his tie and] laughing, 'Joe, I can't yoke you up?'"

In addition to her humor, members appreciated Louise's spiritual presence within the church community. "Spiritually, . . . she was a clue-into-people, people kind of person," one church mother relayed. "She would observe you, see what you needed, and she'd just do it. And people would never know what she did.[25] She'd just pick right up on it. She be standing there looking at you, but she'd be praying too, a very prayerful person, very prayerful . . . and a very gifted singer."

Her obituary remembered her "truly 'gifted hands.' She was a brilliant painter, hairstylist, photographer, interior decorator, construction worker, party planner, seamstress, [and] hat maker." Mother Reeves concurred. "She was a great artist. I mean, holy tuna fish! She was great! And it wouldn't take her long to do it either." Church members took pride in a wall-sized mural she had painted in the preschool classroom at the TDC Christian school.[26] The summer before her passing, at the COOLJC Annual International Holy Convocation in St. Louis, she approached me in the convention center lobby, excited about her most recent work. She beamed, and rightfully so, revealing a beautiful two-foot by three-foot collage oil painting with photographic-quality likenesses of eight COOLJC leaders.

Louise graduated from Manhattan's Art and Design High School but did not pursue higher education in the visual arts. At the time of her passing, she was twenty-five years into a career with the federal government as a contract specialist. Returning to college twice, once in 1990 for an associate's degree and again in 2003 for her bachelor's of science, helped her to advance in her career. One church mother told me, "[She was] very, very smart. She went back to school, got her degree while she was working, bought her house, saved the money, kept them children in school, getting her promotion. . . . She took promotion upon promotion, and they gave her a lot of flack, but this new position is finally where she wanted to get to." She was, in many ways, a success story within the church community.

Louise had a quirky personality. According Bishop Cook, people "had to learn her." She carried an attitude of "If you like me, fine; if you don't, fine." Mother Reeves described her as "a little crazy, too. She had ten attitudes." "She could get to a point where she wasn't always your friend," she recalled. "She'd sometimes . . . just be inside herself, and she couldn't talk. She'd come in and just sit. And you know that's not the day to bother her.

Sometimes I'd just grab her . . . and hold her and hug her and [her] tears would just roll. . . . But she come through so much."

When I first arrived at TDC, the degree to which individuals would engage me varied, but the vast majority were warm and friendly. Louise was different. She was cool. When we saw each other, she didn't always speak. I came to assume she either didn't like me or didn't approve of my research. Then, one Saturday afternoon in July, seven months into my fieldwork, that all changed. Four times a year, TDC and the other Queens- and Brooklyn-based COOLJC churches participated in the Tri-district Diocese Quarterly Convocation. The services, meetings, and workshops ran from Wednesday to Saturday, with the host church rotating each quarter; Brooklyn's Antioch Church of Christ hosted this convocation. Following the afternoon workshops, dinner was served in the church's social hall. I went downstairs; moved through the line of women serving homemade baked chicken, cabbage, greens, mac 'n' cheese, and salad; and found a seat at one of the long folding tables. A few minutes later, Louise came over with her dinner, sat down next to me, and began to chat it up as if we were old buddies. From that point on, she was very friendly and, six weeks later, surprised me with a beautiful handmade corsage for my birthday. I don't know what changed for her.

It wasn't until after her illness that we had another one-on-one conversation. During the last week of October, Sister Holmes and I visited her at home on Wednesday and Sunday evenings after services. On Wednesday when we arrived, in addition to her children, two of her good friends from the church were there. Mother Reeves was in the kitchen preparing meals for the week. We chatted with her briefly; she and Sister Holmes talked through some logistics for the rest of the week—transportation for doctor's visits, grocery shopping, transportation for the children back and forth to church services, who else would be on duty, and phone calls that needed to be made.

Sister Holmes and I then went upstairs, joining Sister Lee at Louise's bedside. Sister Holmes entered first. She bent over the bed and hugged Louise. "Praise Him," they exchanged. She moved into the room. I went over, did the same, and then shifted back to stand in the doorway. There wasn't much floor space in the room. Immediately inside the door to the right an end table was wedged next to the bed. To the left was a narrow walkway between the bed and a large dresser. At the foot of the bed, Sister Lee sat in a folding chair in front of another dresser that was topped with a large television.

On the far side of the bed, clothes spilled out of a large, double-door closet. Louise's seventeen-year-old daughter brought another folding chair and left. Sister Holmes sat, and everyone conversed. Sister Lee got up after a while and went downstairs. A few minutes later, Sister Holmes left the room as well.

I moved to the folding chair next to the bed. We made a little small talk, and then Louise began talking about her medication regimen. She pulled a plastic bag containing pills off the end table and deliberately went through them, detailing when she had to take them and how they made her feel. She talked about doctors' appointments and testing she had been subjected to, all the while interjecting, "But, you know, God is good. He's a healer." At one point she looked directly into my eyes and said softly, "You know it's a lot, it's a whole lot." She looked frightened. During those moments, when I believe she allowed me to be privy to her fear, I was frightened and honored. I wasn't a saint. But maybe that's why she was talking to me in that way. I don't know. She wanted to talk about the ordeal of sickness and medicines and doctors. Then she said, "But God told me, 'You are already healed,' and I believe His promise."

Two nights later, Louise sponsored and attended the Friday Joy Night service as a fund-raiser for the Building Fund, to assist in the purchase of commercial and residential property next door to the church. It was also an Armor Bearers Young People Union service, meaning she had coordinated with children, teens, and young adults to sing, read poetry, speak, and read scripture. Turnout was good for a weeknight at the midsize church. About sixty people came, adorned in pink and black, the colors she had chosen for the night. Members of COOLJC color-coordinate clothing for services, events, and trips all the time. It is an embodiment of spiritual unity—all being "with one accord"—like the disciples, "the women, and Mary the mother of Jesus, and . . . brethren" on the day of Pentecost (Acts 1:14).

For the opening scripture, Louise selected Ephesians 4:1–16, which reads in part:

> 1: I therefore, the prisoner of the Lord, beseech you that ye walk worthy of the vocation wherewith ye are called, 2: With all lowliness and meekness, with longsuffering, forbearing one another in love. . . . 4: There is one body, and one Spirit, even as ye are called in one hope of your calling; . . . 15: But speaking the truth in love, may grow up into him in all things, which is the head, even Christ: 16: From whom the

whole body fitly joined together and compacted by that which every joint supplieth, according to the effectual working in the measure of every part, maketh increase of the body unto the edifying of itself in love.

After the reading, the Praise and Worship Team moved to the front and opened with an up-tempo church favorite, "What a Mighty God We Serve." Following a lengthy and high-spirited praise and worship time, Louise rose and introduced the service, announcing, "We're here to have a good time in the Lord and raise money for the Building Fund."[27] Before she turned the microphone over to the evening's emcee, ten-year-old Sister Yasmine Johnson, Louise told the congregation what she had told me, "I'm nonchalant about how sick I am because I got on the prayer line, and God told me I was healed."

At the time it didn't seem surprising that Louise had coordinated the service and gotten out of her sickbed to attend. It was her service, and she was going to be there. Five weeks later, she was gone.

"LIKE SOMEBODY PULLED THE RUG FROM UNDERNEATH"

It was overwhelming. The pain and grief were palpable. The chatter and laughter normally heard outside of church, as folks gathered before and after services, was gone. Sunday afternoon meals in the dining hall were somber. Gradually, over the next six months, the thick fog of sadness dissipated into a haze. Out of respect for people's grief, I held off asking questions about her passing until the end of summer. She had been gone for seven months, and saints had been working to reconcile God's power to heal and promise to answer prayer with all the unanswered prayers and Louise's passing. She had confessed her healing to the congregation ("God told me I was healed"), which carried particular significance because she was both professing her faith and also testifying about a direct communication with God.[28] Sister Holmes later explained that "people's devastation" was also rooted in the confidence in communal power. "It was a corporate prayer and the powers and the numbers and the unity, and all these things were happening," she said. "And when she passed, it was just like somebody pulled the rug from underneath [everyone]."

Here we will see—through three women: Sister Holmes, Mother Reeves, and Sister Kendra Clark—how church members worked through these theological conundrums. As saints continued to develop and engage the tools of faith discussed above—participating in corporate worship through song, testimony, and prayer, and studying and hearing the Word—they also engaged in intellectual work, biblical exegesis, and evaluation of religious practices.

So how did saints evaluate or interpret the efficacy of prayer if the church prayed for one thing in particular but that was not the outcome? I asked Mother Reeves, "In a situation like this how does prayer work?" "Bishop Cook told us to pray," she explained. "After [Louise] had the biopsy, he told Mother England to get everything in order and to pray that God's will be done. He knew that she was not going to live. He knew that. We might have been praying, *Lord, keep her, heal her,* because we don't want to let her go, but God's will must be done." In Mother Reeves's telling of it, Bishop Cook recognized the conflict between the desire of the saints and God's will, urging supplicants "to pray that God's will be done." In hindsight, she conceded, there was indeed a conflict of will. Mother Reeves talked about her distress, as she worked through the tension in prayer, knowing, yet not able to face, what was to be. "You don't want to accept that," she said, "so you're praying, you're still travailing past that because you don't want to receive that. I'm gonna lose my friend?! You ain't gonna accept that. You're praying and travailing, *Lord, please have mercy!* That was my prayer, *Lord, please have mercy!*" As the realization began to seep in, she shifted her petition to "Lord, please have mercy," no longer asking for a healing. "I woke up at six o'clock that Tuesday morning," she recalled, describing her prayer work, "and got on my knees and I prayed until after seven o'clock. I got up off my knees, and I was crying. God knows I was crying. [She slapped the table repeatedly.] My heart bust open like a big ocean. . . . That was the day she was supposed to go up for surgery." She paused, shaking her head. "Yeah," she went on, "maybe it was a warning to me because I hadn't cried like that for her. Then I got the call later [that day] that she was in a coma, and [my husband] said, 'That's it. She's gone.'"

Mother Reeves conceded that in the moment, "You feel it, but you don't want to hear it, . . . that little voice that speaks. You can just press right over that. And it don't keep telling you over and over." In retrospect, she understood the instructions from Bishop Cook to pray for "God's will," her wailing during prayer, and "that little voice" as three distinct instances of God preparing her for the inevitable. Louise slipping into a coma served as the final divine event to prepare Mother Reeves and the other saints for what was to come. "The whole purpose of her laying there like that [in a coma]," she said, "is [God giving] people time . . . to be able to accept the *shock*. So it wouldn't just knock you off your feet. That's what that was." Mother Reeves was clearly tormented as Louise's final days unfolded. Yet, viewing events through an Apostolic lens provided much-needed comfort. God had been present throughout, preparing her for the unavoidable.

Sister Clark, however, was having a particularly hard time. "It still don't make sense to me," she said. A thirty-nine-year-old minister's wife and stay-at-home mom of three young boys, she had come to COOLJC in her late teens, from a Lutheran upbringing, after some admittedly wild years of drug and alcohol abuse. She and Louise had known each other for years, through church, but had become close only in the past few years. Louise was god-mother to Sister Clark's youngest son. "It seemed like every weekend [Louise and her children] were here for the summer," Sister Clark reminisced. They had also spent significant time together in St. Louis at the Annual International Holy Convocation in August. In a pained voice, she shared, "I'm, like, still dealing. I mean, God gives us strength, but it's not a day that goes by where [she broke off, voice quivering] . . . There is this girl so full of life. I know things come. . . . But I still don't understand. And I get angry. *She should be here!* . . . But you know, we always say, God knows best, and He does." Even though the situation was incomprehensible, Sister Clark tried to find some solace in church teachings ("we always say, God knows best").

While saints pressed to know and do God's will, God's will was also the repository for the unexplainable. Since prayers for Louise's physical healing were not answered, the saints then understood the outcome as the will of God, which was still incomprehensible. Now they had to push to accept it. Mother Reeves shared part of her process. She asked the Lord to help her accept it. She knew it was "only God" because, "if it wasn't, she would still be here." She explained, "See, Satan can afflict your body, but he can't take life, and he can't give it. Only God can do it. So God . . . took that last breath from her. Breath goes back to the God that giveth." Ultimately, trusting that "God . . . took that last breath" brought her closer to accepting unacceptable circumstances, but not completely. "So how do you accept that?" she asked, and answered, "It's *HARD! It's hard.* You're still baffling with yourself. *She's gone? What?*" Continuous supplication provides some answers. "You're still begging God, 'Lord, *please*. Why? Mercy, mercy!' But He did have mercy [because] . . . she didn't want to go through no chemotherapy. She had told Mother England that she didn't want to suffer and go through all that."

Mother Reeves employed the same tools the saints always used to bring their perspectives in line with that which had not yet been internalized but which religious conviction and church teaching said was true. She talked about the ways studying and teaching scripture on predestination helped get her through. "And you know it's already been predested," she said. "Our life and . . . *Halleluuujah!*" She physically shuddered. Her tone dropped. Her voice thickened and quivered, with the touch of the Holy Ghost. She paused briefly and continued, "However it's to go has already been preset. You know, it's just that you got to fall in place." In that moment, when the internalized Holy Spirit reverberated through her body and voice, she received validation and affirmed, "God is good. We may not always agree with it, and we may not always know what we've got to suffer to get through these points, but trust me, you'll get there. We don't always understand, but her time and destiny was already predestined. That's scripture. We just had that lesson in Sunday school [yesterday]."

Mother Reeves had taught an adult Sunday school class the day before—lesson 7 from the *Student Handbook*, titled "Storm Warnings: God in Love Prepares Us for the Trials We Face." It focused on Acts 21:7–17, which tells the story of Paul preparing to travel to Jerusalem, knowing that he will be jailed. Church members were to draw "three important foundational truths" from the lesson:

1   If we pray daily for God to have His way in our lives, then whatever happens that day we can accept as His will at work in us.
2   We know that God is in ultimate control and He has a predestined plan for those who live according to His will.
3   "And we know that all things work together for the good to them that love God, to them who are called according to his purpose" (Romans 8:28). God works with the end in mind and dovetails all things in our lives to bring about our ultimate development into His likeness.[29]

"If we love God and pray for His will to be done in our lives daily," the lesson concluded, "then we can trust that He is working His will out through our lives, and He is using all things to positively develop us in His predestined plan."[30] The Bible works as a living and contemporary text for the saints; hence, Mother Reeves mapped the example of Paul's determination to do the will of God, through suffering, onto the tragedy of losing Louise. Through immersion in scripture, prayer, and worship, in church and at home, saints render biblical lessons into daily experiences and vice versa, thus resting assured of God's control over every aspect of life.

Mother Reeves seemed to find a measure of comfort in the doctrine of predestination. Sister Clark, however, continued to struggle. "I think we could pray, we could fast, or whatever," she said, "but if God says, it's not so, it won't be so. I don't know. I really don't. I'm struggling with that now, trying to understand certain things as far as why my prayer wasn't answered, or is this God's will? *Is it* God's will? I don't even understand. It's just hard." Her struggle was not uncommon. For months after the tragic event, in casual conversations, most saints declared that Louise's death was most certainly the will of God, while their faces and body language suggested confusion.

Sister Holmes offered a more nuanced analysis, distinguishing between what God wills and what God allows. While she held to teachings of predestination, God's will, and the power of prayer, introducing the role of individual choice—what God allows—brought her to a different conclusion. Notably, she seemed to be coping with loss better than the others I spoke with, so many months after Louise's death.

SISTER HOLMES: It's already charted out what God's will is for your life. But He also allows things to happen. . . . And clearly, upon her birth, this could have been God's will for her life. . . . Do I *know* that it was His will? I have no idea. I don't know if it was His will or hers because He gives us choice.

JUDITH: I heard a number of people say this was God's will.

SISTER HOLMES: They don't know that. Plus, that makes you feel better . . . So then you don't have to ask the question, you don't have to answer the question why would she leave her children. Why wouldn't she want to live? She was good. She was a faithful saint. She was a good mother. She was young. She was a diligent employee. She was full of life. She had all the reasons visible to anybody that she should be living. I think people justify it in ways that they need to be able to deal with it. It's one of the ways they define and contain it to have it make sense, to help them get through it.

So I don't know if in her comatose state, because I don't know anything about that medically or spiritually, that she felt it was more peaceful, . . . and she decided she was fine where she was. And possibly [she considered] where she could be going by not coming back here. Hopefully, she was spiritually sensitive enough to have made that choice for herself. Nobody knows what was happening in that silence, in her comatose state for all those days, what she thought, what she saw, [and] what she was feeling. So I thought that she probably decided to transition and God allowed her to do that. . . . Maybe it was her love for herself, and God allowed it to happen. And all the prayers in the world couldn't keep her here.

[Her healing] is according to *her* faith. . . . That's something that I think we forget when we pray, because you want the best for everybody in your life. But it's according to *their* faith. If they can't believe what you're praying for, then you're praying amiss. We forget that because you're thinking, who wouldn't want to be healed? That's a good thing. Who wouldn't want to have that testimony? Who wouldn't want to extend their life like Hezekiah?[31] Some people have a different idea for their life. And I think at points it could change.

Sister Holmes, Mother Reeves, and Sister Clark interpreted the meaning of Louise's passing within the context of COOLJC teachings, yet differently from each other. Sister Clark, although perplexed and angry ("*Is it* God's will?"), confirmed, "God gives us strength." Mother Reeves found a disquieting comfort: "We don't always understand, but her time and destiny was already predestined." Sister Holmes found reassurance in an agentive interpretation, "So I thought that she probably decided to transition and God allowed her to do that." While these three women represent a range of responses, most saints adhered to the interpretation expressed by Mother Reeves. Louise's death, although tragic and painful, revealed the omnipotence and inscrutability of God. Acknowledging the subsequent journey of faith, they worked hard to understand and accept the ways of God. At the time of this writing, some were still working on it.

"SHE'S WITH CHRIST"

We can understand the array of responses to shocking death—the saint with choice (Holmes), the saint at the mercy of God's will and divine providence (Reeves), and the uncertain saint (Clark)—in light of religious expertise. Sister Holmes was a third-generation COOLJC member, raised and active in holiness for close to forty years. Mother Reeves, as mentioned earlier, joined as a married adult and had been active for thirty years, while Sister Clark had been participating for twenty years, having joined as a teen. Of course, there is not always a direct correlation between years "on the job" and expertise. With any work, the commitment to training and the attention to tasks at hand play a significant role in skill development. By my observations, Sister Holmes and Mother Reeves took on more hours of weekly church activity than Sister Clark did, which provided them greater opportunity to hone individual skills, as well as participate in communal exchanges about religious teachings.

In the end, if relief from the grief of loss existed, it was found in the promise of eternal life. Sister Clark struggled to alleviate unrelenting anguish by reiterating church doctrine. "I guess I'm still in mourning. It's just constant," she acknowledged. "I guess you gotta learn how to trust God, that He knows what He's doing," she said. "I'm glad she's, you know, gone on. She made it, hopefully. But she believed in living right, so I believe if anybody made it, she made it." Sister Clark, however, professed her religious teachings with revealing qualifiers: "*I guess* you gotta learn how to trust God," "she made it, *hopefully*," and "*if* anybody made it, she made it." Whereas Sister Clark avoided placing Louise anywhere specific—"She's gone *on*, . . . she made *it*," Mother Reeves and Sister Holmes issued unambiguous proclamations. "As long as you die in Christ, ultimately as long as you're sleeping [in Christ], that's the consolation," Mother Reeves explained. "So it don't grieve you as much because you know that she's with Christ. She's saved. So that gives you peace." Sister Holmes, referencing scripture, concurred, "She's in a better place. And the Bible says that death is the last of the enemy . . . because . . . absence from the body is in presence with the Lord [2 Cor. 5:8]." During Friday's service, the night after Louise passed, Bishop Cook told the congregation, "When we're down, look up. Be glad she died in the Lord. We've got time to get it right. We don't mourn like others with no hope. We lift Him up. Don't feel sad. . . . God never makes a mistake. . . . Thank God she was saved."[32]

On the morning of Louise's death, before many of these issues had been articulated, Mother Reeves's singing, "Thank you, Lord," demonstrated a stroke of religious mastery, as she harnessed COOLJC practices and teachings, and revealed her sense of effective action.[33] Envisioning Louise with Jesus offered a long peace, while singing supplied an immediate balm, in Mother Reeves's body and throughout Louise's house. As noted earlier, women initiated church protocols of "homegoing" and took on responsibility for bearing up the family and wider church community in the days following Louise's passing. At the same time, any death in the church family puts everyone on notice; as Bishop Cook reminded them, "We've got time to get it right." "We need to ready ourselves," he warned. "Can't say how long you're gonna live. . . . Those who live right have a hope in Christ." Grappling with the meanings of death, judgment, and the future state, saints anticipated and worked to manifest a "new heaven and a new earth" (Rev. 21:1). They knew, also, that "the fearful, and unbelieving, . . . shall have their part in the lake which burneth with fire and brimstone: which is the second death" (Rev. 21:8).

What did it mean to be awash in the paradox of divine healing and death, of predestination and the promise of answered prayer?

Through spontaneous song, Mother Reeves stood "in the gap" for uncertain, yet, committed saints (Ezek. 22:30). The prayers for divine healing did not have the anticipated result in Louise's case. Now they needed another healing. Mother Reeves performed a restorative act by sounding the conviction she might not have quite felt in her heart. In the midst of trials and tribulations, a key indication of a saint's religious confidence rests in her ability to thank and praise the Lord. Acquiring and maintaining steadfast faith is a process that has its ebbs and flows. During times of trouble, if a saint feels spiritually weak, praising God and giving thanks becomes a strategy that shores her up.[34] "I'm gonna praise my way out." "The victory is in the praise."

Consequently, the reservoir of techniques used to demonstrate faith is the same one used to instill faith—tools used to show what you have or to get what you need. For Mother Reeves and the saints, the *act* of giving thanks and praise invoked the power of Jesus, which strengthened. With "Thank you, Lord," Mother Reeves signaled conviction and uncertainty, and she knew, from experience, that intoning gratitude would move her to a spiritually stronger place. Ambiguity about the degree of faith being demonstrated levels the spiritual playing field, throwing open an interpretive space that allows anyone to enter, regardless of her spiritual grounding at a given moment. The action of Mother Reeves created a passageway for "her sisters in the Lord" to access "the new heaven and new earth." The lyric was open— "Thank you, Lord. I just want to thank you, Lord"—which let each woman access what she personally needed from the song. Chanting created a sacred space for worship and fellowship, bringing each closer to God and giving comfort. So, whether Mother Reeves was in fact grateful to God at the time she sang the song, or was singing as a reminder to *be* grateful, contemplating gratitude while grieving kept everyone bound up in the religious milieu and close to their spiritual sister who had "gone home."

The saints of COOLJC hold to the promise of eternal life—the final reward of holiness. The indwelling Holy Ghost sanctifies them, sometimes compelling, sometimes prodding, and sometimes leaving them to their own urges, as they "work at living a holy life." Sister Thomas's statement, "Walking with Christ means you decide about how you gonna act all the time," highlighted the individual perseverance at the heart of this community of worshippers. In the process of developing spiritual expertise, saints utilize instruments of faith in communal religious practices and private endeavors. Prayer, praise, worship, and study mutually inform each other, as members labor to bring their dispositions in line with their convictions and doctrine.

The events surrounding the illness and death of Louise opened a window onto several levels of simultaneous religious labor done by these New York–based women. In the chapters that follow, I use different aspects of women's religious lives to focus on particular registers of labor—organizational, emotional, intimate, and aesthetic. The work of COOLJC women resonates with that of many others in Holiness-Pentecostalism, including the wave of late twentieth-century neo-Pentecostals that has garnered recent scholarly attention. The saints of COOLJC, however, organized as a distinct religious group, engaged in the labor of faith, in early twentieth-century Harlem, New York. We now turn to that history.

CHURCH

BUILDING

Mother Carrie F. Lawson functioned as
Bishop Lawson's chief advisor, alter-ego, and trusted visionary.

East Harlem leaves had the red tips of early autumn when Amaryllia (Lillie) Jones ventured down E. 131st Street in 1919 to her neighbors' home for worship services. Addie and Edward Anderson and Ida and James Burleigh had opened their shared brownstone to sojourners from the Midwest— Robert C. and Carrie F. Lawson—who had come to New York to spread the fire of the Pentecost. Exactly how Lillie heard about the gathering is not part of the historical record. Perhaps she was friendly with the Burleighs and Andersons. Maybe she heard the praises to the Lord as she walked by; it was only a block from her home. Lillie joined the worshippers and gave her life to Jesus that same year, being baptized in the East River and baptized in the Spirit.[1]

Lillie had been widowed since 1910, left to finish raising three children—George, ten; Octave, sixteen; and Grace, eighteen. Grace married Herbert Smith that same year but stayed close by, moving only a few doors away and later joining her mother's new church. In 1922, three years after Lillie, Grace, too, found salvation; she was thirty years old, and her daughter, little Ethel Mae, was four years old. Lillie was no doubt unaware that going to that first worship service, and her Spirit baptism soon after, would be the catalyst to bring her daughter Grace, and by extension her granddaughter Ethel Mae, into lifelong service in what would become one of the most prominent churches in midcentury Harlem, the Church of Our Lord Jesus Christ of the Apostolic Faith, Inc. (COOLJC). Grace would be at the center of establishing the "women's auxiliaries," as they would come to be known (see chapter 3). In the mid-twentieth century, Ethel Mae would take up the banner of church work, and her marriage to William L. Bonner, Robert Lawson's successor, would lead to her organizing the wives of the church leadership, in her position as the first lady of COOLJC.

This chapter examines the early twentieth-century western and midwestern roots of COOLJC, its founding in 1919, and the nearly five decades of work of the founders, Robert and Carrie Lawson. It then briefly covers the leadership change and structural reorganization under William and Ethel Mae Bonner after Robert Lawson's death in 1961; the resulting structures are still in place today. The final section examines the establishment of one COOLJC church in the mid-1970s, True Deliverance Church (TDC) in Queens, founded by Crosley J. and Reva E. Cook. The official founding and formal leadership of Black American Pentecostal churches in the larger denominations are understood as the province of male ministers, and COOLJC members embrace this view of formal leadership, as evidenced by written church histories that designate Robert Lawson, William Bonner, and Crosley Cook as founders and leaders.[2] This chapter inserts the pivotal work of their wives. The influential legacies of these women garner some attention in church documentation; however, the role of Black women as "helpmeets" in institution building receives more detailed acknowledgment in oral histories. As a result, "the ways in which women's presence and sensibilities have contributed to and shaped . . . [Pentecostal] religious culture" as cofounders of churches remain understated in printed church histories and undervalued in scholarship.[3] Undervalued, too, are the ways in which women cofounders comprehended the meaning of "helpmeet," which are made clear by delving into the full extent of their work and influence.

Race consciousness played a central role in the foundation of COOLJC as well, evidenced by the civic, political, and social agenda of Robert Lawson. In the same ways that religious leadership has been attributed to men, so, too, have the rhetoric and characteristics of race consciousness been gendered male, thereby obscuring the perspectives of women. This is not specific to cooljc but is the result of complex raced and gendered political histories that have conflated Black with male.[4] Lawson's politically progressive agenda in the early and mid-twentieth century pushes against a narrative of African American Pentecostalism as strictly otherworldly and compensatory, just as its appeal to a female majority membership counters the gendering of race consciousness as male. In addition to his progressive race politics, members were attracted to Lawson's theology that fashioned a distinctive Pentecostal space, which advanced Afro-biblical readings while placing Black women at the center, just as they were in the church itself.

When the Lawsons came to New York from Ohio in the early twentieth century, midwestern Pentecostal communities already knew them to be spiritually powerful. Robert had been making a name for himself within the burgeoning and controversial oneness Pentecostal movement, while Carrie had relinquished her position as a preacher with Pentecostal Assemblies of the World (paw) to start the New York church with Robert. The historical record is silent on Carrie Lawson's (neé Fields) rise to evangelist in paw, but scholars indicate that her ordination took place under Herbert Davis, the pastor of her Leavenworth, Kansas, congregation.[5] Once in New York, Mother Carrie Lawson would gain prominence through radio broadcasts, as "the Praying Mother of the Air," where her praying was "reputed to have stopped the taverns from serving their drinks and made people on the street respond to this godly mother's prayers."[6] Her spiritual acumen was no doubt instrumental in pulling Harlemites to worship services from the beginning. History nonetheless recognizes Robert as the sole founder of cooljc, and his remarkable organizational, intellectual, theological, and political work is well documented. Details about his life before young adulthood, however, are scant.

The church historians of cooljc, Dr. Robert C. Spellman and Mabel L. Thomas, report Robert Clarence Lawson's birth as taking place in New Iberia, Louisiana, on May 5, 1883.[7] After the early death of his parents, he lived with his aunt Peggy (Frazier), who raised him. Lawson reportedly came from at least four generations of ministers; nonetheless, his early career goals did not include the ministry but centered in law and business. In spite of these pragmatic interests, he was bitten by a more creative bug and cut college short to embark on a singing career. Over the next few years, by his own admission, he became involved in "devilment . . . the way of the world . . . [and] gambling."[8]

Travels as a tavern singer took Lawson to Indianapolis, Indiana, where he was hospitalized with tuberculosis. Here his story aligns with many conversion narratives in which a serious illness (or other life-threatening crisis) leads to conversion. A missionary woman ministered to Lawson in his hospital bed, and he reluctantly agreed to attend her church, the Apostolic Faith Assembly (which would later join PAW), led by Garfield T. Haywood. Soon after arriving at the church, in late 1913 Lawson received Spirit baptism. Landing in the Indianapolis-based organization led by Haywood would prove to be the catalyst to Lawson's national profile, as he gained access to influential leaders of the emergent American Pentecostal movement, Haywood being one.[9]

AZUSA ROOTS AND ROUTES

Haywood had come to Pentecostalism in 1908, when two revivalists, Glenn A. Cook and Henry Prentiss, brought "the fire" to Indianapolis after being "baptized in the Spirit" at the Azusa Street Revival in Los Angeles. Teachings of sanctification and evangelical enthusiasm were firmly in place in the United States by the mid-nineteenth century, yet the Los Angeles outpouring marked a new theological and missionary era.[10] Between 1906 and 1909, thousands passed through Azusa Street, then fanned out across the country and abroad to spread the new doctrine of Holy Ghost baptism evidenced by speaking in tongues. Under the pastoral guidance of William J. Seymour, Azusa Street conducted round-the-clock revivals for nearly three years, becoming "the Grand Central Station of global Pentecostalism," as missionaries, evangelists, and ministers brought the message to their home congregations and established new churches.[11]

Along with teachings of the embodied Spirit, Azusa Street provided a radical social model for early twentieth-century American religion, attracting worshippers across ethnicities, nationalities, denominations, and classes. This kind of mixing was extraordinary just ten years after the Supreme Court had sanctioned racial segregation in *Plessy v. Ferguson* (1896), and it appealed to a cross-section of people with a vision that brought spiritual equality before God into alignment with societal equality across lines of race, ethnicity, class, and gender. While this was reminiscent of the race and gender boundary crossings of antebellum Methodism, twentieth-century Pentecostals grounded Holy Ghost infilling and equality before God in scriptural interpretation of specific experiences of the apostles on the day of Pentecost.

All who attended Azusa Street did not, however, ascribe to the divine egalitarian vision. Spectators, most notably the press, came to ridicule. The *Los Angeles Times* gave an account of a "wild scene" in which "pandemonium breaks loose, and the bounds of reason are passed by those who are 'filled with the spirit,' whatever that may be." The reporter described Seymour as the "old colored exhorter . . . with his stony optic" and women congregants as a "colored 'mammy,'" "a buxom dame," and other "black women" who "gurgle," "jump," "gesticulate," and "faint." While the reporter attributed "the strangest harangue[s] ever uttered" to these women, he also inadvertently pointed to the centrality of women to the movement.[12]

At the dawn of the twentieth century, a network of religious Black women, moving across the South, Midwest, and West, had facilitated Seymour's move to Pentecostalism and Los Angeles. From 1895 to 1905, before arriving in California, Seymour traveled about as well. A first-generation free Black from Louisiana, he journeyed from the Gulf Coast area to Indiana, Ohio, and then back down south to Texas. In Houston he met Reverend Lucy Farrow and began attending her church. Farrow introduced Seymour to the doctrine of speaking in tongues, inviting him to learn more about it at a local Bible school headed by Charles Parham, a White preacher from Kansas. Farrow had traveled from Kansas with the Parham family as a governess and was quite familiar with his doctrine.

As early as 1901, Parham had promoted speaking in tongues as evidence of Spirit baptism, which he disseminated through his Bible school, initially in Kansas, Missouri, and Oklahoma and by 1905 also in Texas.[13] Parham's divine revelations stopped short of racial integration, however, as he required Farrow, Seymour, and other Black followers at the Texas Bible classes to engage with the teachings while sitting outside and listening through an open door. They were nonetheless persuaded by Parham's interpretations of the book of Acts and, as the movement that followed showed, took biblical analysis even further, melding the promises of spiritual and social parity.

In that same year, Farrow left her congregation under the temporary leadership of Seymour while she traveled to lead revivals. Neely Terry, a visitor from Los Angeles, happened to attend the church and was impressed by Seymour. Upon her return home, she recommended him to fill an opening as associate pastor at her Los Angeles church. Clearly, Terry was a trusted member; the pastor, Julia Hutchins, accepted the endorsement and sent for Seymour in January 1906. The congregation, however, rejected the theology of speaking in tongues that Seymour promoted, so Terry introduced him to a couple who opened their home to use for church meetings. Within a few months, the gathering exceeded the capacity of the house, and the congregation moved to an old African Methodist Episcopal church building on Azusa Street.

Farrow, along with Seymour, Hutchins, and Terry, wound up in Los Angeles; after serving for four months as "God's anointed handmaid" at Azusa Street, Minister Farrow moved out to conduct revivals and plant churches. In addition to foot soldiers, the Azusa Street newsletter, the *Apostolic Faith*, carried the word of Holy Ghost fire; a free periodical, it reached fifty thousand subscribers within a year. The first issue of the *Apostolic Faith*, in September 1906, reports that Farrow "has now returned to Houston, en route to Norfolk, Va.," a childhood home she was taken from, "being sold into slavery in the south."[14] By December Farrow was making her way up the East Coast and on to Liberia, where she stayed for several months, before returning to Azusa Street. Notably, Hutchins, who had initially rejected Seymour's teachings, accompanied Farrow to the foreign field. Hutchins embraced the doctrine of tongues after visiting Azusa Street; she became a regular participant. Hutchins's husband and niece joined the movement as well, accompanying her and Farrow to Liberia.

By 1909, three years after its inception, the zenith of the Azusa Revival was over. The church remained as a small, predominantly Black congregation, a casualty of the rise of other Pentecostal churches, local segregationist impulses, and internal divisions. Nonetheless, within those same three years, Pentecostalism had spread rapidly, and every region of the United States, as well as Mexico, Chile, Liberia, South Africa, India, Hong Kong, Japan, and the Philippines, felt the impact of the Los Angeles spiritual outpouring.[15] So, in 1908, when Cook and Prentiss carried the message of holy tongues and divine equality to Indiana from Azusa Street, Haywood, and soon Robert Lawson, would become part of a wave with national and international momentum.

THE MIDWEST AZUSA: INDIANAPOLIS

In the wake of the radically inclusive Azusa Revival, American Pentecostal communities grappled with the contradictions of legal and social racism and the message of "brotherhood in the body of Christ." Following the Los Angeles model, Indianapolis witnessed racially integrated Pentecostal worship. The color line that was "washed away in the blood" in Los Angeles, however, soon resurfaced in Indianapolis.[16] Just as the *Los Angeles Times* reports instigated negative reactions to demonstrative, integrated worship with active participation by women, Indianapolis newspapers fanned the flames of ridicule and racism. Reporters identified followers as "gliggy bluks," referring to the "jibberish" of speaking in tongues, and obsessively focused on interracial physical interaction. Black and White worshippers kissed each other "indiscriminately." White women hugged the "dusky necks of negresses." "Bluks" participated in foot-washing ceremonies and congregated at the local creek for full-immersion baptism.[17] The racial acrimony of the press hinted at a deeper race hatred that would soon fully erupt. By the 1920s Indiana was home to the largest Ku Klux Klan organization in the United States, with 500,000 women and men in its membership.[18] As early as 1907, the racial climate in Indianapolis caused Prentiss and Cook to establish separate congregations for Black and White followers because of "safety concerns."[19]

In 1908 Haywood and his wife, Ida, joined the Prentiss mission, and soon after, following Prentiss's unexpected resignation, Haywood took over, began growing the congregation, and brought it into PAW.[20] Haywood already enjoyed recognition as the illustrator for the well-known Indianapolis-based Black weekly *The Freeman*. In keeping with the paper's charge, his illustrations during his seven-year tenure (1902–1909) depicted vital African American concerns—disfranchisement, racial violence, education, employment, and poverty. Haywood's work as an illustrator would, however, soon be dwarfed by his rise to national stature within the Pentecostal movement. In spite of the pragmatic segregation of the Indianapolis church body, Haywood managed to keep White members and maintain alliances with White Pentecostal leaders, making him instrumental in keeping PAW integrated until 1924, after other Pentecostal groups had placed social conventions over theology and reverted to segregated congregations.

In the lead-up to nearly total racial segregation of Pentecostal congregations, White southern leadership began pushing back against having to travel north for organizational conferences. The undue financial burden could be eliminated, they argued, by having separate regional conferences. Tellingly, they proposed two "regional" bodies divided along racial lines.[21] Black leaders balked and roundly rejected the proposal. At the same time, many northern and midwestern White Pentecostals were becoming increasingly soft on expecting southern leaders to defy conventions of Black exclusion. Ironically, the government granted authority to one Black church leader, which slowed Pentecostal segregation. Charles H. Mason, leader of the Memphis-based Church of God in Christ (COGIC), incorporated his church in 1907, making it the only Pentecostal body with authority to legally ordain ministers.[22] In addition to being able to officiate marriages, credentialed ministers received discounts on train travel, essential for poor and working-class ministers eager to spread Pentecostalism across the nation. Ordained ministers also received exemption from military service, which became especially significant in the lead-up to World War I, when some Pentecostal bodies took pacifist stances.[23] Within six years of the founding of COGIC, the groundswell of White ministers who objected to being credentialed by Mason, an African American, came to a head.[24] In 1914 White ministers pulled out of COGIC to form the Assemblies of God (AG).

In the wake of the rise of AG and significant weakening of Azusa Street, Haywood held on to the vision of an Azusa-like interethnic body of worshippers. His vision of Pentecostal unity, however, was further impeded by a major theological schism—the oneness issue. In 1915 Glenn Cook, who had been instrumental in bringing Pentecostalism to Indianapolis, returned with the "new issue" of oneness, which Haywood embraced. The controversial teachings, also called "Jesus-only" or "Apostolic" doctrine, contested the long-held theology of Trinitarians, arguing for a unified godhead, the absolute deity of Jesus, and water baptism done in the name of Jesus, not "in the name of the Father, Son, and Holy Ghost." Haywood's new conviction caused a theological schism between his organization (PAW) and his associates in mainstream Pentecostalism.

With the withdrawal of White ministers from Mason's COGIC to form AG, Haywood remained the only nationally recognized African American closely associated with AG. After accepting the oneness doctrine, he became part of a group of ministers pushing the AG leadership to adopt the new theology. In 1916 the majority of AG leaders roundly rejected oneness and, in a public forum, singled Haywood out for ridicule, stating that the new doctrine amounted to "hay, wood, and stubble," a dual rebuff of the theology and Black leadership.[25] Haywood nonetheless remained fully committed to the new theology and rebaptized his entire congregation (now the largest Pentecostal church in Indiana), including Robert Lawson, whom he also ordained.[26]

Studying and serving under Haywood, Lawson not only was at the center of the oneness Pentecostal movement but also found in Haywood a true "father in the gospel" and a man with whom he had much in common. Both men earned reputations as biblical scholars, powerful preachers, sacred-song composers, and influential religious leaders. Just as Haywood launched his preaching career right after his conversion, so, too, did Lawson. In early 1914 preaching travels took Lawson to the Leavenworth, Kansas, congregation of Herbert Davis, where he met a young preacher, Carrie Fields, and they married before the year was out. Over the next few years, Lawson made a name for himself by establishing churches in St. Louis, Missouri; San Antonio, Texas; and Columbus, Ohio. His religious zeal was rewarded, as he moved up the ranks in PAW. By 1918, of the twenty-one governing field superintendents in the national organization, four were Black: Haywood and Lawson, in Columbus; Floyd I. Douglas, in Louisville; and Alexander R. Schooler, in Cleveland.[27]

Lawson's ascendency in PAW must have made his departure from the organization all the more surprising. His affiliation with PAW ended in 1918 owing to doctrinal disputes with his spiritual father. Haywood approved of women's ordination and believed a presalvation marriage could be dissolved. Lawson disagreed. Lawson also argued for a more conservative presentation of Apostolic women, including covered heads in the sanctuary.[28] Doctrinal disputes were part and parcel of early Pentecostalism, as there was "no meta-model" or established central authority.[29] Pentecostalism has been "too scattered and fluid to support the idea of an original unity," so Lawson leaving Haywood because of exegetical differences may be taken at face value.[30] Nonetheless, as Douglas Jacobsen rightly points out, "Lawson was clearly a better leader than he was a follower, and . . . [it] is telling that [he] was reluctant to join any other existing group" and instead "organized his own new denomination."[31] Perhaps Lawson was also not prepared to adhere to Haywood's silence on the contradictions between racism and Pentecostal theology.

The founding of AG and the public ridicule of Haywood foreshadowed a racial division in Pentecostalism that was in place throughout the United States by 1924. When Lawson split with Haywood in 1918, he was no doubt aware of the changing racial tides within the churches and ready to openly critique those Pentecostal leaders who denounced racial segregation but "tended to collapse the issue of race relations into a broader category of love—an approach that muted the distinctiveness of racism as a specific kind of moral and spiritual failure."[32] Lawson would soon bring a theological critique to racism and racial division in America, which attracted many to the new Harlem-based denomination.

The Lawsons' July move from the Midwest to New York coincided with the bloody "red summer of 1919," when twenty-six cities across the United States erupted in White-led race riots. The optimism of Black soldiers returning victoriously from World War I was promptly dashed by the resurgence of the Ku Klux Klan and increased racial violence, including a spike in lynching.[33] The eugenics movement, which undergirded the violence, had insinuated itself into science, social policy, popular culture, and education. In 1918 Paul Popenoe and Roswell H. Johnson published *Applied Genetics*, advancing theories of the physical and intellectual inferiority of Black people; it soon became the most popular eugenics textbook in the United States.[34] White reactions to Black people's increasing economic, political, and cultural mobilization triggered physical and ideological attacks on Black communities and at the same time strengthened Black resolve to counter repressive forces. In New York the Universal Negro Improvement Association movement, led by Marcus Garvey, was in full swing, with the first International Convention of the Negro Peoples of the World assembling in August 1920 at Madison Square Garden and drawing an overflow crowd of twenty-five thousand.[35] Meanwhile, uptown in the Lawsons' Harlem, a cultural Renaissance was afoot.

In this climate of both racial violence and cultural-political exhilaration in the early 1920s, Lillie Jones, her daughter Grace, and other Harlemites, mostly women, flocked to join the new oneness church of Robert and Carrie Lawson. When they first arrived in New York, the Lawsons briefly joined worship services "in a basement on 40th Street with a precious elderly brother whose name was Glover."[36] From there they went up to the Andersons and Burleighs' home at 56 E. 131st Street, a block from Lillie and her family. As attendance swelled, Lawson opened the "Gospel Tent" at 144th and Lenox Avenue on a corner lot. A photo of the organization's Fifth National Convocation, held in 1924, depicts a few hundred attendees gathered outside the white-top, thousand-square-foot open-air sanctuary, posing to document the occasion. Dark-suited men stand shoulder to shoulder in the first two rows, backed by an array of congregants, mostly hatted women, loosely arranged. The Gospel Tent became the church feeding ground from which the Lawsons launched a successful fund-raising campaign to purchase new quarters. Within a matter of months, the church secured property at 52–54–56 W. 133rd Street; however, the Gospel Tent operated for over three years while needed renovations took place at the new building to accommodate the two hundred–member congregation.

As they settled into the new Refuge Church of Christ, Lawson focused on growing a biblically literate body. He started to "preach up" churches across the greater New York area and in 1926 established the Church of Christ Bible Institute. Evening courses made it possible for women and men in the New York, New Jersey, and Connecticut area to gain proficiency in scripture and doctrine, preparing a religiously educated band to move into other regions and establish churches.[37] Biblical literacy also made it possible for the rank and file to appreciate Lawson's theological writings. "If you want to understand more about the women in the church," Mother Mabel Thomas advised, "you have to read Lawson. . . . Look at *The Anthropology of Jesus*, who was his audience? Look at what he wrote and how he wrote it. Black women had to be able to understand these writings." Then she reiterated, "Yes, you must read *The Anthropology of Jesus* if you want to know more about the women." As I would come to learn, church mothers' reiterations carried multiple meanings. Not only were Black women "able to understand" the writings, but they would also see themselves in his antiracist theology that placed "colored women" at the center of the atonement.

In 1925 Lawson published *The Anthropology of Jesus Our Kinsman (Dedicated to the Glory of God and to the Help of Solving the Race Problem)* and in so doing set himself apart as the first American Pentecostal theologian to link in-depth historical and biblical analyses of race in a critique of racial discrimination.[38] Combining historical, philosophical, and anthropological scholarship and scripture, he sought to overcome "prejudice . . . the greatest enemy of mankind" by digging out the root cause—ignorance.[39] Beyond overcoming prejudice, however, he fought to eradicate White supremacist thought and "the Inferiority Complex . . . in the black race."[40] Marshaling the work of Herodotus, "the father of History [*sic*], an eyewitness"; of Constantin-François Volney; and of Franz Boas, he came to trenchant conclusions.[41] "By the light of modern research," he argued, "it does appear as if white-skinned humanity got its civilization from the black-skinned variety, and even its origin. Volney says: 'To the race of Negroes—the object of our extreme contempt—we owe our arts, science, and even the very use of Speech [*sic*].' "[42] Through Lawson's "corrected racial history of the world" we see a church community participating in early twentieth-century conversations about African diasporic modernity.[43]

Lawson and COOLJC joined James Weldon Johnson, Alain Locke, W. E. B. Du Bois, Marcus Garvey, Loïs Mailou Jones, and other political and cultural activists in unearthing "histories of black contributions to civilization [that] unsettled and decentered Western historical narratives."[44] Along with others in the Black public, they looked to Africa to inform their historical, political, and racial identity. Moreover, fueled by the harsh racial environment, both nationwide and also within Pentecostal churches, Lawson constructed a distinct religious identity by developing a theology grounded in African antiquity. In *The Anthropology of Jesus*, chapters such as "Negro Civilization of Babylon" and "The Hamitic Contribution to the Anthropological Development of Jesus" grant Black people full historical and religious inclusion, countering Pentecostal segregationists.[45] "Our brethren of the white race are laboring under a handicap," Lawson asserts. "Their spiritual condition is deplorable. To see them laboring under the two ideals, once [*sic*] racial and the other spiritual, trying to adjust themselves according to two different principles, makes them cowards in one sense and hypocritical in another."[46] Like many Black theologians and adherents, Lawson identified racism as a moral issue at odds with Christian ethics. By establishing an antiracist theology, he also hoped to eradicate the racist attitudes of White Christian missionaries outside of America—a hindrance to "building the Kingdom." Charging that "color prejudice" had caused the Christian missionary movement to come to a "standstill in India, China, Japan and Africa," he argued that "the darker races" reject "a gospel of love and brotherhood when the denial of their essential manhood by Christian people negatives [*sic*] the tenets which they are asked to accept."[47]

Lawson's central theological argument that placed "the darker races" in the Christian body states that God had deliberately created a mixed bloodline in Jesus—Hamitic, Semitic, and Japhetic. Tracing the Hamitic genealogy of Jesus through the Old and New Testament, he argues that Mary, the progeny of David and the tribe of Judah, descended in part from "two Negro [Canaanite] women," Shuar, the wife of Judah, and Tamar, Judah's daughter-in-law, who bore twins by him. Lawson further identifies Rahab, a "harlot," the mother of Boaz and great-great-grandmother of King David, as "the next colored woman who gave her blood into the royal line."[48] Finally, he identifies Bathsheba, Solomon's mother, as an equally important contributor to the Hamitic lineage of Jesus. Thus, he maintains, "if any race have whereof to boast as touching things of the flesh, relative to our Lord Jesus Christ, the colored race has more, for they gave to the world the two mothers of the tribe of Judah, out of which Christ came. . . . The fact that Christ had Negro blood in him is vitally connected with our redemption through Calvary."[49] If all three races contributed to the ethnic lineage of Jesus, then the atonement was for all, giving equal access to his salvation and blessings.

Lawson's reading of the body of Christ as divinely multiracial struck a blow at "the pseudo-scientific teaching of the day . . . in regard to miscegenation," which had become pervasive within popular culture, social science, and law.[50] Through deliberate intermarriage, he argued, God "intensified" the strong "psychic and spiritual" traits of Abraham, "the Semitic contribution to the anthropological development of Jesus Christ," while Hamitic women contributed their "warm, loving, peaceful, sympathetic, and moral" nature to Christ's lineage. Here Lawson also promoted ideal female attributes that holy women should aspire to, indicating that they were qualities of the one God-Jesus—at once human and divine—which must have had a profound impact on his predominantly Black female following. Not only did Christ arrive via the body of a woman, but his theology also, by racial and gendered association, placed Black women *in* the body of Christ. The "Negro blood" of Jesus flowed by way of women's veins. Black women did not merely have access to salvation; rather, the blood Jesus shed on the cross *was* their blood, placing them at the center of the atonement. (Reprints in the COOLJC organizational journal, in 1949 and 2000, show that Lawson's theology is not just of archival interest but has been carried forward into late twentieth- and early twenty-first-century Apostolic hermeneutics and identity.)[51]

Even though the blood of "Negro" women runs through Christ, Lawson believed that elevation to deacon, minister, elder, and beyond was the province of men. Yet their inability to move into positions of formal power did not dampen women's enthusiasm for Lawson and COOLJC. In addition to his keen intellect and distinctive theology, members were drawn to Lawson's spiritual aptitude. Church mothers raised under Lawson described him as "powerful." "When he walked down the church aisles," one church mother recently recalled, "the Lord would direct him. . . . [He] could just go and lay hands and [people] would start speaking in tongues." The pragmatic and race-conscious social gospel of Lawson also appealed to followers, as he developed and maintained an active political and civic presence that linked theology and racial-economic justice. "In practical Christian technique," he argued, "the approach to one in need of help—and God knows we are all in need of some form of help—should not be with the question where shall one spend eternity, but where shall one spend the night?"[52]

His holistic approach to church building included civic participation and racial economic self-reliance through business ventures that served the Harlem community.[53] Over the course of the 1930s, Lawson opened a printing company and three funeral parlors, and he purchased an apartment building on 132nd Street and a grocery store across the street from the church, the proceeds of which went to "the poor of his parish to alleviate suffering."[54] Members took pride in belonging to COOLJC. "In Harlem people knew who he was," a church mother remembered. "You could walk home at two o'clock in the morning, and they would say, 'Don't bother them, they're from Lawson's church.'" His move to the airwaves in 1932, however, significantly enlarged the COOLJC presence. After short stints on WGBS, WHOM, and WINS, he finally found a home with WBNX, where he remained for over three decades.[55] Radio also elevated the profile of Lawson's wife, Mother Lawson.

THE PRAYING MOTHER OF THE AIR

Dubbed the "Praying Mother of the Air," Mother Lawson became known for holy petitions, a feature of the popular COOLJC Sunday night radio broadcast. Yet, like so many highly regarded women in COOLJC, printed historical material about her life is minimal. Spellman and Thomas devote one and a half pages to her in *The Life, Legend and Legacy of Bishop R. C. Lawson*, describing her as "that prayerful source of strength behind Bishop Lawson . . . a quiet humble woman who you did not see in public that much except for when she was praying on the broadcast."[56] The portrayal of Mother Lawson highlights her life as wife, mother, and "homemaker to the greatest degree." Noting that she "saw much of her role in the ministry as providing for her family," Spellman and Thomas devote most of their ink to detailing the work and attitude of a religious superwoman—rising early to go the market and "carry[ing] the heavy groceries back by herself."[57]

"The Legend of Carrie F. Lawson," as the section is titled, sheds no light on her years before she married Robert Lawson in 1914, except that she "hailed from Leavenworth, Kansas." The census of 1895, however, shows her family living in Tonganoxie, Kansas, when she was three years old, with relatives listed as her father, Kellie, twenty-six; mother, Anna, twenty-one; brothers, Joe, eleven, and George, eight; and sister, Marie, one and a half.[58] By 1914 she was in Leavenworth attending the PAW church where she met Robert, a visiting preacher.[59] Details of Carrie Fields's move to Leavenworth (twenty miles northeast of Tonganoxie), her baptism in the Spirit, and her road to becoming a preacher remain obscure. Spellman and Thomas do, nonetheless, indicate the importance of Mother Lawson to COOLJC. "Mother Carrie F. Lawson," states the penultimate sentence of the biographical sketch, "will always be a giant personality in the history of the Church of Our Lord Jesus Christ."[60]

Church mothers recently remembered her as "a very prayerful woman," "understanding" and "never too busy to where she couldn't listen to you." They were careful to point out her work in building the church. She was "very good in the tarrying room," spending hours praying with those seeking Holy Ghost baptism. One mother offered, "She tarried when my mother got saved." A paragraph near the end of the Spellman and Thomas text highlights other qualities that no doubt directly influenced the ways in which the church operated and, perhaps, also the theological perspectives and the public strategies that Bishop Lawson undertook in building the civically engaged denomination. "Mother Carrie F. Lawson functioned as Bishop Lawson's chief advisor, alter-ego and trusted visionary," they reveal.[61] Bishop Lawson and the church benefited from her "keen insight into the problems and the needs of the saints. She could be seen whispering in his ear or talking privately.... Bishop Lawson would always listen with attention and respect.... She could see things from her vantage point that he could not see."[62] Church mothers shed light on the meaning of "her vantage point." "Mother Lawson was very spiritual—consecrated," one woman recalled. "She always sat in the back of the church," another remembered, "so she could see everybody and what was happening. She had an overview of the church." They noted that that was unusual, as most pastors' wives sit in the front of the sanctuary during services. Too, her specific insight may have come from "never [being] too busy to ... listen" as congregants sought her counsel.

Mother Lawson's influence extended throughout the greater New York area, as far as WBNX radio carried her prayers, evidenced by the public's response to her passing in 1948. Twelve thousand mourners flocked to the Harlem church for the four-and-a-half-hour homegoing service, with most crowding the Harlem streets outside the church.[63] The night before, over seven thousand people came to view her lying in "a copper casket, interlined with white crushed velvet, and covered with a glass top."[64] Everything was white. A white orchid was pinned to the left shoulder of Mother

Lawson's white crepe gown. "A blanket of white roses" covered the lower section of her casket. It took "85 white-robed members" to carry the volumes of flowers out to five funeral cars for transport in the funeral parade.[65] There is no way to know how many of the twelve thousand mourners had ever attended church services, just as there's no way to know how many thousands more had been touched by the "Praying Mother's" on-air petitions and did not come to her funeral. High attendance at the final rites for Mother Lawson reflected her stature in the wider community, while the grandeur showed the honor bestowed on her by the saints. Over the course of the sixteen years that Mother Lawson prayed on the air (1932–1948), while Bishop Lawson engaged the community religiously, politically, and economically, both Refuge Church in Harlem and also the organization expanded considerably.

HARLEM AND BEYOND

The first major project that took the church beyond Harlem occurred in the early 1930s when Lawson opened the Industrial Union Institute and Training School (later renamed the R. C. Lawson Institute) in Southern Pines, North Carolina. His stated mission was "to encourage, promote and disseminate among the people of the United States, West Indies, and Canada racial and such other essential principles as will severally ameliorate their conditions . . . and . . . to enhance their moral, intellectual, industrial and mechanical condition in general."[66] The institute followed in the tradition of the COGIC Saints Industrial School, established in Lexington, Mississippi, in 1918, as well as an earlier training school for girls in Washington, D.C., founded by Nannie Helen Burroughs in 1909.[67] The Southern Pines project, however, in addition to providing religious and technical training, placed race consciousness at the center. It proposed "to unite the race in America, its dependencies, to open branches where all well disposed boys and girls may be taught trades of some kind and improve the general condition of the races everywhere."[68] Uniting "the race" extended past U.S. borders, as church workers moved into the foreign field, territory to which Lawson was eager to bring the message of salvation. By the mid-1930s COOLJC had churches in Saint Kitts, Antigua, and Saint Thomas (in the Virgin Islands), established by Charles Michael; and in Trinidad, started by Sister Frederica C. Johnson. In 1938 Aaron and Pearl Holmes established the first African mission in Liberia.

Lawson and COOLJC enjoyed extensive press coverage as well. His early years of church building in the Midwest may have been pivotal in keeping Black newspapers attuned to his activities once headquartered in New York. Throughout the 1920s and 1930s, articles in the *Negro Star, Afro-American, Plaindealer, Chicago Defender,* and *New York Amsterdam News* no doubt assisted the denomination's expansion, as they reported on the religious, political, and economic pursuits of COOLJC.[69] By the mid-1930s, the *Chicago Defender* reported that the organization had expanded to include ninety-five churches.[70] The W. 133rd Street location, with a capacity of a thousand people, was overflowing. Large numbers of worshippers, unable to fit in the sanctuary, "had to listen [to services] over the amplifier downstairs in the Guild Room."[71] A church mother recently remembered, "People used to come to Refuge just to hear Bishop sing and to hear Mother Carrie Lawson pray." On Sunday evenings, crowds would assemble around six thirty to get seated for the broadcast service that began at nine thirty. In 1945, three years before Carrie Lawson's death, Bishop Lawson secured a large corner property at 124th Street and 7th Avenue (now Adam Clayton Powell Boulevard) from the Loews Theatrical Corporation to house Greater Refuge Temple. The new sanctuary, with two large and five small balconies, held thirty-five hundred worshippers, and twenty-one rooms behind the pulpit accommodated choir rehearsals, prayer rooms, and offices.

Following the death of Mother Lawson in 1948, Bishop Lawson continued church expansion, as well as civic and political activities, until his death in 1961. Unclassified Federal Bureau of Investigation surveillance documents report his participation in a Harlem meeting in 1949 that protested race riots in Peekskill, New York.[72] White mobs had disrupted a scheduled performance by Paul Robeson, the world-renowned Black actor, singer, and renaissance man. At a subsequent mass gathering in Harlem, Lawson stated, "I am going back [to Peekskill] . . . and [will] hold a meeting, because I am fighting the evil that broke out in my home."[73] Lawson was referring to his Scrub Oak residence, six miles east of Peekskill. Along with a family residence, the sixty acres held "a 20-room summer inn, a cattle barn, a grocery store and bungalows."[74] Known as Lawsonville, the upstate New York settlement provided leisure space for Black people excluded from other Catskill-area resorts.

Lawson's repute as a "race man" prompted organizers to request his participation in the Prayer Pilgrimage for Freedom in Washington, D.C., in 1957. This gathering of thirty-five thousand people at the Lincoln Memorial on

May 17 was a precursor to the massive March on Washington for Jobs and Freedom that would take place six years later.[75] The cochairs of the Prayer Pilgrimage—A. Philip Randolph, president of the Brotherhood of Sleeping Car Porters AFL-CIO; Rev. Martin Luther King Jr., president of the Southern Leaders Conference; and Roy Wilkens, executive secretary of the NAACP—called on national religious and political leaders to gather at the three-year anniversary of *Brown v. Board of Education* to "give thanks for the progress to date, and pray for the wiping out of the evils that still beset our nation."[76] This understudied, yet significant, march had civil rights icons Ella Baker and Bayard Rustin serving as organizers. According to the program of events, Bishop Lawson delivered a scripture reading after a solo by gospel luminary Mahalia Jackson.[77]

Just as Lawson valued working with prominent Black political, cultural, and religious figures nationally, he also appreciated making international connections. His first foreign excursion took him across Europe—to England, France, Germany, and Italy—and culminated in a visit to the Holy Land. Throughout the 1940s and 1950s, the work of missionaries in the foreign field afforded him the opportunity to dedicate churches in the Caribbean and to travel to minister to budding congregations in Liberia and Sierra Leone. In 1950 Bishop Lawson embarked on a world voyage that took him to southern Europe, the Middle East, North Africa, and Asia. In India he, "as the representative of 15 million colored people of America," placed a wreath at the grave of Mahatma Gandhi to honor "the most noble" Gandhi.[78]

Travels to North Africa opened the way for an ongoing association with Emperor Haile Selassie. In 1951 the Ethiopian government granted an endowment to Lawson's Southern Pines institute to teach Amharic.[79] Three years later, during a visit to New York, Selassie conferred the Star of Ethiopia Medal on Bishop Lawson, Congressman Adam Clayton Powell Jr., Walter White of the NAACP, Manhattan borough president Hulan Jack, and James R. Lawson (no relation) of the United African Nationalist Movement.[80] Refuge mothers talked about Lawson's civic and political activities with pride. "He was *involved* in the community," one woman said. "He even hosted Eisenhower in 1952 [when he came to Harlem]."[81]

In the midst of all his international and national activities, Bishop Lawson managed to remarry. In 1952, four years after the passing of Mother Carrie Lawson, Evelyn K. (Burke) Lawson became the new first lady of COOLJC. Ironically, like Carrie Fields Lawson, she, too, relinquished her standing as a preacher with PAW to marry. Official church history is silent about Evelyn, but the Refuge mothers were not. One morning I sat with three of them, and they described the second Mrs. Lawson. "The next lady, Evelyn Lawson, she was nice," explained one mother, "but we didn't accept her too much. We could *never* call her Mother Lawson. She was always Sister Lawson," while some of the younger members called her "New Ma." They remembered her as "very intelligent" and "considerate," even as she faced the challenge of "people always trying to compare her [to Carrie Lawson]." They also pointed out "her concession" in giving up preaching in order to marry Lawson. "But," one mother revealed, "on Saturday night she still used to preach after young people's service. She didn't call it preaching. But she said whatever she wanted to say in the way she wanted to say it. She would pray for the people if she wanted to. . . . [And] she was *very* good!"

Evelyn Lawson was so good, in fact, that "other pastors would invite her and she ran revivals." I asked how she could do that, given that COOLJC doctrine prohibited women from preaching (and especially since she was Lawson's wife!). They explained that a woman could speak as "a missionary." One of the women said, "They wouldn't use the term *evangelist*. They would just say, 'She's the speaker,' and then she's got free rein to speak on whatever. But she's *the* speaker of that night. . . . A lot of women did that." Another mother clarified further, "But Sister Lawson wasn't the only woman running revivals. There were others. Well, not at Refuge Temple but at other churches. But they definitely were not the *pastor*. That was the main thing." It's unclear how "Sister Lawson" referred to herself, but a New York newspaper, reporting on a weeklong "successful Salvation Healing Revival and Campaign," identified her as "Evangelist Evelyn K. Lawson, . . . wife of Bishop Robert C. Lawson of Refuge Temple."[82]

The distinction between preaching and teaching is that women may not exert organizational-political authority over men. Preaching is understood as the work of men who have been ordained as ministers or pastors by COOLJC, whereas both men and women can teach. As the activities of Evelyn Lawson show, the boundaries of ritual authority remain ambiguous. Although she had given up being called a preacher to marry Lawson and join COOLJC, women recognized her Saturday night orations as preaching. Perhaps official church history remains silent about Evelyn Lawson because her public persona highlights ambiguities within church doctrine, rhetoric, and practice. Robert Lawson was clear about women being ordained or pastoring churches: it was prohibited. He nonetheless acknowledged and, if his spouses are any indication, valued spiritually powerful women. One of the Refuge mothers explained the ways many women experienced the "Lawson era." "Actually under Bishop Lawson we were very free," she maintained. "We just basically knew what the limits were. You didn't want to go out of the rhythm . . . because you respected yourself. Why would you want to go out of the Word of God? The Bible talks about the place of women and he would preach on it, 'The Proper Place of Women in the New Testament Church.' And you tried to follow the Bible, and you loved him and respected him." That members "basically knew . . . the limits" suggests spaces of complexity and room for interpretation.

SCHISMS, TRANSITIONS, AND NEW STRUCTURES

While many did not "want to go out of the rhythm," some men who disputed points of doctrine or who sought definitive organizational authority did "go out of the rhythm," splitting off from COOLJC to form other denominations. In 1933 Sherrod C. Johnson, the state overseer for North Carolina, charged that Lawson held too liberal a position on women's attire. Johnson argued that the appropriate presentation for holy women meant cotton stockings, no makeup, and unstraightened hair. In contrast, COOLJC allowed women to straighten their hair. Johnson moved to Philadelphia and founded the Church of *the* Lord Jesus Christ of the Apostolic Faith, Inc. (emphasis added).[83] Ironically, in addition to Lawson's objections to the ordination of women, their presentation had been at the heart of his split with Haywood fifteen years earlier. At that time, Lawson argued that women should wear head coverings in the sanctuary, which Haywood did not require.

Other splits occurred within COOLJC in response to Lawson's authority over other men. The first happened early in the church's history. In 1927 Henry Chauncey Brooks pulled his Washington, D.C., congregation out of COOLJC to form the Way of the Cross Church of Christ, Inc. He had taken offense at Lawson's suggestion to merge Brooks's body with another Washington, D.C., congregation, that one headed by Smallwood E. Williams.[84] The most consequential fracture, however, occurred in 1957, when Williams, pastor of the second-largest congregation in COOLJC, and several other high-profile pastors left to form the Bible Way Church of Our Lord Jesus Christ World-Wide, Inc.[85] Exasperated by Lawson's refusal to elevate any men to the bishopric, the dissenters charged Lawson with an "authoritarianism, which could no longer be tolerated."[86] A total of seventy congregations left

COOLJC, which was by far the most substantial exodus, both because of its scale and also because of Williams's involvement; he had seemed positioned to be Lawson's successor. The schism reportedly caused a "deep wound in the heart of Bishop [Lawson]"; nevertheless, he carried on as the sole prelate until his death four years later.[87]

With the passing of Bishop Lawson in July 1961, Bishop William Lee Bonner of Michigan, who was also the executive secretary of COOLJC, took the helm as pastor of the Harlem church, and the organization addressed the replacement of the denominational leadership at the annual convention in August. At that time Bonner recommended, and the organization began implementing, a new governance structure—a form of episcopal polity consisting of a board of presbyters, a board of bishops, and a three-man board of apostles that would oversee the organization. Bonner submitted that Bishop Lawson could not be "duplicated by any personality"; therefore, the new hierarchy was needed to keep the organization viable. As it turned out, the new governance also served particular needs of the minority male population by providing ladders for formal elevation and recognition. All men entered the church as "brothers" and, through service and ordination, could follow the trajectory from deacon, through minister, elder, and bishop, to apostle. Organizing men's operations into boards of presbyters, bishops, and apostles set up the pipeline for men to formally advance. Today, each board benefits from representation on the all-male executive board, the church's highest advisory board to the Board of Apostles—the final decision-making body.

With Bonner's new structure in place, Apostle Hubert Spencer of Ohio was installed to serve as the presiding apostle and did so until his death in 1974, at which time Bonner took the helm. Spencer's greatest contribution, according to Spellman and Thomas, was that "[he] held the Organization [sic] together during its transitional period after the death of Bishop Lawson."[88] They may view Spencer's twelve-year term as "transitional" because it bridged the Lawson governance model and the episcopate of today. Also, Spencer's term was relatively brief, given that Lawson headed COOLJC for forty-two years and Bonner stayed at the head of the organization for over forty years. Bonner held the office of presider until 1995, at which time he established and occupied the lifetime office of chief apostle. The office of presider now carries a three-year term with a two-term limit.

Throughout the 1970s Bishop Bonner conducted a campaign to further expand formal leadership opportunities for the men in the organization.

He subdivided large states into smaller diocese, opening the way for installation of district elders and junior bishops to oversee the new regions. He then appointed administrative assistants to aid each apostle, bishop, or elder heading a department—such as Sunday school, education, and home and foreign missions. The Board of Apostles has since expanded to twelve members, each overseeing a multistate or international region, and five "honorary apostle" positions.

In response to the increase in men's positions, Bishop Bonner's wife, Lady Ethel Mae Bonner, reinvigorated the Ministers' and Deacons' Wives Guild in 1972 to give much-needed support to an increasing population of women with husbands in leadership.[89] Evelyn Lawson had originated the guild in 1956, but it had been set up to serve fewer spouses and was not prepared to meet the needs of women under the new governance structure (see chapter 3). Lady Bonner was well acquainted with the workings of the church and well established within the women's networks. She was a third-generation member of COOLJC, the granddaughter of Lillie Jones, who had joined the church in 1919, and the daughter of Grace Hill, who had served as secretary of the Missionary Department in the 1920s and had co-founded the Women's Council in 1952. Lady Bonner also garnered respect from the women because of her educational achievements, having attended Hunter College High School and then Hunter College, earning a bachelor's degree in the early 1940s. After college she had difficulty finding a job befitting her qualifications, so Bishop Lawson took her into his employ, as secretary and manager of the Church of Christ Bookstore.[90] She met William Bonner when Bishop Lawson hired him as a chauffeur.

William Bonner had not been in New York long. He had been born in 1921 to Emmett and Janie Bonner in the rural, segregated, sharecropping community of Milledgeville, Georgia.[91] Like many children in poor farming families, he and his four siblings attended school for six months each year and farmed during the other six months. Bonner disliked farmwork immensely and found construction work that took him to Atlanta. There he joined a small COOLJC church and soon after traveled to a national convention in New York, where he first encountered Bishop Lawson. Lawson so impressed Bonner that he did not return to Atlanta. Bonner recalls that hearing Lawson speak convinced him "it was God's will that I should be blessed by this man. . . . I attached myself to him and made myself available to him. . . . I was anxious to serve him."[92] And serve him he did.

Bonner became Lawson's driver for twenty dollars per week, chauffeuring Lawson to engagements along the Eastern Seaboard and locally between Lawson's homes in Scrub Oak and Harlem. During his time working as Lawson's chauffeur, Bonner was installed as assistant pastor at the 133rd Street Refuge Temple, and later as junior pastor at a Brooklyn church. Contrary to observations by Refuge mothers that "anybody that knew [Lawson] just loved him," Bonner describes his relationship with his boss as antagonistic, partly owing to Lawson's demanding nature. "I was always at his beck and call," Bonner states. "I could make few plans of my own. . . . Bishop Lawson and I had quite a few arguments about being ready when he wanted to go."[93]

Tensions between Lawson and Bonner intensified when Bonner started dating Ethel Mae Smith, his future wife and Lawson's secretary. He maintains that Lawson encouraged their courtship, then "had a sudden change of mind. . . . I saw Bishop trying to pull us apart. Even Mother [Carrie] Lawson . . . tried to pull us apart. She began saying things like the marriage wouldn't work and we wouldn't get along."[94] A Refuge mother recently disclosed, "Lawson didn't approve of the union because [Ethel Mae] had a degree from Hunter College and [Bonner] didn't have a high school diploma. Not that [Lawson] had anything against *her*. . . . He was a firm believer in education, but he didn't think they would get along. They were mismatched." Perhaps Bishop and Mother Lawson's displeasure was akin to the upset of parents when they disagree with a daughter's choices; Ethel Mae had grown up under the spiritual guidance of the Lawsons. Also, when Ethel Mae and William met, she was engaged to a young man serving in the military. She ended that engagement and, in 1944, married William. Within two years, Lawson appointed him to pastor a church in Detroit, and the couple and their newborn daughter relocated.

Lady Bonner went on to receive a master's in education from Wayne State University in Detroit and a doctor of sacred literature degree from the Christian Theological Seminary in Indianapolis. As an educator, she taught in Detroit public schools and later at the Church of Christ Bible Institute in New York. The Refuge mothers recently described Lady Bonner as "very smart" and "very wise," as well as "a good teacher." "You could learn things from her," one mother said. She then went on to reveal, "She taught her husband how to speak. He was from Georgia, and I didn't even want to hear him talk." After a few years of marriage, Bonner "spoke such lovely English. . . .

She taught him beautifully." The mothers thus unknowingly explained a cryptic line in an issue of the church publication, *The Contender for the Faith Magazine* that paid tribute to Lady Bonner. "As a housewife, pastor's wife, mother, Jr High School teacher [*sic*], and church worker," it begins, "Lady Bonner juggled each role with grace, precision, and style. *She was a strict advocate of excellence in speaking diction.*"[95] Along with being an effective teacher, Lady Bonner proved to be a skilled administrator, as the principal of the R. C. Lawson Institute in Southern Pines, North Carolina, as well as the head of curriculum development and teacher training programs for the R. C. Lawson Institute in Liberia, where she stayed for over two years during the mid-1970s. Known as an advocate for women, she named buildings in the Liberian complex after some who had labored for the church—Sister Isa Winans, Sister Willette Price, Mother Frances Canady, and Margaret Giles Johnson.[96]

Whereas Lady Bonner focused on education and on organizing (and memorializing) women, Bishop Bonner turned his attention to remodeling existing churches, constructing new edifices, and developing new congregations. His first project, "a vision for a new 'Mother Church,'" involved completely remodeling the Harlem Refuge Temple.[97] With new churches constructed in Detroit, Michigan, and Jackson, Mississippi, as well as school-church complexes in West Africa and the Caribbean, "people began to characterize him as the 'great builder.'"[98] As well as constructing new churches, he also served as pastor for a few churches. By the early 1990s, in addition to the Harlem church, he oversaw congregations in Jackson, Mississippi; Columbia, South Carolina; and Washington, D.C. He also continued leading Solomon's Temple in Detroit. One outcome of his overall strategy was a lower national profile for the organization than under Lawson, evidenced by the considerable decrease in print media coverage of the organization. Nonetheless, in the stories that were published, Bishop and Lady Bonner, like Lawson, emerge as promoting Black civic, social, and economic concerns.[99]

Even as Bonner and Lawson operated from like positions of race consciousness, they were very different men. Lawson struck an imposing, cosmopolitan, and outgoing figure, whereas Bonner exuded a more provincial demeanor, less traveled and less intellectually curious. While Lawson had belonged to ecumenical organizations and moved in highly influential circles, Bonner was more comfortable turning the church inward. "I have been invited to join various international groups across the country," he told the church in 1988, "and I have flatly refused." He went on to assert that joining other groups opened the church up to becoming "part of their rule book." He expressed concern that COOLJC would be "absorbed" by other groups if they associated too closely with them.[100]

In conversation, Refuge Mothers Etta Samuels, Jane Peters, and Margaret Batson talked about how they experienced the change in leadership from Lawson to Bonner. (Bishop Spencer, who led COOLJC for twelve years between Lawson and Bonner, according to church history, was a "transitional" leader based on the time he served and the manner in which he bridged the Lawson and Bonner eras.) The mothers detailed shifts in church structure and operations under Bonner—changes not reported in the official church history. What follows is the discussion that ensued when I asked them to describe some of the differences in "sitting under" Bishop Lawson and Bishop Bonner. "Bishop Lawson built souls, and Bonner built buildings," Mother Batson said without hesitation. Mothers Peters and Samuels, speaking at the same time, responded, "Well, *exactly!* She put it right!"

MOTHER PETERS: Souls . . . souls to last.

MOTHER SAMUELS: Bonner's legacy is buildings—build, build, build.

MOTHER PETERS: When Bonner first came in, his influence wasn't as big as it is now. Now it's all encompassing. It's really dictatorial.

MOTHER SAMUELS: When he first started it wasn't like that. He wanted to be the head, but he was not the head for twelve years.

MOTHER PETERS: [Lawson] was not that dictatorial. Everything was done in open meetings. . . . Catechism [for ordination], it was in the open. . . . Now it's all in the back room. You don't know if the person really passed or not. That changed when Bishop Spencer died and Bishop Bonner became the presider. As long as Bishop Spencer was alive, it [continued to be] done in the [sanctuary]. You could learn the questions and doctrine of the organization . . . sitting in the catechism. . . . If there was a meeting of the executive session, the women could participate. You can't do that now. . . . If they had a vote, you raised your hand, and you voted. You could get up, and you could speak. It wasn't just for the men, or the pastors, or the ministers. It was for the whole organization. But now everything is done in a *room.* And when they taught lessons they didn't have any special lessons for bishops. If they had a seminar [anyone could] go in, sit down, take the paper, and ask questions. It was open. There were no secret meetings. And that changed with Bishop Bonner. It changed a lot. Now bishops have their own meetings with themselves. Now elders have their own meetings with themselves.

JUDITH: Why do you think it changed?

MOTHER PETERS: I think they were fearful of the women.

MOTHER SAMUELS: You cannot speak your mind. If you speak your mind, you're in the doghouse.

MOTHER PETERS: And you stay in the doghouse forever.

MOTHER SAMUELS: You never come out the doghouse. Whatever he says goes.

MOTHER PETERS: A lot of people don't want to hear the truth, but *this is the truth*. . . . Well, the truth is the light. This *is* the way the organization ran. . . . The ones who are new haven't lived under freedom. They don't know what it's like to . . . have your own mind.

MOTHER SAMUELS: Bonner is the chief [now], and you have to abide under his rules. . . . But he is *human*. God gives him the message when he gets up there to preach. When the message is over, he is Bonner. Just like I'm a woman, he's a man. You eat the fish and spit out the bone. . . . I know who he is. I respect who he is because you have to respect leadership.

MOTHER BATSON: But there's no closeness. With Lawson you could always talk to him. If he saw you and you looked like something was wrong, he would ask you what's the matter. You could go to his office without an appointment and say, "I want to talk to Bishop." We called him Pops. "I want to talk to Pops."

MOTHER SAMUELS: One time I said to Bishop Bonner, "Do you know my name?" He says, "Ha, ha, ha. I don't have to." And I said politely, "Then I don't have to give you my money either." That was it.

As time passes, the church community will most likely forget the oral accounts of women about challenges in transitioning to new leadership, and its impact on the ways they operate within the organization. Within male-headed Black Pentecostal organizations, women's "oral tradition is militant, [while] their written tradition is indulgent, eschewing overt conflict."[101] The church code of behavior demands that saints "abide under [the bishop's] rules . . . because you have to respect leadership." When they disagree with leadership, they "assert their economic and structural importance" by reducing financial support, as Mother Samuels indicated.[102]

These Refuge mothers represent a portion of membership dissatisfied with the leadership of Bishop Bonner. Most members, however, loved Bishop Bonner and held him in the highest regard. Under Bonner's stewardship, COOLJC grew, although an accurate count of churches has been difficult to ascertain. The COOLJC website states that, under Bonner, the denomination grew "from 155 churches in 1961 to over 500 churches and missions throughout the world."[103] Spellman and Thomas state that in 1961 "approximately 217 churches" belonged to the organization. Their analysis of church growth between 1961 and 1983 (the publication date of the text) relies on COOLJC minute books, the annual convocation reports. They conclude that in 1983 "there were close to 300 churches in the body."[104] Fourteen years earlier, however, on its fiftieth anniversary in 1969, COOLJC reported three hundred churches in twenty-seven states.[105] According to the minute books between 2004 and 2012, the number of churches in the organization has fluctuated between 272 and 343.[106]

From 1961 to 1974, Spencer maintained much of the status quo, which may have stabilized COOLJC immediately following the death of Bishop Lawson. Bonner, on the other hand, opened up administrative positions, addressing the grievances of disgruntled male leaders who had left the organization. His vision of a restructured body may have prevented further splits; however, an in-depth analysis of local, regional, national, and international church documentation that could shed light on COOLJC growth patterns over the past nine decades is beyond the scope of this study. Whether or not the organizational restructuring and new leadership style implemented in the 1970s promoted, hampered, or had no impact on the growth of the denomination remains unclear.

Nonetheless, COOLJC is now the third-largest U.S.-based Black oneness denomination, reporting 55,000 members.[107] The highest membership, 1.5 million, is claimed by PAW, with a third in foreign congregations, while International Bible Way Churches of Our Lord Jesus Christ is the second-largest oneness group, with 300,000 members in the United States.[108] We can also understand the significance of COOLJC by the numbers of denominations tracing their lineage back to the organization. While International Bible Way (above) is the largest, others include Way of the Cross Church of Christ (founded in 1927 by Brooks), the Church of the Lord Jesus Christ of the Apostolic Faith (founded in 1933 by Johnson), and Bible Way Church of Our Lord Jesus Christ World-Wide (founded in 1957 by Williams).[109] As well, numerous independent churches trace their religious roots back to Robert Lawson.[110] As of 2000, U.S. Black Apostolic or oneness Pentecostals totaled over 2.9 million and are projected to number over 4.9 million by 2025.[111] Black Trinitarian members in the United States numbered 7.6 million in 2000 and are projected to reach 11.6 million by 2025.[112] Growth in Apostolic adherents can be seen in independent churches, as well as those belonging to the various denominations. Also, as we will see, individual churches have continued to be built up under the banner of COOLJC. We now turn to one in Queens, New York.

TDC

Bishop Crosley J. Cook founded TDC with his wife and "helpmeet," Mother Reva E. Cook, in 1975. "When Mother Cook and I started True Deliverance," he explained, "we had a little [money] and invested everything." They had sold their deli-grocery store in Queens, New York, and were "retiring to Florida."[113] On the drive down, "the Lord told me to . . . come back to New York and start a ministry." Mother Cook told him that he could count on her support "as long [he] stayed in the Lord," so they "turned the car around." The Cooks found suitable property, situated on a busy commercial Queens thoroughfare, acquired thirty-year financing, and "burned [the mortgage] in nine years." It was a storefront with gray cement floors and roll-down gates over a glass-windowed front. They brought in metal folding chairs to accommodate worshippers. The cement floors are now dressed in burgundy carpeting, while matching seat cushions cover rows of oak pews that can seat over two hundred worshippers. Burgundy curtains hang on brass railings on the front of the elevated dais, which holds, at center, an oaken pulpit lectern. Elaborate high-backed chairs are positioned behind and to the left of the lectern, and choir pews (which cover the baptismal pool) are on the right. Directly in front of the choir pews, on the sanctuary floor, sits a full drum set and Hammond B-3 organ. A grand piano sits on the left side of the sanctuary, opposite the organ.

The two-story storefront has undergone extensive renovations over the years. Yellow-brick facing has replaced the full windows and metal gates. Over the double-door main entrance, a seven-foot by three-and-a-half-foot lit cross announces, "True, Apostolic Deliverance Church," with the first two words running vertically and the second two running horizontally. Below the cross and immediately above the door, a large painted sign asserts, *"The Church with the Old Time Power"—Blessings • Miracles • Healings • True Love; Pastor and Founder, Bishop Crosley J. Cook; Chief Apostle, Bishop W. Bonner; Establishmentarian, Bishop R. C. Lawson; Christian School opening September 2003—Day Care (3 months) to 7th Grade (12 years).* "True Deliverance grew," said Bishop Cook, "from zero . . . to what it is today," which is 110 tithe-paying adult members, while saved and unsaved children add significant numbers to the congregation. On big holidays, such as Resurrection Day (Easter), Pentecost Sunday, and Watch Night (New Year's Eve), worshippers can number over 250, with the overflow sitting in folding chairs in the aisles and side foyer.

After purchasing the church building, the Cooks continued to acquire properties in the surrounding neighborhood, increasing the assets of the church to over $5 million.[114] In addition to the church, real estate holdings include three multifamily residential properties, a commercial-residential property next door to the church, and, a few blocks away, a $1 million Christian school facility, built from the ground up, housing preschool through eighth-grade students. Members noted that the church acquired most of its property "because of Mother Cook," who passed away in 1995.[115] "She would see a 'for sale' sign and come back and tell Bishop Cook, 'Oh, we've got to get it,'" recalled Sister Stephanie Dean, vice president of the Usher Board, who came to TDC in her teens. For nearly thirty years Sister Dean had witnessed "God bless[ing] the church . . . because [the Cooks] were a team, . . . they pulled together." Her observation of the couple's teamwork described how Bishop and Mother Cook had been operating from the beginning of their relationship.

Crosley J. Cook and Reva E. Straghn met at Bethel Church in Corona, New York, in the mid-1950s. She had come to New York from Miami Beach, Florida, in 1947, when she was twenty-three years old. A few years after her arrival, she joined Bethel and received the Holy Ghost. Crosley hailed from Darlington, South Carolina, a World War II veteran and college graduate. ("I studied science," he said. "I wanted to be a doctor, but the Lord didn't have that in mind for me. He let me know.") Dismal prospects in the South pushed him to New York, where he secured a job with the Veteran's Administration. There he met Brother Lytle, who had received the Holy Ghost a few years earlier, "listening to Mother Lawson praying over the air." Brother Lytle brought Crosley to Bethel Church, where he first met Reva.

Crosley and Reva made no connection at that time but met again a few years later at Zion Church. "That's where I was saved, at Zion Church under Bishop Shields," he said. "That's where our relationship developed. She wouldn't marry me until I was saved. She tarried with me to be saved." During his initial "infilling," unbeknownst to him, "I was preaching in the Spirit [in tongues]." Reva had the gift of interpretation and later "told me I would preach." She also told him to prepare himself by attending the Church of Christ Bible Institute, which he did for almost four years. He was ordained in 1963.

The Cooks' decision, over a decade later, to start a church instead of retiring felt wise, of course, because it was God's will but also because they both had a sense of what each brought to the endeavor. Saints described Mother Cook as "a soul winner." "If you were hungry, she fed you. She would clothe you." "She was a go-getter." "She had the young people right there." Sister Martha James, a church usher, said of Bishop Cook, "When push comes to shove, Bishop lives the right lifestyle. I don't want to be somewhere where the leader isn't doing the right thing. It's hard enough to live holy. I would leave if the truth was not taught or if the leader was not living right." In the early days of the church, conveying those qualities to attract new members took "a lot of legwork." Sometimes it required the Cooks to make home visits to "introduce themselves [and explain] what they wanted to bring to the community." One member explained that when she was a child, her older sister brought her to TDC only after their parents had "drilled" the Cooks. "My sister came home and told my parents about [a new church in the neighborhood]." Her sister wanted to attend, "and the first thing my mother says, 'Well, I want to meet these people,'" she recalled. "So Elder Cook and Mother Cook came to the house. My mother . . . wanted to know what [name] did you baptize in, what did you believe in, do you believe in miracles, and all this, because she came up in [Refuge] Temple under Lawson." The Cooks answered satisfactorily, and the girls joined the church.

Members who joined the church in the beginning talked about the Cooks' labor, building a church that started as a bare-bones space. They would see Bishop Cook outside in his overalls working on the property. Mother

Cook would "bake or fry chicken and have bake sales [to raise money], and every Saturday she was out there giving out tracts." Both of them conducted prayer services, tarried with souls, and taught Bible classes for "the very handful. But the people started coming." Members appreciated the Cooks' "vision and great business sense." Sister Dean explained, "They both had it. I mean, Mother Cook didn't go to college and all that, but she was no joke. She had some kind of business mind." Mother Cook was equally successful negotiating with bankers, realtors, and city officials as she was cajoling church members, friends, and people in the surrounding community to donate, and then buy, food and crafts for fund-raising events. Bishop Cook described his wife as "a 'jack of all trades.' She sold real estate. She sold clothes. She was a faithful woman and wife. We were compatible."

By all accounts, Mother Cook possessed the qualities of an ideal pastor's wife. She was kind to everyone, "not stuck up." "She had a PhD in wisdom. She was smart *and* wise." "You can't talk about working," said one long-time member, "or having an unction to do something without mentioning Mother Cook, because she started it all." Bishop Cook remembered the first Sunday after the church had been "dedicated back to God" by Apostle Bonner. Bishop Cook told his wife that they "might not need to go, since it was the first day. She said we should, and . . . the church was full of people. In that first year, we did hundreds of baptisms. God was saving left and right." Others remembered Mother Cook as "fun-loving" and "encouraging," as well as "the motivator."

In 2005 the *Thirtieth Anniversary Journal* for TDC depicted Bishop Cook as "a man with a vision, humbly leading the people of God, at the 'Church with the Old Time Power.' " Saints attested to his spiritual power. "I suffered with migraines, and Bishop laid hands on me, and it moved right out of my face, and it was gone." "Bishop's prayers freed me from my fight with evil spirits." They also described him as spiritually discriminating, thoroughly vetting any guest preacher or speaker. "[A visiting preacher] will not just be coming up in True Deliverance laying hands on Bishop's people," Sister Dean said, "no, no, no." She explained that touch is one way to transmit evil spirits. "Then he got to pray whatever you put on them, off."

Bishop Cook was a quiet man (except when preaching), yet demanding in the ways of holiness. He pushed saints "to keep their houses in order" not only spiritually but also intellectually and financially because God's children are "the head and not the tail." He represented the generation of race men born in interwar America, promoting education and economic self-sufficiency ("Black men should own their own [businesses]"). He organized educational workshops for the congregation on life and health insurance, living and final wills, and investment. He also held classes on public assistance, likening it to "a slavery-type mentality." He told members who were on public assistance to get off, asserting, "You should love yourself enough not to want to be supported by the state." Congregants appreciated his balance of personal responsibility and historically informed race consciousness. One church mother affirmed that Bishop Cook's racially conscious all-encompassing approach to holiness was "very important" because he wanted each member to "take pride in yourself." By attending to a range of needs, Bishop Cook fulfilled congregants' expectations of a "father."

Sister Thomas, a grandmother in her sixties, further explained the importance of having a spiritual father, "When you don't have a covering over you," she said, "which is a pastor, then you're almost on your own. . . . [There's no] pastor . . . watching out for your soul . . . no protection." Protection cuts both ways. Saints considered it their duty to shield him as well. "Never point out your pastor to a stranger," Sister Dean instructed the ushers. "If someone comes in the church and asks for him, find out what they want, and take them to another minister. *Never* take them to Pastor. You don't know what people are really up to."

In spite of doing all they could to protect Bishop Cook, the congregation could not slow time. As he aged, they faced the prospect of transitioning to new leadership. By the end of 2005, his health had deteriorated and he was hospitalized; formulating a plan for selecting his successor took on new urgency. By this point in time, the church had grown to include five ministers, none of whom was an assistant pastor, so there was no heir apparent. While each minister had strong qualities, none, according to many saints, had the spiritual maturity, intellectual aptitude, *and* business acumen of Bishop Cook.

In considering candidates' qualifications, congregants also talked about the part that marital status and the first-lady-to-be would play in their deliberations. "He would be [good]," one woman said about a candidate, "but he don't have a wife." I asked whether having a wife was required or something customary that made people comfortable. "I don't know if the Church of Our Lord Jesus Christ would prefer that he have a wife," she said. "I think it's something that people [in TDC] would be more comfortable with. *I think* a man needs a wife because he needs help. . . . [It's] very much so a package deal. You're more complete when you have a wife." She explained further, "She influences her husband. Mother Cook was very important. She was Pastor Cook's eyes and ears." In thinking about a successor to Bishop Cook, saints said they were evaluating the potential pastor *and* his wife. As one member confided about a candidate, "He would be good, but no, because of his wife. And that's a shame to say that," she concluded, "but that's real."

CONCLUSION

The men of COOLJC, as "the heads," receive official credit for founding churches, yet the spiritual acumen, work ethic, and personality of pastors' wives can determine the success of any ministry. Worshippers coming to a church that is in the process of being built assess the leadership to determine whether or not to join. When the Lawsons came east to start the Harlem church, which would become a denomination, Bishop Lawson provided the public face, moving nationally and internationally in religious, civic, political, and intellectual circles. Mother Carrie Lawson became her husband's "eyes and ears" in the church and skillfully parlayed her devalued ordained status to become a broadcasting "soul winner" as "the Praying Mother of the Air." Thousands of early and mid-twentieth-century Black women and men found resonance in "the absolute deity of Jesus" and the mixed-race suffering body of the Christ descended from "Negro" women, which was advanced in a politically progressive Black milieu.

With its sociocultural and theological identity in place by midcentury, COOLJC yet had to weather the death of its founders and the Bonner-led transition into an expanded chain of command. Established ministries transitioning into new leadership afford members the opportunity to scrutinize potential successors and highlight the qualities they deem necessary to expand the church. As COOLJC looked toward the horizon of late twentieth-century existence and their potential for growth, Bishop Bonner's proposed hierarchy provided men a clear route to advancement and, perhaps, assured congregants of protection from future ruptures. Lady Bonner was a third-generation "Refugee," and her religious pedigree, education, and attention to the needs of wives certainly augmented the "package deal" put in charge of steering the organization into the future.

As the Cooks' story shows, building individual churches in the late twentieth century relied on much of the same strategies as did the Refuge Temple and the denomination, but on a smaller scale. The Cooks started TDC as a team, with Mother Cook providing the public face for bankers, realtors, and the local community, and Bishop Cook teaching congregants the skills needed for a stable quality of life. Both of them attended to the spiritual needs of members—praying, tarrying, and teaching the Bible. During the thirtieth-anniversary celebration, Bishop Cook repeated the story of building TDC, detailing "how the Lord blessed us in our dealings with Chase Manhattan . . . and building inspectors." He went on to sing the praises of "my companion, Mother Cook. . . . She would always go. She was a go-getter. Then her health deteriorated. The saints worked her to death. She would never say no."

Church cofounders Reva Cook, Ethel Mae Bonner, and Carrie Lawson each preceded their husband in death. Each rigorously toiled, with their husbands and parishioners, to build up the "body of Christ." Each woman's church labor began, however, before she took on the responsibilities of a pastor's wife. Each had been a "sister" in the church, working in horizontal women's networks that became known as "the women's auxiliaries," the primary labor force driving the organization.

CHURCH

SUSTAINING

Man is the head and the woman is the neck
that turns the head. The head cannot do without the neck.

Mother Gladys E. Woodley, missionary

In 1923 the women of the Church of Our Lord Jesus Christ of the Apostolic
Faith, Inc. (COOLJC), began to arrange the already existing, cross-cutting
webs of local, regional, and interstate networks into formal units in order
to sustain and grow the church. Known as "the three women's auxiliaries,"
the International Missionary Department (IMD; founded in 1923), the
International Women's Council (IWC; founded in 1952), and the Ministers'
and Deacons' Wives Guild (MDWG; founded in 1956) continue as the primary organizing vehicles for women today. Each auxiliary has its own principal focus: *missionary* is a licensed position concerned with the spiritual
well-being of the church and with "bringing souls to Christ"; the Women's
Council, whose primary focus is education and evangelization, is open to
any woman in "good standing"; and the MDWG is reserved for spouses and
widows supporting the male leadership. This examination of women's inter-
secting organizational and spiritual labor within auxiliaries shows that formal
and informal management by women at microlevels (re-)creates doctrinal

notions of Black religious female personhood. This, in turn, shores up regional, state, and national male hierarchical structures that were introduced four decades *after* women's horizontal webs of labor had begun servicing the overwhelmingly female congregations.

As detailed in the previous chapter, with the death of COOLJC's leader, Bishop Robert C. Lawson, in 1961, the church implemented a new form of episcopal polity, which today consists of boards of apostles, bishops, and presbyters and a decision-making executive board composed of representatives of the male leadership. The vertical male hierarchy was constructed over women's horizontal auxiliary operations, which had sustained the church up until that point. Auxiliaries provide women with a formalized means to function in almost every arena of church work, without an expectation of lifelong, church-wide titled recognition or representation on the executive board. Eschewing permanent titles, women reinforce desirable feminine qualities—to be humble, nurturing, and submissive to authority and to be workers for Christ. Holding office within auxiliaries provides a mark of distinction for a woman over the long term, but only insofar as she is effective in the position. Once she ends the term of appointment, her title returns to "sister" or "mother." Many women see this as beneficial, insisting they are able to accomplish more, because "titles don't mean anything," and "with titles come egos."

Unlike women in auxiliaries, men, once elevated, retain titled positions in the overarching hierarchy. Men's titles thus become markers of identity from young adulthood on. For women, however, public naming does not mark their progress over the course of their church life, and a woman is not considered eligible to rise to the title of mother until her senior years. "See, all the brothers need to become deacons or ministers, eventually," a church sister explained. "As a woman, you're just a sister." Women's cross-cutting webs of operation made it possible for Bishop William L. Bonner to establish a vertical hierarchy for men without upending church operations. The episcopate of COOLJC provides a system for men's distinction and elevation in rank that circumvents, yet depends on, women's networks of labor to sustain the institution.

In early interviews, my attempts to clearly demarcate positions and responsibilities in women's auxiliary work hampered my understanding of the fluid system. While each auxiliary operates hierarchically, with rotating presiding officers (president, vice president, secretary, and treasurer) at the local, regional, and national (now international as well) levels, women may hold membership in all three units at once and therefore be operating in multiple positions across the local church and national organization. For example, lifelong church member Mother Jessie England was a licensed missionary and minister's widow; she served as the president of the MDWG, the vice president of the IMD, and a general member of the Women's Council at True Deliverance Church (TDC) in Queens, but she held no organization-wide office.[1] Independent of the auxiliary structure, she had been elevated by the local pastor from sister (the title of all female members) to mother, an official title granted to older churchwomen who have exhibited years of consistent spiritual and organizational leadership. As a church mother, she wielded extensive spiritual authority in TDC. No national auxiliary or board, however, represents church mothers.

Women like Mother England have significant authority locally because daily operations at TDC, like in other COOLJC churches, fall under the auspices of the home church auxiliaries. At TDC, women initiated, planned, and developed strategies for projects, although final approval for major initiatives rested with Bishop Crosley J. Cook, the pastor. Unless a woman moves into auxiliary leadership nationally, her organization-wide influence remains limited. "We [the local church] as a whole deal with state, and state deals with international," Mother England explained. "There are local planning sessions for the quarterly meetings with the auxiliary heads [from each church]. At the Quarterly Conventions every auxiliary has to be represented . . . and then in July a report is made so it can go in August [to the international convention]."[2]

At the international level, the Apostle to the Women's Auxiliaries oversees the women's units. Formal male supervision of women's auxiliaries is most apparent when the overseer offers words to the assembly at organization-wide convocations. Male oversight is also marked in printed journals, which catalog the organizational structure and official titles. The *Beacon*, the official journal of the IMD, often includes a message from the overseeing apostle "thank[ing] God . . . [for the] Spirit-filled, dedicated and well informed devout women capable of leading other women in the church both administratively and spiritually."[3]

The approach taken by COOLJC women to administrative and spiritual labor within auxiliaries not only produces and reinforces notions of Black female religious identity, while bolstering a male-headed institution, but also demonstrates the particular salience of "Jesus-only" theology. Through practice and rhetoric, women assert the inseparable relationship between the perpetuation of COOLJC as a Jesus-centered denomination and women's qualities (and perspectives) of divine personhood, which align with qualities of the indwelling Christ—working under submission to authority in service to God. The ways in which women articulate each unit's mission in *The Discipline Book*, and carry out their work, highlight the importance of their humility, "touch," and "labor as helpers."

INTERNATIONAL MISSIONARY DEPARTMENT

On September 8, 1923, the IMD became the first COOLJC women's auxiliary, organized "for the purpose of aiding this church as an organism, to perpetuate the doings of the saints in the beginning of the church; that is, to make an opportunity for the missionary women to be helpers together with our ministers and pastors in bringing souls to Christ."[4] Carrying forward the work of the "saints in the beginning of the church" connected the women's charge to both the second-century New Testament church, on which Apostolic Pentecostal theology is built, and also to women in the Bible who labored with men to spread the message of Christ.[5] The stated purpose of IMD, "to *make* an opportunity" for women (emphasis added), is, however, somewhat misleading. Women had been working "together with . . . ministers and pastors" since the church's beginnings in the early twentieth century. The first services that laid the groundwork for COOLJC took place in 1919, "in the home of two . . . precious saints . . . [and] faithful women," Ida G. Burleigh and Addie Anderson, "who with their husbands . . . welcomed the blessed shepherd [Elder Lawson (and his wife, Carrie Lawson)]" into their Harlem, New York, home.[6] The budding congregation soon outgrew the "Cradle of Refuge," as it is now remembered, and within four years had purchased and relocated to new quarters a few blocks away (see chapter 2).

Church growth between 1919 and 1923 also seems to have spurred missionary women to spell out their particular responsibilities and organize as an official "functional unit" of the church. Mother Elizabeth Brown served as the department's president from its inception in 1923 until 1931, yet today the IMD recognizes Mother Carrie F. Lawson, the first wife of Robert Lawson, as missionary president from 1919 to 1923.[7] This retrospective installation of Mother Lawson as the first president of the missionaries (before the official body existed) speaks to the ways in which missionaries see Mother Lawson specifically, and their early work generally, as integral to the very existence of the church. The women further cemented their place in the organization by establishing "missionary" as a licensed position, giving them the opportunity to be officially recognized for their invaluable work as "helpers."[8] To become part of the missionary unit today, a woman must be "baptized with the Holy Ghost"; exhibit "some fruit of the spirit in [her] own life"; be "obedient" to local, regional, and national church authority; have two years of service in her local "Social Mission Work Band"; attend all missionary functions; and be recommended by her local pastor. It is customary for the president of the local Missionary Department to make a recommendation to the pastor, who will make a recommendation to the IMD. It, in turn, issues certification. Licensing, in addition to establishing qualifications within the church, expands the missionaries' ability to "comfort those in need, . . . [and] give godly counsel in the fear of God," by providing access to people in hospitals, nursing homes, homeless shelters, domestic abuse shelters, and prisons.[9]

The church therefore views the IMD as the most vital of the women's auxiliaries for its work within churches and surrounding communities. The conventional view of a missionary as the evangelist venturing to distant lands seeking to bring people to salvation does not represent the majority of COOLJC missionaries. Although some missionaries do labor in the foreign field, that work is conducted under the auspices of the Global Missions Initiative. The vast majority of missionaries serve at the local level, focusing on the spiritual well-being of the church by linking COOLJC biblical exegesis to everyday life, in order to encourage members, "rescue the fallen," and attract new converts.[10]

Along with bringing individual "souls to Christ," the church presses missionaries "to labor together with the brethren in establishing churches, . . . as those women in the churches of old were helpers of Paul."[11] The history of women's church planting in the first half of the twentieth century attests to the many COOLJC missionary pioneers who convened prayer bands or Bible study groups that grew into churches—such as Mamie Martin of Pennsylvania, Ada Washington of West Virginia, Essie Ross of Florida, and Addie Keith of Kentucky.[12] As late as 1974, religious undertakings by women spawned congregations. "Through the initiation . . . of a student body Bible Class at Northeastern University," graduate student DyAnne Moultrie started what would become the Mission Church of Our Lord Jesus Christ in Somerville, Massachusetts. Mother Moultrie and her husband, Apostle H. A. Moultrie II, as cofounders, continue to preside over the successful congregation.[13]

Some pioneers, too, labored *ahead* of the brethren to establish churches. During the 1950s and 1960s in Halifax County, North Carolina, "the missionaries ran our church," Dr. Ruby Littleton recalled. (Dr. Littleton is a church mother and missionary; however, once a member receives a doctorate, the church uses her academic title.) "We did not have a full-time pastor, a male pastor," she explained, "until maybe two years before I went off to college [in the mid-1960s]." Dr. Littleton's church shared a pastor with a Virginia congregation, so their "main service used to be on Saturday because he had his Sunday services in Richmond." A part-time pastor nonetheless did not mean part-time services. "We had regular Tuesday night Bible study, we had a regular Friday night evangelistic service, we had Sunday school on Sunday, we had ABYPU [young people's service] on Sunday afternoon, and we had an evangelistic service on Sunday evenings."

Dr. Littleton's story shows the ways in which women channeled spiritual passion, day in, day out, and week to week. "The missionaries ran everything," she reiterated. "I saw them clean the church [and] bring their unsaved husbands to make repairs on the church. I saw them, then, change into the Sunday school teacher or the missionary president. I served in Sunday school under my mother as Sunday school superintendent. I served in the Missionary Department as a junior missionary with my mother as missionary president. A sister played the piano. They did so many different jobs." Dr. Littleton pointed out the shifts women would regularly take to run the church. From roles as domestic workers ("clean[ing] the church") and as wives ("bring[ing] unsaved husbands to make repairs"), the missionaries around her would "change into" teachers, superintendents, presidents, and musicians. Having been "called . . . into holiness and sobriety, and charity," missionaries "administer any and all help, as we have opportunity, whether spiritual or material," and therefore, by necessity, carry out religious, domestic, professional, supervisory, and administrative duties, especially when a full-time pastor has not yet been assigned to the church.[14]

Dr. Littleton's Halifax church also highlights the ways in which a male-headed national organization could not structurally keep up with the religious zeal of its overwhelmingly female majority membership. The state bishop would come "occasionally, very occasionally," but the church was, in fact, a missionary operation. "You know there weren't . . . ," she hesitated briefly, and then said pensively, as if it were a revelation, "Boy, there were no men in the church." On the one hand, she brings to light the extent to which women-controlled religious life seemed commonplace. On the other hand, she suggests a structure in which part-time pastors and visiting bishops relied on women's evaluation of each other when granting missionary licenses. It's difficult to determine how many COOLJC congregations over the past nine decades have functioned like Dr. Littleton's church. Hers was rural and "modest," and as soon as they could, the national body installed a full-time pastor. The women in the church probably appreciated becoming a "healthy body in Christ" with "a head," regardless of any challenges they may have faced in transitioning to full-time male oversight. Perhaps, too, the new pastor appreciated the years of women's labor that had readied a congregation for his charge. Perhaps he would have agreed with sociologist Cheryl Townsend Gilkes: "If it wasn't for the women," she observes, "you wouldn't have a church."[15]

In addition to sustaining sacred communities, religious multitasking by missionaries across the domestic and professional spheres has shaped wider community perceptions of women's abilities, as well as women's sense of their own and each other's potential. Mother Ada Washington was one such woman. She moved with her husband from Depression-era York, Alabama, to Welch, West Virginia, where he found work in the coal mines and she in the homes of white families (including then mayor John W. Blakely). Within the church, Mother Washington moved through the ranks, serving as the local Sunday school superintendent for twenty-eight years and then as state mother of West Virginia. During an interview with the *Welch Daily Newspaper* in the 1950s, she stated, "I never thought I'd reach such a status."[16] As state mother, Mother Washington organized statewide quarterly meetings of all West Virginia churches. She also joined other representatives at national convocations, where they brought local and state concerns to the larger church body and gleaned information to take back to the saints at home. Such organization-wide gatherings also "immersed [the saints] in fervor, prayer, [and] fellowship . . . for a protracted period of time."[17] Mother Washington had the responsibility of both relaying discrete information back to her congregation (such as doctrinal issues or news about church growth) and also, equally important, carrying the spiritual "refreshing" from the convocation to "fire up" members back home.

Perusing any recent edition of the *Beacon* gives the reader a sense of the scope of the work of a "Mother Washington" as it is conceived and implemented today at the local, state, national, and international levels. The missionaries of COOLJC can be seen organizing prayer breakfasts, providing a church with "100 new hymnals" and donating "beautiful embroidered . . . communion linen," collecting toiletries to take to homeless shelters, producing religious tracts, organizing and overseeing Junior Missionary departments, establishing educational programs (religious education, after-school tutoring, and computer training), creating regional and state directories, and managing state, national, and international committees, departments, and events. Modeling a religious posture and work ethic for girls and women, who make up the majority of the church's workforce, missionary activities transmit what Suzanne Carothers calls "concrete learnings" and "critical understandings" to current and future generations of religious laborers.[18] Writing on the ways in which Black mothers influence their daughters' female identity, Carothers explores teaching and learning processes between mothers and daughters in home-centered work, identifying specific task-oriented skills (concrete learnings) and broader concepts and values (critical understandings) derived from culturally specific approaches to work around the home.

Mother-daughter home-centered work teaches values of give-and-take that shape daughters' notions of responsibility to the family unit, which, in turn, extend to "a conscious model of social exchange" within the wider Black community.[19] "Beginning in early childhood," Carothers argues, "the wider social context in which Black children are raised usually involves not only their mothers, but also many adults—all performing in a variety of roles in relation to the child, the domestic unit, and the larger community."[20] Dr. Littleton spoke about social values gleaned from watching and working with missionaries in the wider community. "At least two Saturdays out of a month," she said, "we would cook big things of Brunswick stew and barbecue to sell to support something in the community." These assemblies of the wider Black community took place at a local lodge. This was significant since the church, as a self-segregating religious body, "didn't do a lot of fellowshipping with churches outside of holiness churches." The desire to worship separately cut both ways. The practice of speaking in tongues marginalized Holiness-Pentecostals from the mainline Black religious community, and oneness theology further stigmatized Apostolics within Pentecostalism. Neighborhood fund-raisers organized by missionary women therefore proved important for strengthening the Black public sphere by building bridges across religious differences; at the same time, these gatherings presented occasions for saved and unsaved family members to enjoy time together in a communal environment.

Dr. Littleton gave credit to the missionaries of her childhood church for her ability to network across various communities while upholding strict standards of holiness. Growing up in a sacred world that, by her description, ran with a cooperative ethic conceptualized by Black women, she acquired specific skills that have served her well over the years. As an adult, she has risen to prominence within the COOLJC international body while remaining active in educational and civic initiatives in her New England community. Additionally, she spent eight years as the president of a national interdenominational women's group. "I didn't know the word then," she stated, "but they were multitasking. I saw that. I lived that. I learned to do that." She asserted that a full-time pastor would have altered the ways in which missionaries worked. "If there had been a pastor there," she said, "many of things that they did, and things that I learned, I wouldn't have because he would have, you know, stepped in."

Dr. Littleton knew that specific initiatives would have relied on the approval of the pastor and, more importantly, that the cooperative ethic would have been subject to his oversight. While she probably would have learned to multitask in any case, a pastor could have curbed the ways in which women approached leadership in the church and activities in the wider community. The women in the Halifax church taught Dr. Littleton to presume women capable of decision making and institutional control. One church sister stated plainly, "How you function and move around at the local level depend[s] on the mind-set of your leader, [his] expectations, and commitment to tradition and doctrine."

The individual pastoral "mind-set" notwithstanding, the independence and leadership history of the IMD continues in the church tradition; it is the only auxiliary that organizes regular weekly instructional services. During the early days of COOLJC, missionary services provided the teaching vehicle for men who wanted to move into the ministry. Initially, Bishop Lawson was the principal biblical instructor; however, as the church grew, he looked to studied women for assistance. "When men in New York, New Jersey, and Connecticut wanted to go into the ministry, Bishop Lawson would tell them to go to missionary meetings," Mother Pearl Norris explained. "He told them that the missionaries were prepared with topics, and they were qualified to expound on the Word." She went on, "When I was coming up a lot of the men were trained by the [missionary] women." During the 1960s and 1970s (after Lawson's death), men's attendance at missionary services decreased, and enrollment in the Bible colleges increased. "Now you can hardly get men to go to a missionary service," Mother Norris stated, somewhat annoyed. "They hardly know they're there."

Still, the teaching work of missionaries remains indispensable to the viability of the church. Similar to Sunday school and Monday night Bible study, which help members gain proficiency in the Bible and learn doctrine, missionary services also foster a space centered on women's biblical interpretations. It was during a Wednesday night missionary service that Sister Cheryl Brown pressed the women gathered "to be like Jesus." Quoting from Matthew 28:19–20, she exhorted them, "Go ye therefore, and teach all nations. . . . Teaching them to observe all things whatsoever I have commanded you." She expanded on the text, "We are saved to serve. We have a commission to go into the world. [Jesus said], 'Go ye into all the world, and *preach* the gospel to every creature'" (Mark 16:15; emphasis added). In a stroke of rhetorical brilliance, she then turned *preach* back into *teach*, reinforcing church doctrine that prohibits women from preaching as she recognized divine authority in teaching. "To talk and teach the gospel," she explained, "you must have power. You must have the anointing. You must have the Holy Ghost. God was manifested in the flesh, justified in the Spirit. Jesus is God. I'm standing on the name of Jesus. There's power in the name." One sister later explained, "You got to search yourself to be like Jesus. . . . It's your job to study the Word for yourself. It's not necessarily anybody else's responsibility to teach you the words of the scriptures." Moreover, she pointed out that an essential part of one's responsibility is to attend teaching services in which the meanings and daily applications of scripture are explained. The legacy of teaching runs deep as the heart of missionary labor, molding missionary identity and contributing to so many COOLJC women's ability to "rightly divide the word."[21]

As Dr. Littleton's Halifax church showed, along with teaching, everything needed to start a COOLJC church and keep it going fell under the rubric of missionary work, including the critical task of fund-raising. "I always saw them [financially] support the presiding bishop, . . . [and] education and . . . foreign missions," Dr. Littleton recalled. "I've seen that all my life." Women's tithes and freewill offerings, and the proceeds from special services organized by missionary departments, kept the church doors open. Through special services, banquets, dinner and bake sales, "change" campaigns (members saving and donating their change), and block parties, women continue to keep churches operating and drive institutional growth, while modeling missionary conduct. A missionary's sense of self shapes and is shaped by the networks created to sustain the church. Upholding fund-raising, serving, organizing, and teaching as highly desirable spiritual gifts, she moves across those networks with holy comportment, in "submission to authority," fueling the organization.[22] For example, owing to the religious zeal and fiscal savvy of the IMD, in collaboration with the Women's Council (discussed below), a Milwaukee, Wisconsin, congregation purchased a new building in 1987, with the women's groups donating $25,000, cutting the mortgage in half.[23] Three and a half decades before the Milwaukee women realized the new sanctuary, a New York saint envisioned the Women's Council, the group that would partner with the IMD to bring the building project to fruition.

THE INTERNATIONAL WOMEN'S COUNCIL (IWC)

In 1951 Delphia Perry, the IMD president and state mother of New York, "received a vision for a council of . . . women workers," operating under the theme of "Unity" and with the goal of "Glory," who "would share in helping to foster the gospel, evangelizing, encouraging and educating man kind."[24] Mother Perry's National Women's Council (now the International Women's Council [IWC]) would be unique because, unlike in the IMD, membership was fully inclusive and automatic. "Any adult female member in good standing with a local church," the proposed IWC constitution now states, "is a member of the International Women's Council."[25] Mother Perry presented her idea at the annual meeting of the State Mothers' Council, and they determined she should go to Bishop Lawson for approval. Her vision, according to church history, was God's answer to a ten-year prayer by Bishop Lawson for an auxiliary "that would include all the women of COOLJC." In 1952, with the assistance of Mothers Miranda Beane, Grace Hill, and others, Mother Perry convened the first National Women's Council meeting in Petersburg, Virginia.

Printed church history does not, however, convey Mother Perry's spiritual magnetism. "She used to do a good mean preachin'!" recalled one Refuge Temple church mother recently. "I mean, we don't have women preachers," she clarified, "but in today's economy, if they heard her . . . She ran a revival in Washington, I think it was. Seventy-two souls got saved. How many men you know do that now? You know what I'm saying? She had such a gift." The church mother continued, "She was a pretty woman, too. And she was such a beautiful person. She used to beat up on me all the time [when I was a youngster] . . . telling me [what] I wasn't doing right. You know, correcting me. But she did it in such a way that it didn't chase me from her. I loved her to death."

Mother Perry translated her unction to evangelize and mentor young women into an organization-wide network (serving as its first president from 1952 to 1968). By making each woman a member of the auxiliary, the IWC provides a means by which all women become integrated into church structure—which is important for an organization that depends on women's labor to sustain it. The IWC's stated purpose "of uniting women of [COOLJC] as workers for Christ both at home and abroad" is carried out through education, evangelism, and foreign and home mission work, with particular attention to women's education and health. The council's constitution outlines four objectives: (1) evangelizing and supporting home and foreign missions; (2) promoting religious and secular education; (3) assisting the sick and seniors in health care, and educating members about good health practices; and (4) supporting the financial goals of the presiding apostle.

For the vast majority of women, work at the local level translates into the international body, most immediately as financial donations. Within the first year of its existence, the council donated $500 and supplied library books to the R. C. Lawson Institute in Southern Pines, North Carolina.[26] Today, COOLJC expects local councils to raise funds from individual churches and state-diocese councils, which flow to the international body. Local and state IWC groups contribute funds from "standing" (permanent) programs and short-term initiatives. Yearly awards and banners presented at the IWC Annual Convention encourage local councils and state dioceses to compete to raise the most funds. Groups receive recognition for accomplishments such as "report[ing] the largest amount of finances," "add[ing] the most lifetime members," "recruit[ing] the most Boosters [official male supporters]," "recruit[ing] the most women between the ages of 20 and 40," and "report[ing] the largest attendance."[27]

While financial support by women in the IWC has an immediate impact on the organization, over the long term the IWC benefits individual women and the institution as a whole by providing women encouragement and spiritual and organizational training, by means of sponsored services and special programs throughout the year. The IWC Annual Convention at the national level and Annual Women's Day programs at the local and regional levels exemplify events run by and for the women of the church. As in Black churches across denominations, the COOLJC Women's Day programs come out of the tradition initiated by Nannie Helen Burroughs in 1906 at the National Baptist Convention.[28] Burroughs conceived of the day, "not . . . as a scheme for raising money, but primarily for raising women," to build leadership, communication, and organizational skills among women.[29] As we will see, within COOLJC, the day for "raising women" is also a time in which particular understandings and experiences of Apostolic Black female identities are created, expressed, and reinforced for women and girls. Program elements, focusing on women's education and the spiritual and physical health of women, families, and the community, offer a course of action designed to strengthen women's resolve to remain steadfast in holiness. Annual Women's Day also draws attendees from across the region to the host church, to "have a good time in the Lord," fortifying bonds between congregations—all of which builds up individual women and the organization.

Women's Day at TDC takes place on the third Saturday in May, which adds another day to the church schedule. Sandwiched between Friday Joy Night service (which can go until eleven thirty or so at night) and Sunday services (which for many begin with Sunday school at nine thirty in the morning and end at the seven-thirty evening service), Saturday is a precious day to "get every chore done." In addition, many of the members attend Monday night prayer service and Bible study class and the Wednesday night missionary service. Nonetheless, women and girls, as well as a few male "boosters," eagerly assemble for the Annual Women's Day. Over the course of my fieldwork, I attended three Annual Women's Day services. Each involved a celebratory atmosphere; saints and their families and friends from throughout the region came together as speakers, soloists, and attendees to honor and inspire women. Women donned the IWC uniform— white dresses or skirt suits that fall below the knees, white stockings, purple shoes (black or white shoes are permissible as well), and a glorious array of deep-purple head coverings—"crowns" of all sizes with glitter, ribbons, and flowers. ("White is symbolic of our purity. Purple is symbolic of royalty. We are the King's daughters!"[30]) Instead of hats, most young women and girls donned purple "chaplettes," round lacy head coverings between five and eight inches in diameter, held in place by a bobby pin. Before the service begins, young girls cluster in the ladies room, excitedly primping each other and admiring new outfits, because "within the confines of a strict moral code" dressing for Sunday and special services is rife with "experiences of playfulness and joy."[31] In the foyer or downstairs social hall, they can be seen putting the final touches on an original poem or anxiously rehearsing a recitation.

Each program followed a similar structure and protocol. The all-day event, running from noon to six in the evening, followed by dinner in the social hall, was divided into sequential young adult and adult sessions and designed to address the "spiritual, educational and social needs of women."[32] In the first session, girls and young women, ranging from elementary-school age to their thirties, ushered, delivered the welcome address, emceed, read scripture, recited poetry, and offered orations and musical performances. Incorporating young girls into Women's Day affords them the same attention and respect as adults, while educating them in the ways of holiness, church protocol, and public performance. The emcee's profile of each presenter highlighted educational and career goals and accomplishments and, for young girls, favorite school subjects—reinforcing the IWC's directive to encourage its members "to pursue education to the greatest extent possible."[33] The young women's session concluded with adult presentations—an "inspirational speaker" from TDC and a "guest speaker" from a regional church.

Five months before the big day, the local leadership of the Women's Council assembled a planning committee to bring the program together. A key part of each year's planning is selecting the theme, topic, and focal scriptures, from which everything else in the program flows. Examples are "A Woman with an Issue: Desperate for Healing" (Matthew 9:20, Mark 5:25–34, and Luke 8:43), "Is There Anything Too Hard for God? He Kept His Promises . . . Did You?" (Genesis 18:11–14, 21: 1–3), and "Victory in the Praise: Praising My Way Out!!" (Jeremiah 33:1–11 and Acts 16:25). The theme-topic-scripture structure charts a scripture-based, general-to-personal approach that speakers follow. The theme summarizes the broad message of the scripture, and speakers use the topic as a catalyst to render a testimony, tying the general to the personal.

"Victory in the Praise," for example, captures the messages of Jeremiah 33:1–11 and Acts 16:25. In the first story, God promises to reward the praises of Jeremiah with health and freedom. In Acts, Paul and Silas are released from a Philippian jail by the power of prayer and sung praises. At the service, women testified about the power of praise in their own lives, with many focusing on physical health. One woman testified about the stroke she suffered a few years earlier. "I was sick unto death!" she exclaimed. "I'm praising God because He gave me victory! That's what today is about!" A visiting first lady (pastor's wife) from a regional church praised God for recently ending a demanding medication regimen, and the visiting guest speaker, Sister Rose Carpenter, tied praise to self-esteem and sociopsychological healing of Black women.

After the emcee's introduction, Sister Carpenter rose from her pew and energetically moved down the center aisle of the sanctuary. Clapping her hands, she exhorted, "Praise the Lord, saints!" A chorus of "Hallelujah!" sprang from the congregation. Her voice filled the sanctuary as she moved to a floor podium below the raised pulpit, the area designated for women speakers. She did not need the microphone but used it, intensifying her presence. "Praising my way out, praise is what I do!" she proclaimed. "Praise is expressing appreciation of each aspect of His work. . . . Praise for providing . . . [He's] a way maker . . . a healer." She then began to sing a beautifully meditative gospel hymn: "Praise is what I do / When I want to be close to you / I lift my hands in praise / Praise is who I am / I will Praise Him while I can / I'll bless Him at all times."[34] The gathering of fifty women and girls and three men joined in. As the song ended, Sister Carpenter launched into her lesson based on the story of the imprisonment of Paul and Silas. "Praise expands our vision of who God is," she affirmed. Connecting the biblical to the personal, she asserted, "The enemy wants to close our mouths. [There are] frustrations at work, with our families, and even in church. The enemy wants you to sit in church like a bump on a log." Quoting and performing Psalms 47, she clapped and cried out, "Oh clap your hands, all ye people, dance, play instruments!" She then merged Bible time with the present, warning, "The enemy tries to strip us of our joy, [telling us] we're too big, too fat, [our] hair's too kinky, [fostering] low self-esteem. Well, I'm gonna praise my way out. Praise is a weapon. There's victory in the praise!"

Sister Carpenter's oration linked the theme of the day, "Victory in the Praise," to the broader IWC directive to "gain knowledge and deal with issues which relate to women and society."[35] Even as she adhered to the protocols of gendered space by speaking from the floor podium below the pulpit, Sister Carpenter specifically addressed societal denigration of Black women's bodies and offered a spiritual weapon for countering psychological defeat. In so doing, she communicated that the sociopsychological and religious goals of COOLJC women worked in tandem with male-headed vertical structures.

Printed materials that every participant received also underscored the message of Sister Carpenter and the IWC mandate. The packet of registration materials opened with "The Fruit of the Spirit . . . Walking in the Spirit," listing examples of "Fruit" (positive qualities), "Fruit Robbers" (negative behaviors), and "Insecticide" (scriptural "cures"). An anonymous poem, "Realization," followed "Fruit of the Spirit" and was recited by a young woman early in the service:

Who am I?
I'm an African American Woman.
What makes me strong?
My heritage.
What makes me weak?
My fears.
What makes me whole?
My God.
What keeps me standing?
My faith.
What sustains my mind?
My quest for knowledge.
What lifts my head high?
My pride.

Photocopied clippings from secular magazines instructed women on ways to "find happiness every day" and "count your blessings." The latter reported a study in the *Handbook of Positive Psychology* that linked keeping a journal of things to be grateful for with improved physical health.[36] The packet included practical information as well. "Important Phone Numbers" listed dozens of local government, civic, and community resources, including hotlines for AIDS, cancer, suicide, substance abuse, and physical abuse. The New York Foundation for Senior Citizens contributed "Safety Tips for Seniors" and "Bedroom Safety," which included a warning against smoking in bed. The packet ended with a brief poem-synopsis titled "Books of the Bible" and a reminder of daily "prayer at noon" services at TDC.

Beginning with "Fruit of the Spirit" and ending with an outline of the Bible and the church prayer schedule, the order of printed materials transmitted a message, God first and God last, which spoke to IWC's "focus on teaching and encouraging women to be holy, . . . as spoken of in the Word of God."[37] At the same time, by offering a wide range of resource materials, the IWC showed appreciation for everyday challenges faced by holy women. The church prohibits smoking, drinking, dancing, and other "worldly" indulgences, but materials that warned against smoking in bed or provided resources for dealing with substance abuse recognized saints' close relationships with family and friends who are not church members, as well as substance challenges they themselves may be facing. By supplying contact information for civic and community groups, the IWC also acknowledged and encouraged the participation of church members in local and regional affairs.

A good deal of effort goes into preparing a program that communicates the religious ethics and values of COOLJC women. The planning committee schedules speakers and presenters, selects and assembles materials for the registration packet, selects items for and assembles gift bags, decides on bouquets for the sanctuary, and plans, shops for, and prepares the evening meal and cleans up afterward. Presenters meditate on selected scriptures to prepare orations; singers prepare songs; and poets write poems. Everything that goes into making Women's Day successful involves work that, on its face, might not be thought of as religious. Mothers make sure "the whites are white" (sometimes shopping for new outfits for daughters), their hair is freshly coiffed, and children's homework is mostly done. All of the labor required for Women's Day—maternal, domestic, therapeutic, administrative, performative, and exegetical—models religious behavior for girls and young women and sustains "the presence of a woman-centered perspective in the life of the church."[38]

Through local and regional Women's Day programs, the yearly IWC convention, and other special events and services, the IWC affords all COOLJC women "in good standing" a means to participate in church operations. Augmenting the teaching and oversight of the IMD, the IWC works to ensure that all female members receive practical training in the ways of holiness, regardless of their age, length of time in the church, or calling.

MINISTERS' AND DEACONS' WIVES GUILD

While the IWC provides an all-inclusive unit for COOLJC women, the MDWG is the most exclusive auxiliary. Established in 1956 under the leadership of Mother Evelyn Lawson, the second wife of Bishop Lawson, the MDWG limits membership to the wives and widows of COOLJC deacons or ministers (unless the widow has remarried). By definition, this unit is destined to have the fewest members of the three women's auxiliaries. As with most Pentecostal congregations worldwide, in COOLJC women make up over 75 percent of practitioners.[39] Therefore, in all probability, less than half of female COOLJC congregants will ever be married to a deacon or minister. As a result, local chapters of MDWG have few members. At TDC, for instance, five deacons, four ministers, and Pastor Cook served the 110-member congregation, and two of the men were widowers.

In spite of the inevitability of many small local chapters, Mother Evelyn Lawson deemed the unit necessary. According to MDWG history, the guild was formed to "instruct young wives in their roles as leaders, helpmeets to their husbands in the work of the ministry."[40] When current members of the guild spoke about their work, the position of their husband colored the ways in which they viewed the work of the auxiliary. The wives of deacons reflected on the fund-raising activities of the unit, while wives of ministers emphasized the forum the MDWG provides for learning ways to support their husbands. "It teaches the wives their role in the church, what they should be doing, how they should carry themselves, and how to pray for their husbands," one woman explained. All of the wives stressed the importance of praying in the moment, whether a spouse is praying over others or preaching a sermon. "When he's praying for people," another wife said matter-of-factly, "I have to be prayerful for the bad spirits that my husband could pick up." During a sermon, wives pray for God to reveal his word through their preacher-husband. The wife of the preaching minister will also most often be the first in the congregation to stand during his sermon—to support, witness, and physically testify.

In addition to bearing up a companion through prayer, other indications of her support call for self-examination. Is she performing the appropriate role and carrying herself properly? While all women in the church are concerned about behavior and comportment, wives of male leaders face additional considerations. Women married to ministers operate under dual tenets of obedience as it relates to spouses—submission to the husband and submission to the man of God, in the same person. One church mother put it this way: "I always say, 'Lord, teach me how to be a helpmeet to my husband and not be a hindrance to his ministry and to keep myself under subjection that I don't become a hindrance to God's work.'" She explained that asking for God's guidance in these matters was "just normal." "My role is to support my husband," she said, "and that will never change for me. I will always be a prayerful partner. . . . [Prayer is] something I have to do for myself anyway just to stay saved. You should live a godly life irrespective to whatever the calling of your husband is." Independent of any benefits men may derive from women's role, this church mother pointed out the intrinsic values of being supportive of and submissive to male authority. She understands subjection in terms of its value to God's work, and she links submission to her "own personal salvation," which is inextricable from her role as helpmeet.

Guiding wives "in their roles as leaders . . . [and] helpmeets to their husbands in the work of the ministry" became more fully developed fifteen years after the guild's initial formation by Mother Evelyn Lawson. In 1972, under the leadership of Lady Bonner, wife of Apostle Bonner (the COOLJC presider), the MDWG drafted and ratified a new constitution, spelling out the nature and goals of partnered ministerial leadership. "The Ministers' and Deacons' wife is called to be part of the total ministerial service of her husband," the constitution asserts, "as together they pursue the will of God, the development of their leadership skills, and their opportunity to serve humanity."[41] Positioning the work of a wife in "ministerial service" as a counterpart to that of her husband can be read in light of Mother Bonner's reputation as one who "championed the cause of women's rights within the church and in the secular world."[42] The significance of women in an effective COOLJC pastorate, however, harks back to the beginnings of the church, because, as Dr. Littleton explained, wives were so crucial to effective ministries that "Bishop Lawson did not ordain pastors that were not married" until the late 1950s. Mother Bonner came of age under the first generation of Refuge Temple saints, so her late twentieth-century understanding of a wife's importance to the ministry of her husband was shaped by Bishop Lawson. Too, her sense of Black Apostolic womanhood was shaped by church pioneers such as her mother, Mother Grace Hill, secretary to the first IMD in 1923 and cofounder of the Women's Council in 1952 (see chapter 2).

Just as Mother Hill and the first missionaries asserted a particular gender equivalence in spiritual work, "to labor together with the brethren," so, too, did Mother Bonner, in crafting the MDWG constitution, harness language associated with the advancement of men into spiritual leadership. According to the document, a wife "is *called* to be part of the . . . ministerial service."[43] In most instances, couples marry before men receive the call to preach, which might contradict the notion of a wife's call. Yet women understand their calling within the framework of predestination, because one may not know "what office God [will] put you in or allow you to be in God," one minister's wife stated, "[but God] saw me as that type of person." God had a "call on her life."

In addition to validating the calling of wives to "ministerial service," the constitution declares—for the edification of the entire church—the value of a wife to the marital partnership and congregation. It states, "The **touch** that the woman brings to her husband's ministry is inestimable and irreplaceable. She provides the ingredients for enrichment and fulfillment, which can inspire, motivate, enlighten and strengthen the very fabric of the spiritual life of her minister-deacon husband and the congregation he shepherds."[44] Without receiving a title, without moving through the organization's vertical channels of authority, the wife brings her invaluable and unquantifiable "touch" to catalyze "the spiritual life" of the sacred environment and all within it. The constitution, moreover, details some of the intangible, yet "essential," feminine attributes wives bring to their partnership, their congregation, and the wider organization. "The wife," it asserts, "provides the balance, discernment, sensitivity and nurturing essential for growth and blessing."[45] On the one hand, the MDWG constitution can be seen as a bold assessment of ministerial wives over the preceding half century, what the women drafting the constitution in 1972 knew to be true. Church "growth and blessing" are unimaginable without the "balance, discernment, sensitivity and nurturing" of wives. On the other hand, expectations run high. When women move into ministerial service based on the trajectory of their husbands, they are compelled to build on feminine qualities perceived by church culture as inherent and to acquire those qualities they lack.

Women spoke about the increased pressure and religious work they encountered as their husbands moved from deacon to minister. "As my husband becomes a minister, . . . I gotta do more, pray, more work as unto the Lord," Mother Geneva Reeves said. "If he has to go minister, I have to be sure that I'm there with him to support him." Her husband was not the pastor of a congregation, so would be called to preach at other churches and events.[46] Accompanying him carried a set of expectations because "you have to have this husband-wife thing that people expect for you to have." She avoided detailing exactly what she meant, but I took her to be alluding to negotiating the natural ups and downs of any relationship, under the eye of church folk. Excursions of this sort also required additional wifely duties on her part. "I always make sure that he has a certain look. When he steps out the door he's gonna be looking a certain way. That's just me. Like if he's up there praying for people, I know that he's gonna need a change of clothes." The additional labor Mother Reeves spoke about represented one transition, from deacon's wife to minister's wife. By most accounts, the MDWG affords women a forum with practical and emotional support, which helps them manage the shifts. When a husband is installed to pastor a congregation, however, pressures on wives increase even more and are exacerbated by the status afforded by the position.

In what follows, I detail my conversations with wives of pastors, bishops, and apostles who generously shared sensitive information. More than once, "I shouldn't be saying this" preceded a story or bit of information, but, without exception, they wanted to talk about their lives and labors as wives of clergymen because "there's a lot, it's hard." I have therefore decided to provide neither biographical information nor a name for any of the women. As a group, they represented both women who had moved into the position recently and those with decades of experience. They all had children and jobs outside of home and church. Their education level ranged from general education development (GED) diplomas to advanced degrees. Some had navigated life successfully, some fared OK, and some weathered bouts of "deep depression." Regardless of the differences in education, class, and years and quality of experience, they all found that the MDWG could not adequately address the range of issues they faced that were particular to the position of pastor's wife.

According to the MDWG bylaws, the pastor's wife presides over the local auxiliary, a dynamic that can isolate her from others in the group. Owing to the counseling relationship between the pastorate and the congregation, pastors' wives are hesitant to bring concerns to the group. "I've learned that in being a pastor's wife you can't share things with people," said one woman, "even if you think they're your friend. You have to tell God." As a result, the MDWG provides less support for women married to pastors. "Sometimes you may go to a workshop and hear something, but there's really not that much [support] out there," another observed. The wives tended to cobble together resources, with the only established support being a Sunday morning prayer conference call. Pastors' wives from around the country would call in to pray and ask each other for prayer support as they struggled to take on additional responsibilities and emotional labor.

Women needed support transitioning into more internal spiritual work: "you have to pray more," and "you have to be more humble." Practicing humility and patience helped women manage relationships with parishioners. One woman who married into an established church "had to be patient" with older congregants "trying to boss me around." She had always been active in church, but in the new situation, she said, "I had enough sense to know that I couldn't go and take any jobs from anybody, and all the jobs were taken." Eventually, she was able to "become active" and "well respected by my husband's people." She said they were always "very nice to me for the most part"; however, while she waited to become fully integrated, she relied on "scripture that says your gift will make room for you."

While some women married into the position at new churches, others married within the church they had called home since childhood. "I had to talk more to [the members]," one wife reported, "to be friendlier, to be more understanding." The levels of self-expectation were based on the examples of pastors' wives they had "come up under," as well as the real demands of shifting relationships with people they had known for years. "More people were reaching out to me," another woman said, "asking, 'Will you pray for me?'" She continued, "[Before, if] I didn't come visit [when they were sick], they were like, 'Oh, [it didn't really matter].' But now they say, 'You know, the pastor's wife didn't come visit me.'" Whereas she was being treated as the pastor's wife almost right away, another woman found that in her home church "people can't see you [as the wife of the pastor] when you grow up [in front of them]." Church members resisted acknowledging her as "mother" or "first lady." "They didn't want to give me that respect," she recalled. She said it had taken years, "up to this day . . . to feel comfortable with these people that I grew up with. I feel comfortable now, but I know I'm not to take ease. I know to arm myself and protect my heart."

Women also spoke about protecting their heart in marriage. "You have to give your husband to God and to the people." Jealousy could become an issue. "If he has to give a lot of time to [a female parishioner] and if you don't understand, . . . if you don't look at it in a spiritual realm and just see it in the natural realm, you could destroy your marriage and you could destroy yourself." One of the newer wives addressed the issue, but not from personal experience. "We had a Women's Council meeting," she said, "and there happened to be only pastors' wives there, so we did have a chance to share a little bit. I'm a newbie. . . . They've been pastors' wives longer, and they seem to face some God-forbidden challenges, a lot more challenges than I face." She avoided going into detail but said it had to do with "counseling women." Then she talked about a situation with her husband. "My husband had to counsel [a woman]. He pulled out a chair, pulled out a table, and had me there with him, and I guess some of the other pastors' wives may not do that." Her husband had her attend the session because he felt uncomfortable with the potential dynamics. "We're friends," she said. "He really respects me."

The ways in which a husband shows respect for his wife before the congregation can determine her interaction with parishioners. The woman who said it had taken "up to this day . . . to feel comfortable with these people that I grew up with" explained that for people to properly acknowledge the pastor's wife, "the pastor himself has to convey that." It wasn't until her husband spoke directly to the congregation (some time into the pastorate) that she felt her relations with members improve. She recalled, "He said, 'My wife is not your mommy, but she is your spiritual mother, because she is my wife. So don't say you can't call her mother. She is the mother of the church.'"

These women's work as spiritual mother, natural mother, and wife demands more time than they actually have. "How do you fit all of this in?" one asked rhetorically. "My prayer life has to take priority, but how do you do that? I've got to take care of home, take care of children, and still work. I've got to be a good wife, a good mother, a good pastor's wife, a good mother to these people. And we *always* have engagements to attend." A woman who lived in a different town from where her job and church were located said that for a long time "we visited our home and lived at church." They would go home to get clothes, and clothes matter for the wives. Another woman pointed out, "This is part of the work [of a pastor's wife], too. I have to look better." She considered sartorial demands work but clearly took pleasure in that aspect of her duties. "I know that other people are looking," she went on, "'cause I used to do the same thing, and I still do it when I look at a pastor's wife. I want to make sure she looks good." Yet another wife, who was inclined to simple dress, protested, "[People] want to dress you. . . . They want you to wear all these colored hats." She explained that she was speaking literally and figuratively. Before she took to a dressier style, congregants criticized, "You don't look like a pastor's wife." There were larger implications in that, she claimed: "People want to control you. . . . They like to make you into what they want you to be, instead of letting you be what God wants you to be."

Wives of pastors reported new responsibilities that brought mounting pressures and isolation from the communal ethos experienced in the IMD and IWC. According to the MDWG constitution, one of its primary objectives is "to address itself to meeting the psychological needs of wives of ministers and deacons that are not adequately met through instructions for wives of laymen."[47] In practice, wives of deacons see the MDWG as a fund-raising unit;

ministers' wives see it as a forum for learning how to support their husbands; and pastors' wives find it unable to address the complexity and specificity of many of their psychological and relational needs.

As men are elevated to become pastors, their wives draw their most consistent support from personal relationships with experienced older women. "She gave me a book." "She talked to me, and she encouraged me about being the pastor's wife." One woman spoke about being mentored by Mother Bonner and one specific day that "saved my marriage." She recalled:

> Mother Bonner took me to her apartment—everything was so dainty, so nice—she said, "This is what people think pastors' wives do. You entertain, and everything is really nice and fun." And she said, "I want to share with you what some of the advantages are going to be of being a pastor's wife," and she did. All morning we ate and talked and laughed, and she told me all the nice stuff. You get to travel, and people will say, "Oh, this is Pastor's wife." And she said, "You'll feel so good, and then the next two years you won't know who you are. All you will be is Pastor's wife. And if you have children, you'll be their mother and Pastor's wife, and you won't know who you are. You will have lost everything that you came into that marriage with unless you develop a ministry of your own." That was the most valuable thing that she could have ever given me.

In telling her mentee to "develop a ministry of your own," Mother Bonner may have saved more than the woman's marriage. "Pastors always outlive their wives," the woman said matter-of-factly. She revealed that most pastors in her home state are "on second or third wives." Of all the pastors' wives she had worked with statewide in "the ministers wives' group, it's only two of us remaining with our original husbands [out of about fifteen]. . . . I mean every one of the women that I was working with in the state are dead, except one."

"Why do you think that is?" I asked.

"I don't know," she responded and then said, without pausing, "I, I honestly, I do know. Honestly, I do know. They don't know how to handle the stress of being the preacher's wife because they came into it without the benefit of knowing what to expect and how to handle it. . . . I wouldn't be here now if it wasn't for Mother Bonner." She went on to explain that Mother Bonner told her that clergy couples can "make it look like it's a perfect world, what you see in the church and around convention, but it's not." She continued, "Mother Bonner said, 'They will honor and worship your husband as the man of God, but you know him as the meat man with smelly feet and dropping clothes around the house and you gotta balance all of that. You support your husband. You don't burst their bubbles, but you keep yours clear.'"

In keeping with the broad mandates of the IMD and IWC to equip holy women to "arise and build" a house for the glory of God (Nehemiah 2:20), Mother Bonner had expanded the MDWG in 1972 to more directly address the needs of ministers' and deacons' wives, but her one-on-one mentoring seems to have been most effective. "It is not a casual endeavor," the MDWG constitution warns. "The Ministers' and Deacons' wife has a special call to the service she renders. The clear need of the church today is for spiritual leadership which can inspire confidence to accomplish the divine mandate: 'Go make disciples.'"[48]

CONCLUSION

The three women's auxiliaries serve as anchors within the horizontal webs of church operation. The movement of a woman into official (titled) leadership is temporary; after her term in office, she cycles back into general membership as a mother or sister. The system keeps women who possess extensive leadership abilities and spiritual authority close to the ground of local operations, which serves the religious agenda of holy women—to model, promote, and monitor a "standard of holiness." At the same time, prohibiting women from attaining permanent structural elevation supports the male hierarchy and reinforces gender norms, also part of the COOLJC religious agenda. "The only thing that women can be president of," Dr. Littleton explained, "are the three women's auxiliaries, and they can be directors of initiatives where you have to raise money, such as Global Missions or Home Missions [departments]. You can be the director under that man, but you do all the work." She went on, "Believe it or not, that really doesn't bother me because I have always had the attitude that, growing up in holiness and it being frowned upon so much, I'm going to stay in it and I'm going to make it the best that it can be, and that has been my attitude. That's why I work wherever I need to work. I don't care who the leader is. I will help get the job done."

WOMEN'S

WORK

You have to have the power to submit.
Everyone can't do it.

Sister Cherisse Walker, COOLJC

"Apostolic [religion] is controlling," Sister Addie Thomas said matter-of-factly as she poured hot water into my teacup. "It's good for a man 'cause the men are on top, and that's a beautiful thing 'cause you need to have men on the top." Sister Thomas spoke from over thirty years as a saint, having come to Pentecostalism as a young adult in the mid-1970s. Within three months of her being saved, her boyfriend joined the church, and they married. They raised four children; the youngest, in her early twenties, still lived at home. One son had been called to the ministry, while her husband rarely attended church. "[The] man has a lot of say in this [church] realm," she continued, "even though the women are the ones pushing the church and lifting, and everything, doing most of the stuff."

Since the foundation of the Church of Our Lord Jesus Christ of the Apostolic Faith, Inc. (COOLJC), women have worked in cross-cutting networks of women's auxiliaries—"pushing," "lifting," and "doing most of the stuff"—to develop and exercise spiritual-organizational authority and build up the church. The male-headed hierarchy depends on the female majority's spiritual-organizational acumen and labor for its very existence. The ideology and institutional structure, which privilege spiritual authority while excluding women from permanent incorporation into decision-making bodies, rely on a "politics of incomplete male domination" for their coherence.[1] The gender politics of COOLJC women, a politics of righteousness, is forged at the nexus of religious practice, church-familial relations, American race politics, Black women's labor force participation, and the impact of these realms on women's sense of self. In negotiating gender relations in the church, at home, and in the world, women develop a range of emotion management skills, grounded in holiness practices, which they then judiciously utilize during each shift.

Mother Geneva Reeves, for example, had recently retired from the position of assistant vice president of sales with Chase Corporation, where she handled multimillion-dollar portfolios for private clients. Recalling her rise to upper-level management, she said, "The obstacles and the challenges that you face in a corporation as a Black female[,] . . . that glass ceiling. . . . I mean, when I got to where I was, I should have been there like ten years [earlier] actually. But[,] . . . being a Black female, forget it. . . . [E]very door was closing." She explained that God kept her "focused" because, after three decades in the church, she had a finely developed religious regimen. By her telling of it, she successfully navigated the systemic forces of on-the-job racism and sexism because of daily "six o'clock [morning] prayer. Prayer works. You cannot bend from God in the life of Jesus." On its face, Mother Reeves's demanding career in a secular world may seem to contradict her commitment to a religious organization with such conservative scriptural interpretations of gender roles. Yet her statements point to the emotional labor (no doubt left out of the job description) that she performed through a religious, gendered, and raced self-awareness. Members of COOLJC promote racial advancement, in keeping with mainstream Black traditions where women have insisted on full societal inclusion, even as church doctrine prohibits permanent elevation of women into titled, formal leadership positions.

This chapter first examines the *emotional labor* of COOLJC women as they work through seeming contradictions and real conflicts at the intersections of religion, gender, and race in the church community and at home, where they navigate religious tenets of submission and obedience in order to (re-)produce women-driven patriarchies. It then considers emotional labor in the workplace and positions of institutionalized power, as women confront the challenges of their existence in the worldly labor force, all the while bolstered by a religious community that promotes Black women's struggle for full societal inclusion. As they move between supporting and resisting patriarchal systems, self-identification as sanctified shapes, and is shaped by, the areas women deem oppressive or empowering in the church community, at home, and in the secular labor force. The women of COOLJC (re-)create complicit, resistant, and assertive strategies for righteous living as they move through the world wrapped in a legacy of Black political culture while wearing "the breastplate of righteousness."[2] Therefore, for Mother Reeves and other COOLJC women, "not bend[ing] from God in the life of Jesus" means operating imbued with the power of God, fully authorized to rise to titled leadership in the workplace from a home and church base with "men on the top."

"LET THE MAN LEAD"

In adult Sunday school class, Mother Esther Pea, the ninety-two-year-old senior mother of True Deliverance Church (TDC), lectured about the ways in which women could keep in their "proper place." Charged with training women in the ways of holiness, Mother Pea told them, "Let the man lead. Don't push ahead. Stay in the background. God made woman a great thing. A lot of women don't know how great they are. God made man first. Let him be first. Let him know he can make it." Telling women to consciously work at letting men lead promotes a concept of women's agency that does not "disrupt existing power relations," which resonates with Saba Mahmood's consideration of what it takes for pious women to "undertake particular kinds of moral action."[3] Citing the relationship between an apprentice musician and her master teacher, Mahmood notes that the apprentice musician's "agency is predicated upon her ability to be taught, a condition classically referred to as 'docility.'"[4] Like the virtuoso musician, holy women acquire skills over time through "the regime of disciplinary practice."[5] Successfully following the dictates of Mother Pea to not "push ahead" and "stay in the background" requires deliberate "struggle, effort, exertion, and achievement" by COOLJC women.[6] Training, negotiation, and contestation, too, require significant emotional labor and emotion management.

In 1983 Arlie Russell Hochschild opened a new field of study, coining the term *emotional labor* to describe the ways in which airline companies compel flight attendants to engage customers—for example, by training them to "smile like you really mean it."[7] Initially, analysis of emotional labor focused on duties perceived as part and parcel of paid positions, such as the work of flight attendants, lawyers, and fast-food workers; employees' effective person-to-person contact with the public depended on them managing their own emotions to create or shape emotions in clients and customers—the commodification of feeling.[8] Since that time, as a result of the increase in and the wide variety of face-to-face and person-to-person service employment, analysis of emotion management has expanded to include a broad range of interpersonal relations in the workplace and home, as well as explorations of gendered and classed distinctions in what emotion work is required of whom and how demands are handled.[9] Women's emotional obligations at home as well as "boundary-spanning emotion management" across family and work roles have deepened the field of study.[10] Yet much of the literature evades in-depth examinations of racial and ethnic social power relations from wider society that are carried into workplace relations. Failure to integrate the "social locations" of workers "has limited the knowledge which has been gained about the range of emotion work which is required" of people across social experiences.[11] Using the prism of emotion management shows the ways in which the emotional labor of COOLJC women encompasses negotiations of gender and race, while spanning multiple boundaries between church, home, and the secular workplace. Moreover, church obligations, in and of themselves, mirror *both* job—representing the institution—and "family."[12]

Gendered power negotiations within the church are part of a long "tradition of conflict" waged in an environment "where the operating metaphor and ideology for human relations is family."[13] Members develop intergenerational familial relationships, with all the attendant emotional obligations, expectations, and closeness. Given the male pastor (father) and the unique position of church mother, scholars have mapped a nuclear family model onto patriarchal Black American Pentecostal church organizations.[14] While the nuclear family model remains the ideal for church members' domestic relations, it fails to adequately capture the complexity of the interpersonal relationships and webs people weave to distribute spiritual and material resources within COOLJC. Social organization in COOLJC falls more in line with African American "kin-structured local networks," in which households have "shifting membership," including, on average, three generations, as well as primary networks that extend beyond the residence.[15] The nuclear family model accurately depicts a "one church mother and pastor" relationship but does not explain the organization of many COOLJC churches that have multiple mothers, whose work and influence cuts across various operational spheres.[16] Thus, it is more accurate to think of these churches as "women-centered" kin units in which "women's centrality is characterized less by the *absence* of husbands and fathers than by the significance of women."[17] While titles of "mother," "sister," and "brother" are common, young people refer to each other as "cousin" and call their parents' peers "aunt" and "uncle." The church family also includes blood relations; adult members may be siblings, cousins, spouses, in-laws, or second- and third-generation family members (with parents and grandparents still in church). These kin-unit relations color the ways members interpret and adhere to the rules of submission and obedience.

Church members use the language of submission and obedience, men in relation to God, and women in relation to God and men, yet the rhetoric of women's submission to men, while generalized in discourse, is specific in practice.[18] Doctrine requires women to submit to formal male leadership within the church polity and to their husbands, yet both arenas of submission are quite nuanced. The opening epigraph from Sister Cherrise Walker, "You have to have the power to submit. Everyone can't do it," in many ways encapsulates women's negotiations of gender politics. The "power" of Sister Walker is the power of Jesus that controls holy living. As God-in-flesh, Jesus demonstrates the power of submission and obedience through the crucifixion and resurrection. Having "the power to submit" includes having the wisdom to know when and how to submit, wisdom that is cultivated through a working relationship with God. Having "the power to submit" also points to an interpretive gap between church tenets of submission and obedience and the spiritual practices and authority of women. In relationships with men in the church community, women actively promote male leadership and engage in what I term "leading from the background" and "acceptable disobedience" to avoid open clashes with leadership.[19] Such practices and associated emotion management help women model a complex holy womanhood for girls and young women and, at the same time, keep "men on the top."

To keep the church hierarchy in place, women fashion an environment that encourages male leadership, especially for boys and young men. During a Sunday evening service, young Carter Houston, the eleven-year-old son of one of the ministers, delivered a brief recitation. It was unusual, since his regular participation in services consisted of singing in the children's choir (as do all the children) and playing drums at the beginning of the service, until an older drummer arrived to unseat him. As he spoke, Carter's self-possessed demeanor and clear presentation pleasantly surprised the saints, and they cheered him on throughout. "Yeah, yeah!" "That's right!" Saints always voice support for young people, so the response was to be expected. As Carter made his way back to his seat, one church mother took the urging to another level. "All right, Bishop!" she called. It caught on immediately. Other women, enthusiastically clapping and laughing, joined in, "Amen, Bishop!" "That's right, Bishop." Women are on task for this kind of impromptu reproduction and endorsement of community assumptions that men will move into leadership. Directing congregational emotions and setting off the group's "elevation" of young Carter to the bishopric, the church mother's expression of genuine delight highlighted the "extra emotion work" for which women take responsibility, "especially emotion work that affirms, enhances, and celebrates the well-being and status of others."[20]

Ironically, women's active encouragement of a male-headed polity may, in fact, contribute to the disproportionately low adult male membership. The contrast between the high numbers of boys and low numbers of men within COOLJC churches is striking. A longtime church member, Sister Gladys Ricks, claimed, "These churches do a disservice to men. You can have a church with fifteen women and one boy, and they'll say [to him], 'You're going to be the pastor one day.' . . . It's a disservice because [maybe your] spiritual gift [is to] be a teacher. A woman will take [that] easier, . . . but [for] a man, something's wrong with being a teacher after twenty years." The "pressure" on males to rise to leadership, according to Sister Ricks, contributes to them leaving the church once they reach young adulthood. This concern also garnered attention during an international convention, with a workshop series entitled "Just a Brother: Helping Laity Find and Appreciate Their Place and Functionality in the Ministry." The facilitator asserted that "too many brothers" were "pushed into pulpit ministry," causing "men to believe that unless they have a title they are of less value to the assembly and the body of Christ" and, as a result, to leave the church.[21]

Yet, for all concerned, attending to the emotional and spiritual harm to male members "pushed into pulpit ministry" in no way means the church should rethink its prohibition of women in pulpit ministry. At the same convention, a church apostle spoke in a large general assembly to the female majority about keeping the pulpit a male domain, "regardless of what other churches may do"; COOLJC must keep "the standard," because "it's according to the scriptures." Amid women's affirmations of "Amen" and "Thank you, Jesus," one mother spelled out her reason for supporting the policy to those within hearing distance. She did not reference scripture. "Huh!" she said sarcastically and with a slight laugh. "They can have it. We do enough! I don't want to have to do any more than I already do." As she saw it, not increasing women's workload was one pragmatic consequence of keeping men in formal leadership positions. Too, if the active push to make men leaders drives many away, another outcome is the perpetuation of a "women's movement" within the male-headed structure.[22] When Sister Adele Lee reflected on the small number of men in church, she laughed and asked rhetorically, "And how many [men] do you need? HA! How many do you want to be in there? Do you want an equal amount?" Then, in line with the official position, she added, "No, you need them all." Although most women bemoan low male attendance, practices and off-the-cuff remarks indicate that the disproportionally high female membership might not be so problematic. Perhaps the "imbalance" serves women's interests in the day-in and day-out operations of the church, in that it reduces managerial and emotional labor. Practically speaking, fewer men means fewer whom the women are expected to "let lead."

One young woman recently elected to auxiliary leadership described some of the extra work women perform to let men lead. A second-generation COOLJC member, she explained that church mothers "had a lot of patience" and that she now understood how critical it was to women's church work to "persevere." She went on, "I see that we can do so much, but because of traditionalism a lot of times women don't want to overstep men, which we shouldn't. But sometimes we don't execute on ideas that we do have. So women's labor of love, sometimes you can labor and good results don't come from it." She said moving into leadership required her to spend more time in prayer, so she could accept that some projects are "open-ended" and "never closed." In attempts to get "good results," COOLJC women bring practical tactics and emotion management into gendered negotiations, as they "undertake particular kinds of moral action" to work out church tenets of obedience and submission, avoid conflict, and try to accomplish work they deem important.[23]

LEADING FROM THE BACKGROUND

To reduce the emotional labor that can come from letting men lead, women will lead from the background, a strategy by which women can advance their priorities and keep church polity in place. I was unwittingly involved in one such incident. Over the course of my time at TDC, I participated in the New Converts Sunday school class, which was team-taught by Mother Jessie England and Minister Edwin Lee.[24] (The name of the class is somewhat misleading; it is for any adult newcomer, whether converted or not.) Minister Lee was one of five ministers under Bishop Crosley J. Cook, while Mother England, a lifelong Apostolic, held executive offices in local auxiliaries and, more importantly, exercised a great deal of spiritual and organizational power in TDC. During one class, Minister Jeffrey Anderson, the Sunday school superintendent, approached me during the lesson. "Next week I want you to move to the young adults class," he instructed. "Monica and Jeffrey both work on Sundays now, so they need more people over there." I nodded in agreement, of course, and he walked off. Immediately pausing her lesson, Mother England told me, "You're staying here," then continued teaching. I nodded in agreement, of course, thinking, "How is this going to work?" Apart from concern about my perceived dilemma, I found her semipublic override of Minister Anderson enlightening. She did not seem concerned that the other ten class participants, including Minister Lee, had heard the exchange.

After the lesson, I was standing next to Mother England, with Minister Lee a few feet away, when Minister Anderson returned. "Be sure to go over to the young adults next week," he reiterated. Not knowing how to respond, I gave him a slight smile. As he walked off, Mother England said, "Don't worry about that. You come back here next week. I'll let him know." In a mildly exasperated tone, she continued, "You don't belong over there. He should know that." Minister Lee remained silent throughout but nodded in agreement with Mother England's last statement. At the time of this exchange, I had been attending services for a year. Six months earlier, Bishop Cook had told the congregation I was an anthropologist conducting fieldwork. It was common knowledge that I was not saved, thus Mother England's exasperation with Minister Anderson's directive.

At issue was the prioritizing of administrative business over spiritual business. As the administrator of Sunday school, Minister Anderson was concerned with keeping the young adults class viable. As a spiritual leader, Mother England knew I should stay in the New Converts class until after I was saved. According to procedure, she graduated students out by letting them know it was time to move on to the young adult or adult class (depending on their age). In overriding Minister Anderson, Mother England did not "disrupt the existing power relations."[25] She was not challenging his position as a minister or as the Sunday school superintendent; she was exerting her own spiritual authority. After a year in the church, I understood Mother England to have greater spiritual and operational authority than Minister Anderson, so the next week I returned to the New Converts class, as she had directed. Minister Anderson never raised the issue with me again, and our relationship stayed intact; he seemed to have expected me to follow Mother England's background leadership. I was not, however, privy to any exchange between them and do not know the details and tenor of the negotiation. Mother England no doubt finessed the exchange to avoid any tension. There are times, however, when operating in the background with male leaders proves insufficient for women. Women do push the bounds of submission and obedience in ways that can be acceptable to church authority.

ACCEPTABLE DISOBEDIENCE

One Sunday evening after services, early on in my fieldwork, I accompanied Sister Ruth Holmes and her three children to the home of Minister Robert and Sister Kendra Clark. They tended to have an open-door policy (in fact, their door was rarely locked), so young people frequently gathered in their Queens home. Along with the stream of visitors, the couple's three young sons ensured the house was always a whirlwind of activity. On this evening, Camille Roland and Anna Highland, both in their mid-twenties, and sixteen-year-old Tamara Jones were there. Minister Clark was holding court in his recliner. Stocky and strong from years of construction work, he was a gregarious and opinionated man who loved to "witness" about Jesus.

Minister Clark had not given the sermon at services that morning; Minister James Thomas had preached. Describing Thomas's fiery and direct style, one of the young boys said, "He keeps it real." On this day he had preached about temptation and staying holy, specifically "keeping your body," and his message became the topic of conversation. Minister Clark disapproved of the way Minister Thomas had used a personal situation to illustrate the message. The young, single Minister Thomas was attracted to a female co-worker, and she to him. By his testimony, it was an intense physical pull that he fought hard to resist. Camille, Anna, and Sister Holmes all vehemently disagreed with Minister Clark, arguing that transparency in the pulpit had a greater impact on the congregation. While the substance of the debate lends itself to an analysis of leadership transparency and notions of power, I would like to focus on the manner in which the young women debated with Minister Clark. They had no qualms about raising their voices or interrupting him to make their points. They never backed down from their position. Nor did he seem to expect they would. Given the rhetoric of female submission, (and my assumptions about what it meant) I was surprised by the level playing field in the debate.

As Mother England's strategy with Minister Anderson shows, in church the women exercise prudence when disagreeing with leadership. Yet the women in Minister Clark's home were outspoken and direct. This is understandable in the context of a few variables. First, the women challenged his opinion—not a directive. Too, being outside the church building may have allowed them more leeway in communication. Next, all the women were personally close to Clark. Sister Holmes and Minister Clark had known each other since they were teenagers, and the younger women alternated between calling him Uncle Bob and Minister Clark (depending on the circumstance). Last, the women's achievements in the world imbued them with "a sincere belief in their own competence and capabilities," which included debating effective preaching strategies with a minister.[26] Sister Holmes held a master's degree and had occupied various leadership positions with the New York City Board of Education at the local school and citywide levels. Anna was a graduate student, and Camille enjoyed a successful career in corporate management. Like Mother England, each woman claimed lifelong active membership in COOLJC and dedication to the ways of holiness. The women's assertiveness demonstrated disobedience to tenets of submission that was acceptable, not only to them, but to Minister Clark as well.

"A HELPMEET . . . NOT A SLAVE"

In interactions with male church leadership, women lead from the background and exercise acceptable disobedience to assert their positions and perspectives. Women are also required to carry religious rules of deference to male authority into marriage. Women implement the same strategies with husbands as with church leaders when they deem it fitting. As the exchange between the sisters and Minster Clark suggests, although they advance the doctrine of submission and obedience, women in COOLJC do not view themselves as subordinate to men. By extension, in marriage, they do not see themselves as inherently lower than their husbands or secondary in importance.[27] During a service on "family relationships," Mother Reeves instructed, "Marriage . . . is designed by God, not man. God gave [Adam] woman to be [a] helpmeet, . . . not a slave, not a housekeeper, not someone subservient, but equal partners." She then emphasized men's duty to be providers. "Don't marry someone who's gonna lay on your mama's couch," she warned. "It's solely man's responsibility to take care of his wife and family, but a wife can decide to work if she has the desire to work."[28]

As the service came to a close, Bishop Cook addressed the congregation. "I'm from the old school," he stated. "Man should work, and the wife shouldn't." Then he said, matter-of-factly, "My wife wanted to work. So she did." Public exchanges like the one between Mother Reeves and Bishop Cook let members know that wives' deference to husbands occurs on negotiated terrain that both men and women acknowledge. Of the approximately 110 members in TDC, there were ten married men who regularly attended church services with their spouses—four ministers, four deacons, and two "brothers." While men maintain formal hierarchical authority, the dynamics of power between spouses are always in play. Both spouses participate in the social and political networks of the church and are accountable to formal and informal authority, understanding that "the influence of the female members may tip the balance of power at a given moment."[29]

Sister Lee, the wife of Minister Lee (the New Converts Sunday school teacher), described one example of the balance of power that spanned home and church. Now in her mid-forties, she had been baptized in the Holy Spirit at the extraordinarily young age of five and had remained deeply committed to the church ever since. The Lees had been married for over twenty-five years and were raising two children. Sister Lee explained that "the wife has a big role" in matters pertaining to the official advancement of her husband in the church. Before her husband was elevated to deacon, "[Bishop Cook] came to me and said, these are not his exact words, but, is your husband ready to be a deacon?" she recalled. "Is your husband deacon material? That's not exactly what he said, but that's what he meant." He asked what her husband was "doing in the home." She reported that he was "a good husband" but that she would like for him to go to church regularly.

"He didn't go to church like I did," she said. "When we first got married, although he was saved, he didn't have that zeal that I had." Sister Lee and women like her are spiritual gatekeepers to institutional leadership; the formal elevation of her husband partially, possibly primarily, depended on her assessment of his readiness. The Lees were no doubt both fully aware of the impact that a negative report would have had on the timing of his trajectory. Behind-the-scenes evaluation of men by women happens all the time. When male church leaders call on wives to assess their husbands for formal elevation, women contribute background leadership that is critical to church operations, while their emotional labor increases.

To explain the reasons "the highest degree of emotion management [within the family and church] is performed by women," Sister Lee fused the Bible, women's ongoing output, and biology.[30] "Even though the woman was made from that man and came out of that man," she asserted, "it takes a strong woman, a strong mother, a strong wife to really help that man, help that husband, help that son." She went on, "But it does say in the Bible that women are the weaker vessel, but we're the weaker *stronger* vessel! We're strong in that we can take more. That's why a woman bears children and the man doesn't. We can take more and be under rule more. Even though we have a hard time."

Women "take more" of the emotional burden to keep church and home running, as they carry out boundary-spanning emotional labor and develop strategies at the intersection of church and home, all the while managing the particular demands of each domain. What did it mean for Sister Lee to have to "report" on her husband's readiness? On the one hand, she told the story so that we can understand the direct influence of wives on the church's chain of command. On the other hand, she hinted at potential stresses involved. Giving an overall positive account, she was "able to say" he was a "good husband" and "good provider" who needed more religious "zeal." A negative report would have generated internal emotional conflict (and possibly conflict at home) as she weighed the desire to see her husband promoted against the good of the church. Sister Lee's "weaker stronger" vessels, then, are self-aware women who perform high degrees of emotional labor that bridge church and home, while they keep up an admittedly submissive role in the marriage.

Within this environment, men are expected to live holy, too. Wives resist submitting if they believe the wishes of their husbands run counter to the will of God. Given the intimate relationship between each saint and the

Holy Spirit, this opens a significant space for women to work out the meanings of submission and obedience. In other words, if spouses disagree, the woman's assessment of both her own and also her husband's relationship with God factors into the extent of her compliance with his wishes. This was especially relevant for women who, navigating a range of circumstances, were married to men not in the church. Women spoke about the challenges of being "unequally yoked," often the result of women being saved after marriage.[31] One woman talked about the difficulties in trying "to be a companion" to an unsaved husband, as changes in her values caused tension between them. He charged that she "let that church dictate to you what you're doing." Wives, then, negotiate between the church doctrine of wifely submission and determinations of what we may think of as "acceptable disobedience," which may also be acceptable to the church community but unacceptable to husbands. Yet, once in the situation, most women stay married and stay at the altar, praying for their spouse to come to Jesus.

Some husbands were "backsliders"—converted individuals who had left the church. That was the case for Sister Jeanette Allen, who was born and raised in a Holiness family in a South Carolina sharecropping community. Sister Allen came to New York at seventeen, and at the time of our interview had been married for nearly forty years to a husband who left the church. Her situation was particularly poignant. During the early years of their marriage, Sister Allen and her husband "were always in church together." Once he stopped going, he wanted to control her participation, insisting she could go only when he gave express permission. She refused to obey. She also received pressure from an uncle, who had raised her and was the pastor of the family church in South Carolina. He told her to listen to her husband and stay home. In this instance Sister Allen had to decide to "disobey" not only her husband but also her uncle-father and (in the same person) her former pastor-father. In the end, she told her uncle, "I'm sorry, [but] . . . I want to go to church. I might be disobedient, but God forgive me."

I asked whether she felt her uncle was saying that obedience to her husband was more important than obedience to God. She explained that, without a full biblical understanding, one could mistakenly think that obedience to her husband *was* obedience to God. Paraphrasing scripture, she said, "Like the Bible said, 'wives be obedient,' you know, 'obey your husband in the Lord,' which is right. But then also [the Bible said] 'husbands must treat your wife right.'"[32] Referencing Ephesians 5:22–29 was also a way for her to introduce the physical abuse she suffered at the hands of her husband. Sister

Allen's decision to go against the demands of her husband, based on what "the Bible said," held dire consequences. "Every time [I] would go home [from church]," she explained, "my husband would treat me so bad—kick me, bite me, beat me, put a water hose on me and everything." She said someone had told her she could avoid the mistreatment by just staying home. Knowing that was not the case, she opted to go to church and have "a good time with the Lord."

As it turned out, Sister Allen's husband used "any reason" to justify the assaults. "So if the dinner wasn't right, I didn't iron his shirt right, he would, you know, do anything. So you know . . ." She trailed off and sat silently for a moment. "Well," she continued defiantly, "I would be disobedient," and she resolved to stay in church. "God have to forgive me," she determined, "because I feel as if, as a wife, I do the wifely duty. . . . I do my housework and take care of my family. . . . Why should I be penalized and stay home?" She told her husband, "I go to work every day, so why should I listen to you?" She was living holy and fulfilling her responsibilities, while her husband was neither going to church nor treating his wife right.

Sister Allen's circumstance was exceptional within the church, and her decision to "be disobedient" was acceptable to members. In fact, Mother Pea took it even further. At the end of a missionary service in which Sister Allen testified about her home life, Mother Pea, in her concluding remarks, emphatically told her, and in essence the entire congregation, "If you had gotten a pan and slapped him upside his head, he would have backed up off you! You was too easy. But thank God, He delivered you and kept you." Mother Pea's public declaration that Sister Allen should fight back, like the earlier statements of Mother Reeves and Bishop Cook, serves notice to the membership that wives can stipulate the parameters of submission and obedience. Thus, Sister Allen operated from a position of acceptable disobedience, complicated by her repetitions of "God forgive me."

Sister Lee and Sister Allen, both lifelong Pentecostals, carried out boundary-spanning emotional labor to manage the converging duties of church and home, employing different strategies in differing contexts. Sister Lee suggested that spiritual authority validated her background leadership. Certainly, Pastor Cook calling on her to assess the readiness of her husband for promotion was confirmation. He sought her appraisal because she was authoritative. Sister Allen brought biblical knowledge and authority of scriptural interpretation to undergird the emotional labor of negotiating doctrine and the conditions of her home life. Notably, for Sister Allen, her participation in the workforce and her position as coprovider and manager of the home ("I go to work everyday. . . . I do my housework and take care of my family") also fueled her determination to "be disobedient." With this she pulls our attention to the complex boundary-spanning emotional labor of most churchwomen, which bridges church, home, and paid employment. When situations beyond the sanctuary call for women to address issues of their full inclusion in the workplace, they bring a distinctive religious, race, and gender consciousness to bear on emotion management strategies that bridge religious and secular experiences. Yet, in the workplace, women push against forces restricting their promotion into titled leadership.

"THE HEAD AND NEVER THE TAIL"

The women of COOLJC neither shun public titles nor assume men should be "on top" in their professional lives. Many have advanced degrees and careers that place them in supervisory positions over male workers.[33] They carry on "a tradition of a militant assertion of personhood and a sincere belief in their own competence and capabilities in the larger society" like that found among other women in the larger Black American Holiness-Pentecostal body "who sincerely believe that preaching is a man's province (and sometimes even more among such women)."[34] Self-affirmation as a holy Black woman in the workplace demands significant emotional labor, "the often invisible dimension of relational work," that goes far beyond the job description.[35] When women push against on-the-job racism and sexism, this is acceptable resistance, as no legitimate doctrine of submission and obedience exists.[36] Members see race, gender, and religious discrimination on the job as illegitimate, based on a commitment to meritocracy in the wider world.

Mother Reeves, a minister's wife, cracked "that glass ceiling" at Chase Corporation, and her success in that setting demanded she hone particular emotion management skills. Her "belief in [her] own competence and capabilities in the larger society" was also crucial in the journey from agrarian life to urban corporate culture in a major New York financial institution.[37] In 1970, while in her mid-twenties, she moved from rural North Carolina to New York City with her husband and four young sons. The daughter of sharecroppers, after the age of ten she spent school breaks working the fields, mostly picking cotton ("I had to get that two hundred pounds of cotton per day") and sometimes vegetables and fruits. Mother Reeves always thrived in school, yet she gave up two full-tuition college scholarships to marry. She had completed some college and was working as a substitute teacher when the family ventured north.

Once in New York, she secured a secretarial position at Chase Bank. "Blacks had just begun to . . . become tellers," she remembered. "[Management] didn't trust 'em with the money and stuff. [Most Black people] had the background, cleaning the mail room, all that kind of good stuff." Even though her prospects looked limited, she secured a copy of "a book" on the job "that would teach me anything that I wanted to know" about the world of banking. She said, "[It] became my lunch every day." It was her only avenue for learning the internal workings of the bank because "I found out that nobody was gonna teach me anything because I was Black." Through diligence, by 1988 she had ascended the ranks of the corporation to assistant vice president, which meant surpassing primarily White male managers and negotiating peer relationships that changed as she moved into supervisory positions. Along with proficiency in banking, Mother Reeves developed emotion management skills to cover her frustration with discriminatory practices in White male corporate culture.

Mother Reeves explained emotional labor and its yield, as she climbed the corporate ladder, in the context of holiness. "God, He makes that possible," she said, referring to her corporate success, "because He keeps you, to break the chains that hold you. . . . Because not only do you have the White managers that don't want you to be there, you got your everyday coworkers." To become a successful manager to former coworkers, she had to "stay humble," and "God keeps you humble" through prayer. She let humility guide her management strategies, style, and ethics. Going out of her way to teach coworkers all she had learned, she helped them advance in their careers, which, by her telling, ran counter to corporate culture. Supervisors told Mother Reeves that she was "not rigid enough," "not cold-hearted enough." But she persisted, refusing to adopt strategies "not of God." She said management wanted her "to do the wrong thing. When with God," she explained, "I can't just tell you lies." Sister Karen Gordon had similar experiences. She spent twenty years at Goldman Sachs on Wall Street, starting as a clerk in the early 1980s, right after she joined the church. As she ascended the ranks, she, too, found that management rejected her ethical approach to the job. After over fifteen years of steady promotions, she was in line for a supervisory position, "but, because of my Christian background, they knew I wasn't going to undermine anybody, or lie on anybody." Her sentiments echoed those of Mother Reeves about being duplicitous. "I can't look at you," said Sister Gordon, "knowing I'm writing you up, and I'm gonna get rid of you. I can't do that to people."

Mother Reeves and Sister Gordon significantly expand our understanding of the interactive spheres of emotion management by bridging the religious and secular realms of devout Black women. Both women handled feelings of "frustration and aggravation in the professional workplace" known to many Black people, nonreligious and religious alike.[38] Bringing holiness principles into the corporate world compounded Mother Reeves's and Sister Gordon's already fraught political positions as African American women. They nonetheless implemented particular strategies developed through years of church work. Mother Reeves built a successful career but thinks her refusal to compromise holiness principles, along with "being Black and female," delayed promotions and "held [her] back from accomplishing [her] goals long ago." Sister Gordon feels the response of management to her Christian ethics permanently stalled her career. Being less direct about the race and gender politics at Goldman Sachs, she simply stated, "There were only, like, two Black people [who worked] in my area, so you know . . ."[39] Even though she stayed for twenty years, Sister Gordon "didn't fit in" with an overwhelmingly White corporate culture of backbiting and deceit. She acknowledged, "That wasn't my world. It wasn't for me."

An interesting distinction arose with COOLJC women in the workforce outside of corporate positions. Those working in fields considered an extension of "women's work"—health care, teaching, and other social service or service-sector jobs—reported that employers valued certain Christian ethics brought to the job, such as honesty, caring, and sharing.[40] Here we see Christian ethics merge with "a long history" in which "women should be more altruistic than men."[41] Mother Evelyn Baker, a recently retired registered nurse, explained, "Management at the hospital liked me because I would do extra things even if it was past my shift time, because, for me, it was the right thing to do. They knew a lot of patients liked me, too, because I would pray with them if they wanted." She said all that was fine with the supervisors as long as she did not "talk about Jesus." Whether employers approved or disapproved of the ways women brought religious conviction to the job, women across occupations drew strength from their faith practices while displaying a "militant assertion of personhood" fashioned by years of labor in the church.[42] In addition, regardless of their occupation, women were committed to a meritocracy in the workplace. Sister Gordon believed she "deserved" the supervisory position at Goldman Sachs. Once that had been denied, she stayed at her final position for a few more years to reach the twenty-year retirement mark. Throughout, she drew solace from "laying it all on the altar." She told herself, "God has saved me, and God has delivered me. Don't go back to Egypt." Sister Gordon explained that worship services and prayer work kept her free from bondage ("Egypt"), meaning she could trust God to manage any aggravation until she reached the goal of retirement.

Mother Reeves insisted "that six o'clock morning prayer" assured her success at Chase Corporation. "God brought me the best of clients, and I managed the best of monies," she recalled. "I had a portfolio of $163 million [and] a client base of 685 souls or clients, households that I managed. . . . [There were] fifty-seven branches in Manhattan, and I always ranked in the top five [of branch managers]." As she explained it, race-gender power structures collapsed in the face of holy power. "If you're a White male and I'm a Black female [and] . . . if you want to feel that [you're superior], that's fine," she said.[43] "But what brings me there is what I do. . . . God will make me the head and never the tail, and I always told them that." She then went on to bolster her position with additional scriptural references: "Woe unto you! You might as well have a millstone around your neck as to hurt me, because you really don't know what you're doing! I've seen God move all the managers, just move them, away from me. Turn it all around."

Mother Reeves employed biblical imagery to channel the anger that, many Black professionals argue, "is never appropriate" for them to show in the workplace "and [that] thus should be concealed."[44] She walked a fine line between what she could and could not say. She felt secure citing a portion of Deuteronomy 28:13 to managers (which she "always told them"): "And the Lord shall make thee *the head and never the tail*; and thou shalt be above only, and thou shalt not be beneath; if that thou hearken unto the commandments of the Lord thy God." She paraphrased Matthew 18:6–7, however, for my benefit, so I could better understand the resources she brought to bear on the conflict: "But whoso shall offend one of these little ones which believe in me, it were better for him that *a millstone were hanged about his neck*, and that he were drowned in the depth of the sea. . . . *[W]oe to that man* by whom the offence cometh!"[45] She ended by referencing the words of Jesus at the crucifixion, as recorded in Luke 23:34: "Then said

Jesus, Father, forgive them; for *they know not what they do*." She invoked the millstone to harness workplace foes with God's retribution and begged the Father's forgiveness for the ignorance of the crucifiers, while she became one with the suffering Christ. But, with the managers, she kept that to herself.

Corporate professionals are generally "encouraged to mask emotion, a norm described as 'detached concern,'" because corporate culture sets the dispassionate as authoritative.[46] Within these types of settings, "women will suffer most when the display norms . . . emphasize emotion neutrality" because of gender-specific socialization.[47] For Black professional women, the historical legacy, and also the contemporary setting of "wear[ing] the mask," compounds emotional masking.[48] Since openly talking about the wrath of God would no doubt have antagonized her supervisors, Mother Reeves exercised prudence when citing scripture to both mask her true feelings and also handle the emotions of others.[49] At the same time, adopting a religious posture and "staying humble" with coworkers as she moved up the corporate ladder kept her coworkers from feeling as though she was no longer a peer. Weaving scripture throughout workplace narratives points to the ways in which COOLJC women perform yet another layer of work; they stay in a Bible-time frame of mind that continuously reveals the "living Word" and joins religious labor with workplace emotion management. By refusing to relinquish holiness standards, they understand themselves as spiritual authorities in the labor force.

"YOU'RE SUPPOSED TO BE SUCCESSFUL"

As women push for full societal inclusion, church teachings further fuel women's perspectives on spiritual power, race, and gender and drive approaches to resisting on-the-job oppression. During a Sunday sermon, Bishop Cook, pastor to Mother Reeves and Sister Gordon, told the congregation, "[We have to] fight against the system that thinks a Black man can't be successful in the Lord. . . . [You're] supposed to be successful in life because God is blessing you. [You're] Holy Ghost–filled!" The pastor's call to the "Black man" to "fight . . . to be successful" was meant and understood as specific to Black manhood and general to "the race." After Bible study one Monday night, he used an opportune announcement to encourage women and men to "move higher" in education and careers. "The Building Committee met with the lawyer[,] . . . a young, smart Apostolic woman," he said. "It's good that women are really going someplace. I was telling the men to go back to school. True Deliverance has about fifteen women with [advanced] degrees and two men. . . . I would feel very proud to have [more] men with master's degrees."

Around the same time of Bishop Cook's announcement, the official magazine of COOLJC, *Contender for the Faith*, published an issue focusing on the "Inspiring, Prominent, Productive, Pentecostal Achievers in COOLJC." Corporate executives, attorneys, college professors, medical doctors, and doctoral candidates grace the front and back covers. Of six saints featured on the front, half are women, and of the nine on the back cover, six are women.[50] This signals the ways in which women's educational and career advances translate into religious and racial progress, modeling the success-ful "Holy Ghost–filled" church member and validating the religious man-date of the organization.

Nonetheless, when Bishop Cook held up the "young, smart Apostolic woman" as an example of success, he did so within a realm of ongoing gen-dered tension. While women plow through structural and interpersonal trenches on the job, with the official support of the church, some individual men can meet public recognition of women's successes with ambivalence or hostility. A church sister later confided that the men were "not happy" about the public "encouragement" by Bishop Cook. Some of them were "pretty upset," she said. Black women's lives in the labor market carry a fraught his-tory of debasement, survival, and accomplishment as they continue to navi-gate the dynamics of de jure and de facto racism and sexism.[51] At the same time, the achievements of COOLJC women always carry the potential of sparking the always smoldering intraracial gender tensions that are part and parcel of church life.[52]

Balancing between personal effort and community representation be-comes even more complicated for women when church leaders direct them to use their spiritual leadership and expertise from worldly success to im-prove the conditions of men in their lives. On Mother's Day, Bishop Cook delivered a sermon titled "The Wisdom of Mothers," in which "mother" referred to natural mothers and spiritual mothers. "There is a conspiracy against the Black man," he told the congregation. "A wedge has been driven, but the mother can break that yoke. Help your son to be successful in life. Teach your son how to be a man, not a weakling! . . . Many Black women have been successful. . . . [T]each [men] that they can have leadership. . . . It's gonna take the mothers, the women, to bring the men out." On the one hand, this called into question women's submission to men. On the other hand, Bishop Cook sought to bring (return) men to their "natural" position as the head of women. He was nonetheless confident that women possessed the skills and insight to help men. Emotional and organizational skills that women hone in church and on the job, such as leading from the background, training leaders in order to let them lead, masking, and navigating strategies of acceptable disobedience and acceptable resistance, if passed on, may result in men cultivating much-needed emotion management skills for the workplace.

CONCLUSION

The women of COOLJC develop complex emotion management skills as they slog through the myriad demands of laboring activity, always staying "on business for the Lord." Self-awareness as boundary-spanning workers, at church, at home, and in the workplace, buttresses their sense of righteousness in the world. Even so, translating an Apostolic-centered ethical standpoint into the workplace can increase the emotional labor demands on Black women in secular labor systems. At the same time, women draw support for on-the-job self-assertive strategies from a religious organization that promotes the full inclusion of Black women in society. They therefore must develop skill sets and devise strategies to handle the incongruity of moving between patriarchal systems they promote and those they resist, as they hammer out a politics of righteousness that requires a particular kind of women's work.

This type of boundary-spanning emotion work is carried out solely by women. There are other spheres of churchwomen's labor, however, that have become gendered over time. Intimate labor at the altar to bring new souls to Christ is one, to which we now turn.

HARVESTING

SOULS FOR

CHRIST

Working around the altar . . .
that's really a labor of love.

Mother Lucille Grayson, COOLJC

Sunday morning altar call at True Deliverance Church (TDC) in Queens, New York: "If you need prayer, come. If you're sick in your body, come. If you want to be filled with the precious gift of the Holy Ghost, speaking in tongues as the spirit of God gave utterance, come. If you want to stand in the gap for someone, come." The organ, bass, trumpet, and drums punctuate each of Bishop Crosley J. Cook's calls as he closes his sermon and invites congregants to the altar. Mother Jessie England and Sister Ruth Holmes move from their seats in the third pew and position themselves at the first pew. Standing on either side of the center aisle, they create a gateway to the five ministers who have come down from the dais to the floor to pray for those in need. Sister Daphne Morgan, a member of the choir, begins singing, "Come to Jesus." Following her lead, the band segues from their up-tempo vamp into her meditative hymn. Supplicants form a "prayer line" down the center aisle of the sanctuary. Deacon John Highland anoints the forehead of each petitioner with oil. As congregants reach the gateway to the altar,

Mother England and Sister Holmes direct each to an available minister for personalized prayer. With prayer, some congregants "come under the anointing"—contracting, bending, jerking, whirling, running in place, "shouting" the holy dance, crying out, and speaking in tongues. Others move forward to the curtained railing separating the raised pulpit from the altar area, where they remain deep in prayer; some "tarry"—spending concentrated time praying specifically for baptism by the Holy Ghost. Others immediately return to their seats. As the altar becomes populated, four additional altar workers make their way to the front, attending to individual worshippers as needed.

After Minister Robert Clark prays for Veronica, she stays at the altar, joining about twenty other worshippers; she prays, crying with arms outstretched and palms up. Veronica, a social work graduate student, first came to the church about six months ago, with a good friend who is a longtime member. Her sporadic attendance has grown into regular worship on Friday evenings and Sunday mornings, and she joined the New Converts Sunday school class. At every service over the past few weeks, Veronica has answered the preacher's call to "come for prayer."

The last in line has received prayer. Sister Holmes moves from her position at the "gateway" to Veronica and stands just off of her left shoulder at a diagonal. She plants her feet about a foot from Veronica and leans her upper body forward, speaking into Veronica's left ear. Never touching, Sister Holmes's body comes as close as one can without making contact. She rocks slightly, in and out, so that her body and voice create physical and sonic waves. "Yeah, yeah, yeah." "Call His name." "He knows your heart." "Praise Him." "He's right there." "*Oh, Halleluuujah!*" Tears and perspiration stream down Sister Holmes's face as she urges and prays. After about fifteen minutes, Veronica's intensity diminishes, and she emerges from her prayerful state. They embrace. Veronica returns to her seat; Sister Holmes wipes her face and neck with a paper towel while moving to another supplicant. At the front of the altar, just off the base of the raised pulpit, Mother England is bending over a teenage girl who is kneeling, "tarrying" for the Holy Ghost—crying out to Jesus. Soon Mother England kneels beside her.

It is nearing three o'clock, and both Mother England and Sister Holmes have been in church since nine thirty this morning, Mother England to teach the New Converts Sunday school class and Sister Holmes to attend adult class, then lead devotional, the congregational singing that precedes the eleven-thirty worship service.[1] How long they remain in the sanctuary this afternoon depends on the "move of Spirit" and the souls that need encouragement. After altar work, they'll retire to the downstairs social hall for dinner and relaxation until four o'clock, when an hour of corporate kneeling prayer commences in the sanctuary. They'll stay for the Sunday evening service, which runs from five thirty to seven thirty—depending on the move of Spirit and the number of souls who come to the altar. God willing, before the long day is over, someone will elect to be water baptized or will push through to Holy Ghost anointing—"speaking in tongues, as the Spirit gave them utterance" (Acts 2:4).

INTIMATE LABOR

An altar worker performs a kind of dance, winding in and out of praying and anointed congregants, impelling each to "go deeper" and "praise Him." She knows how long to stay and when to shift to another "soul." When a soul comes under the anointing, the woman must stay just close enough. Sometimes placing her hand lightly on the back or arm, she moves in the rhythm of the embodied Spirit. If a worshipper is "slain in the Spirit" and falls, the job requires quick reflexes and strength for altar workers to catch and ease the woman to the floor. Altar work is physical and spiritual, a type of *intimate labor* that yields individual and communal rewards—bringing a soul to Christ, honing the altar worker's missionary skills, building the earthly church, and building the Kingdom by expanding the saintly "family in Christ."

This chapter delves into women's labor at the altar, "harvesting souls for Christ."[2] Mother England, Sister Holmes, and other altar workers attended to the spiritual needs of the saved and unsaved who came to pray; however, here, *harvesting souls* names the specific labor of bringing people fully into the religious community—conversion.[3] I look at altar work through the lens of intimate labor, an approach that brings together and builds on studies of the emotional, caring, and reproductive labor of women. Scholars of intimate labor aim to broaden our understanding of "work that involves embodied and affective interactions" and its relation with market forces.[4] Bodily or emotional intimacy is characterized by workers' "attentiveness" to the "intimate needs of individuals . . . [that] would include . . . bodily upkeep, care for loved ones, creating and sustaining social and emotional ties, and health and hygiene maintenance."[5] Intimate labor covers a wide range of working conditions and interpersonal relationships involving "interactions . . . [that] depend on particularized knowledge received [by], and attention provided by," the worker.[6] Providers of intimate labor may be privy to "shared secrets, interpersonal ritual, bodily information, [and] awareness of personal vulnerabilities."[7] Strategies of attentiveness may include "terms of endearment, bodily services, private languages, [and] emotional support."[8] Using skilled attentive strategies, altar workers in the Church of Our Lord Jesus Christ of the Apostolic Faith, Inc. (COOLJC), become privy to the intimate processes of embodied spiritual transitioning as they address the "intimate needs of individuals" for spiritual upkeep.[9]

Studies of intimate labor show particular concern for the ways in which caring labor and personal services can be understood in relationship to commodification—whether actually paid or unpaid. For example, elder care provided by a visiting nurse is compensated, yet similar work by a family member rarely is.[10] Intimate labor demonstrates the numerous ways in which money and intimate life converge, in both formal and informal economies. For example, the immigrant worker who incorporates prayer into her client's end-of-life care provides spiritual care beyond the formal job requirements.[11] Attaching dollar values to certain care work troubles scholars concerned about the impact of commodifying relationships, that is, directly linking love and money.[12] Most saints would agree; you cannot (and should not) put a price on the Lord's work.[13] Nonetheless, bringing the religious labor of women into the conversation on intimate labor calls attention to work that has not been perceived as having market value. With altar workers we see women who do not receive direct financial compensation, and thus are considered unpaid. Yet labor at the altar directly produces more church members who are committed, and tithes and offerings from members finance church operations. Church members remain cognizant of the religious institution's economic dependence on the intimate labor skills and practices of women, as well as the direct monetary contributions of women, because, as one church mother told me, "the women are the ones who carry the church, financially and all."[14]

At the same time, altar work broadens conceptual frames of intimate labor by crosscutting two spheres perceived as distinct in intimate labor scholarship—"unpaid care in intimate settings and unpaid care in economic organizations."[15] Altar workers carry out unpaid duties in many settings, blurring a divide between intimate settings and economic organizations. Women work outside of the church with potential saints and spend innumerable hours in prayer at home, at church, on the job, and in the car—

mandatory for effective work. We may also think about the spiritual register in which the work takes place as an intimate setting. Moreover, the kin-based religious environment of the church itself blurs a neat divide between intimate and institutional (see chapter 4).

The intimacy of altar work depends on networks of women who pass along practices through an apprenticeship model, cultivating new generations to take up the mantle of harvesting souls, for the benefit of the individual seeker and the institution of the church. These intimate practices tie church members to each other, while bolstering allegiance to the church community and doctrine. While this study focuses on COOLJC, examining conversion processes as intimate exchanges offers new analytical possibilities for exploring the exponential growth of global Pentecostalism as the religious movement attracts millions of followers, 75 percent of whom are women, across geopolitical, economic, ethnic, and religious terrains.[16] In efforts to deepen our understanding of individual and communal religious identity, Pentecostal scholars give us numerous perspectives on what motivates newcomers to convert. Two key queries drive many studies: what are the circumstances under which people convert, and what are the implications for subjectivity, community, and society?[17] This chapter departs from previous studies by asking, what are the contours of women's intimate labor as they (re-)produce the culture of "bringing new souls to Christ" through altar work?

Embedded in my question about altar work are particularities of COOLJC theology and practice that may not be present in other forms of Pentecostalism. Specifically, full transition into the church requires being born of the water (full-immersion baptism "in the name of Jesus") and being born of the Spirit ("speaking in tongues as the Spirit of God gave utterance"). Except on rare occasions, saints in this study had chosen to be water baptized before they sought Spirit baptism. Going down in the "liquid grave" symbolically ended the old way of life and began a new life in which one, having repented of one's sins, took Jesus Christ as one's personal Savior—accepting the redemption of the crucifixion and the resurrection's promise of eternal life. After going down in the water, the baptized began "tarrying" for the Holy Ghost—the transitional practice of intense, focused prayer that leads to Spirit baptism. Some began tarrying immediately; others held off for weeks, months, and sometimes years, depending on their readiness to fully commit to Apostolic Pentecostalism.

The church offered seekers numerous opportunities to pursue Spirit baptism, including an altar call after each worship service and separate prayer services throughout the week. As a denomination, COOLJC came out of a Holiness-Pentecostal tradition in which "prayer bands" were the heart of prayer services and were "one of the foundational practices of the women's work."[18] Prayer "warriors" would come together, praying and singing, "to increase their personal spiritual discipline and communal focus."[19] Those seekers with "their mind made up" to pursue Holy Ghost baptism made their way to prayer meetings to tarry. By and large, the faithful in COOLJC received the Holy Ghost after participating in church services and actively tarrying, most often at the altar with the support of altar workers.[20] Spirit baptism could be sudden or come after long periods of seeking.

Although saints, as opposed to seekers, overwhelmingly populated the altar at most services, altar workers indicated in conversations with me that they paid particular attention to bringing new souls to Christ. The undertaking required working in close proximity, as they encouraged seekers to open up and "let Him in," and to "loose" their tongues by rapidly repeating "Hallelujah" or "Jesus." Techniques designed to help the seeker mentally, physically, and spiritually surrender are said to allow the spirit of Jesus (the Holy Ghost) to enter the seeker and baptize him or her. The opening narrative revolved around Veronica, a yet-to-be-saved seeker, and the work carried out by Sister Holmes, Mother England, and others possessing the "talent to break the yoke," attending to seekers and helping them to "push through" to Holy Ghost anointing.

In what follows, I examine the intimate labor of altar workers across three generations. The eldest group—the founding mothers and missionaries of COOLJC—I accessed through the narratives of the women they mentored and through church literature. With the founding women we will see the work of social reproduction as they encouraged and trained the next generation. The middle generation came of age as altar workers in the mid-1950s and is represented by Mother Lucille Grayson. Through her we learn details about technical skills required for effective, intimate altar work. The youngest generation of women, represented by Sister Holmes, received training from the middle generation and came of age in the late 1980s. Sister Holmes viewed the caring-reproductive labor of altar work through the lens of midwifery, offering a compelling analogy for the work and its change over time. These women represent those with a lifelong commitment, who were mentored by older women. Some women, however, come to COOLJC and altar work later in life. The final narrative, that of Mother Ida Lester, sheds light on the route taken to gain authority as an altar worker through prayer groups. To fully appreciate the importance of altar workers, before delving into their stories, we will explore the placement and significance of the altar call within its religious setting.

GETTING TO THE ALTAR

The liturgy at TDC, as in the vast majority of Pentecostal worship services, displayed an ideal trajectory toward the sermon and altar call. Bishop Cook's invitation to come for prayer, healing, or Spirit baptism, or "to stand in the gap for someone" (to intercede on someone's behalf to petition God), opened the way for congregants to move forward into the "holy of holies" within the sanctuary space and receive personal prayer and a touch from a man of God. The saved and unsaved alike carried joys, burdens, prayers of gratitude, and petitions for relief to the altar. The altar call and other liturgical elements, however, have different shapes and significance across Pentecostal communities. Writing on South African Pentecostal women, Maria Frahm-Arp divides the worship service into "preliminaries" and "the main event," which is the sermon. The altar call follows, attracting "anyone who had been moved by the sermon" to join group prayer.[21] "After the sermon," as she describes it, "those with particular needs could go into one of the side rooms for prayer or pray with someone in the area in front of the stage."[22] In these South African churches, the altar call appears to be less significant than in COOLJC churches. This may well be attributed to a theology that does not require speaking in tongues as definitive evidence of conversion.

In St. Simon's Island, Georgia, at the Church of God in Christ, speaking in tongues is part and parcel of religious practice, yet the altar call takes a different form than at COOLJC. Instead of forming a prayer line, the congregation, en masse, "kneel[s] or stand[s] around the perimeter of the lower pulpit . . . and [prayer] is directed more specifically at healing," with the pastor asking God for general communal well-being.[23] On occasion, the pastor may be specific; moving throughout the congregation, he "lays on hands, [while] others . . . may also 'lay on hands' at this time."[24] The "power of the spirit" falls, and some come under the anointing—"shouting," "dancing," or speaking in tongues.[25] If an unsaved worshipper appears to be seeking the Holy Ghost, "core women . . . of spiritual influence . . . will group themselves around the individual" to urge them on.[26] Peter D. Goldsmith names this "the intervening time" between the sermon and the benediction.[27] In a familiar academic stroke, both Frahm-Arp and Goldsmith interpret the altar call as an incidental segment of worship that is catalyzed by the sermon. But I would argue that, within COOLJC, the altar call and altar work are essential components of the worship service and worthy of in-depth investigation in their own right. Even beyond its proximity to the sermon, the significance of the altar call, and thus of altar workers, can be better understood through the Black call-and-response atmosphere of worship services.

From the opening devotional through the altar call, congregants activate worship by way of the temporal thrust of call-and-response, the "basic [non-linear] organizing principle" of African American cultural expression.[28] Each element of the service responds to the layers of call-and-response that have preceded it. At the same time, within each segment of worship, call-and-response occurs in multiple directions—congregant-congregant, musician-congregant, preacher-musician, congregant-preacher, and so on. With regard to sermons, scholars pay particular attention to call-and-response through preacher-congregation interaction, hence the tendency to view the altar call as catalyzed by the sermon. An effective sermon, however, depends on the "interactive network . . . of verbal and non-verbal" call-and-response throughout the service, in order to join the participants "in a unified movement" to Jesus.[29]

Consequently, the outcome of a sermon is "related to temporal circumstances beyond . . . the immediate circumstances of [the sermon]."[30] Too, the temporal thrust of anticipatory call-and-response extends the sermon as it flows into the altar call, thereby making the altar call *critical* in evaluating the efficacy of the sermon. The conventional microview of the supplicant's trajectory to the altar (and thus salvation) as catalyzed by the sermon alone obscures both the multiple pathways and also the guides that bring people fully into the religious community. Looking at the cumulative intent of Sunday morning worship and Sunday evening evangelical services, Diane J. Austin-Broos details the processes by which Jamaican Pentecostals bring new members into the fold. Bible lessons, group "vocal prayer," a sermon, congregational singing, and testimony draw the unsaved into the religious environment. An altar call concludes both morning and evening services, which gives saints the forum to pray for members, seekers, and visitors. "Though the pastor is prominent here," Austin-Broos notes, "so also are other saints."[31]

While souls saved at altars in Jamaica, South Africa, and the United States may most certainly be the direct result of a preacher's sermon and altar prayer, here I want to delve deeper into the "other saints" laboring in close proximity to the sermonic event—altar workers. Sister Holmes, Mother England, and their coworkers in COOLJC carried responsibility for realizing the sermon's effectiveness, as its intent reverberated from the pulpit to the altar and beyond. Moreover, charged with the spiritual upkeep of the church, they served as links throughout the week, keeping seekers connected to the charge of the church from Sunday to Sunday and from week to week.

Altar workers in COOLJC are usually church mothers and missionaries. Church mothers wield a great deal of power within local congregations but have no organization-wide representation. The missionaries of COOLJC, however, have their own department that was established in 1923, four years after the founding of the church (see chapter 3). While there is an international component to its work, within the local context the Missionary Department oversees the spiritual health of the church. In large measure, the department was created to "make an opportunity for the missionary women to be helpers together with our ministers and pastors in bringing souls to Christ."[32]

Altar work is not women's work per se, yet women make up the majority of altar workers. "That's because the men didn't establish the network," explained Dr. Ruby Littleton. She went on, "Women set up a system to train each other for altar work. The men didn't." Men, having been "called by God" to preach, pray with tarrying souls. Women, too, insist that they receive the prodding of the Spirit; mothers, missionaries, and other women who "have a love for souls" may become altar workers, without a title or auxiliary affiliation, even as any man can move into altar work. But it's "highly unusual, vary rare," one sister explained, for "brothers or deacons" to be altar workers. Thus, altar workers are understood to be women. Men working at the altar are assumed to be ministers. "That would be a correct assumption," the sister affirmed. We now turn to the histories, training, and labor of the women altar workers across three generations.

THE EARLY DAYS

Mother England (who aided seekers in the opening of this chapter) served at the local level as the vice president of the Missionary Department, the president of the Ministers' and Deacons' Wives Guild, a member of the Women's Council, and, as mentioned earlier, the teacher of the New Converts Sunday school class. The oldest of three girls, she grew up in Harlem, New

York, next door to Refuge Temple, the mother church of COOLJC. When she was seven, her parents began sending the girls to church; her sisters were four and five at the time. Both parents had been raised in church, but, as adults, Sunday became precious time for them. Her father endured a six-day weekly work schedule, and her mother cared for the family and took in other children for extra income. Each Sunday, when the girls returned from church, the family would sit at the kitchen table, where her parents expected them to explain what they had learned from Sunday school and the sermon. To the girls' delight, their mother and father would join them in church on the "big days" of Easter and Christmas, and if they were in a play. This arrangement continued for seven years. At fourteen, Mother England decided to be water baptized and within the year received the Holy Ghost, which seems to have been a catalyst within the family. One of her sisters decided to get water baptized, and both parents joined the church and were baptized.[33] Within a few months, her mother received the Holy Ghost and joined the choir.

In the 1940s and 1950s, when Mother England was coming up, altar workers, by all accounts, provided the organized, day-to-day push to salvation. Mother Grayson attended Harlem's Refuge Temple during that time and, like Mother England, was saved during her teens. She recalled, "My godmother . . . she was lame. One of her legs stayed straight. She could never bend it. But that didn't stop her, she was in church every time the door was open." Her godmother was one of the founding "prayer warriors" of the church, who kept prayer bands operating throughout the week. In addition to the "grace and mercy of Jesus," Mother Grayson credited her godmother and another close guardian, "Auntie," with bringing her to Christ because "Godmother and Auntie would always come and tarry with me at the church."

Mother Grayson was the youngest of six, born in New York to parents from Antigua and Barbados. Her parents belonged to "Old Refuge on 133rd Street," she said, with a certain satisfaction that came from having a COOLJC pedigree.[34] Sometime before her fifth birthday, Mother Grayson's father took her five older siblings to the West Indies, supposedly to "give my mother a rest," and never returned. Soon after, Mother Grayson went to live with her godmother, who "didn't work a job" but took care of children from both the church and also wider community networks. "It seems like that was her ministry," Mother Grayson said, "the children, helping whoever had troubles. I remember Willamina and Katherine. They stayed [at

Godmother's] with me. Willamina's mother was abused." Mother Grayson stayed with her godmother between the ages of five and eleven because her mother's "trouble" was being a single parent with a work schedule that made childrearing nearly impossible.

Back then, according to Mother Grayson, "everybody worked," and women did "day work and stuff." Census data tell us that as late as 1960, wage labor by African American women was concentrated in certain spheres, with over 62 percent working as domestics in private homes and institutions (like hotels) and another 15 percent working in manufacturing.[35] To survive, parents with low-wage, long-hour, and long-week jobs depended on neighborhood women like Mother England's mother and Mother Grayson's godmother to perform "the double duty that black women so often undertook without leaving home."[36] Recent studies of these types of "highly localized" caring networks highlight the indispensable role of women in regional, national, and global economies.[37] Doreen J. Mattingly's analysis of late twentieth-century U.S.–Mexico domestic-service work networks shows middle-class women hiring low-wage domestic workers who, in turn, depend on lower-wage or unpaid familial networks to care for their loved ones while they work long hours. Low-wage and unpaid workers facilitate the careers of middle- and upper-class women, which, in turn, support increased living standards for middle- and upper-class families. The caring labor of Mother Grayson's godmother supported wider economic networks in Harlem, the greater New York metropolitan area, and probably beyond.

Her godmother intended for her work to provide for the well-being of the children in her charge and also to build the institution of the church because, according to Mother Grayson, "if you stayed with her, you were going to church!" But going to church did not mean you participated fully. "[Without the Holy Ghost] you couldn't do anything," Mother England recalled. "You couldn't usher. You couldn't sing. All you could do is come to Young People's service and Sunday School and morning service and missionary service." Stating that "you couldn't do *anything*," except attend four church services per week, Mother England reminisced from the perspective of young seekers eager to fully join the religious community. Mother Grayson's remembrance of the pivotal role of "Godmother and Auntie[,] . . . always com[ing] and tarry[ing] with me at the church," highlighted the ways in which altar workers stoked the enthusiasm of young seekers throughout the week.

"I got the Holy Ghost on a Saturday night right after the Youth for Christ Service," recalled Mother Grayson. The "Young People's" or Youth for Christ Service was held on Saturday night from seven thirty to ten o'clock, and it was particularly important in bringing seekers and altar workers together. Some of the older saints remembered that it was always crowded and that "if you didn't get there early you couldn't get in" because it was "the biggest service in town." After the service, the Saturday night prayer band gathered to tarry with seekers. Mother Grayson explained that "Godmother and Auntie and all those prayer warriors, . . . it was mostly women and more missionaries than mothers, they would line you up across the altar [and work with you] on a one-to-one basis." Altar workers would sit in metal folding chairs with their backs to the altar, and one seeker would kneel in front of each to fervently pray for Spirit baptism. In these moments, altar workers prayed for their own spiritual clarity, for seekers to keep focused on the quest, and for the Holy Ghost to indwell seekers. Workers encouraged seekers to pray out loud, pushing reticent ones to "open your mouth and speak." A returning seeker, familiar with the protocol, often followed the lead of her altar worker. "Now, if that person is saying, 'Hallelujah,'" one mother recalled, "[You] say, 'Hallelujah.'" Others may instruct, "Call His name. Say Jesus." Altar workers would "stay all night long" if necessary. "When I was seeking the Holy Ghost," one mother recalled, "it didn't matter how long you stayed. [It was] somewhere between one and four in the morning when I got saved."

This first generation of COOLJC altar workers encouraged seekers throughout the week and accompanied them to multiple prayer services, modeling the ways of an altar worker to (re-)produce workers in the next generation. To be an altar worker, according to Mother Grayson, a saint must have "a love for souls and a desire to see souls saved." She explained, "Working around the altar . . . that's really a labor of love."

THE LABOR OF LOVE

The "labor of love" that Mother Grayson spoke of straddles the boundary between private and public, as theorized by scholars of caring labor. According to Evelyn Nakano Glenn, on the one hand, White women's *obligatory* care work within the family has historically been "mythologized as love, rather than labor . . . and . . . natural to women."[38] Familial obligations in the private sphere distanced women from obligations of citizenship in the public sphere, and by extension made them unfit for participation in social and political arenas constructed as male. On the other hand, Glenn argues, women of color have lived a long history of *extracted* care labor in the homes of other people. It is clearly labor yet is relegated to the private domain outside the purview of legislative or juridical protections.[39]

It is important to point out the ways in which the evolution of American labor studies erases the experiences of Black, poor, and immigrant women (an erasure that scholars like Glenn help to mitigate). False dichotomies of private-public, unproductive-productive, and female-male have been firmly in place within the dominant American social, economic, and legal systems since the mid-nineteenth century and until recently were embraced by economists and labor scholars across the disciplines.[40] Nonetheless, Black enslaved and poor agrarian women always already disrupted ideologies that set public-productive-male against private-unproductive-female. The legacy of Black women church workers, building the first public Black American institution, further invalidates a labor model of public-productive-male set against private-unproductive-female.[41]

The scholarly focus on production shifted during the interwar period, as leading women economists turned to analyzing women's at-home consumption of goods produced in the market. Viewing women in this way reified dichotomies in which women were still perceived as unproductive. The mid-twentieth century witnessed increases in women's labor force participation, piquing scholarly interest in women's productive labor (the creation of goods and services in the market) *and* their reproductive labor (work within the home and family). This led to scholars acknowledging that unpaid work in the household undergirds social reproduction.[42] The shift from focusing on women's consumption patterns to including their productive and reproductive labor nevertheless showed a continuing preoccupation with the patterns of White middle-class women.[43] Evolving out of reproductive labor studies and gaining purchase in the late twentieth century, analysis of caring labor has focused on work that incorporates an ethic of care and contributes to social reproduction, within the family, the market, and the state.[44] Late twentieth-century interest in and institutional validation of caring labor as an area worthy of study simultaneously speaks to the power of the market—as service economies become increasingly important to globalization—and the marginalization of racialized and feminized labor. Caring labor is both conceptually and also demographically "women's work," and it remains tethered to global racial-ethnic hierarchies.

From a history of care work across family, church, community, and society, Mother Grayson and other altar workers understood full well the complexities and depth of meaning in the phrase "labor of love." While she spoke of her godmother's devotion to the religious development of those in her charge, Mother Grayson also linked that caring work to the mission of the church. "I think [altar work is] the most serious job in the church," she declared, "because those are souls. You tryin' to win them to Christ." Like many Holiness-Pentecostals, COOLJC altar workers operate with the theological urgency of the imminent Second Coming of Jesus Christ, "like a thief in the night" (1 Thess. 5:2). The church anticipates the Rapture in "the end times," when the saints will be "caught up in the air" and saved from the ensuing apocalypse.[45] The salience of COOLJC oneness theology, however, cannot be overstated. The church teaches that one God exists as the Father through creation, as Jesus for redemption, and as the Holy Ghost for regeneration. The incarnation of Jesus *was* God on earth—"the Word was made flesh," and he rose "in all the fullness of the Godhead" (John 1:14; Col. 2:9). The descent of the Holy Spirit on the day of Pentecost, and each subsequent Spirit baptism, is the fulfilled promise of God to "pour out my spirit unto you."[46] Altar workers look to usher God himself into the seeker, connecting the innermost recesses of the seeker, her soul, to God as the indwelling Holy Ghost. For seekers to be filled with the power of Jesus, "they need somebody to help pray them through. . . . And if nobody takes time to work with them," Mother Grayson explained, "they're never going to come through." She expanded on what it means to "take time to work with" seekers. "You can't rush," she said. "A lot of people, they don't want to bother with the altar because it's time consuming and it takes a lot out of you, because you're praying for a soul."

But, as Mother Grayson pointed out, it takes more than love, patience, and stamina. "Altar workers have to have *know-how*," she said emphatically, "to know what they're doing, . . . to know about praying. You know some people might think you keep yelling in the person's ear. [But] you're there to encourage that person. You know, [and here her tone became blanket-like, soft and warm] *press your way. I know you can do it. Say Jesus.*" "Know-how," as she described it, is just that—*know*ing what to say and *how* to say it. She then went on to explain the ways in which altar workers must be attuned to the dynamics of tarrying. "Once they get to a certain point," she said, "you have to know when to stop telling 'em to say Jesus and just encourage them to just start praising the Lord. You know, start praising, say, *Thank you,*

Jesus! It's different little words you say, just to encourage, because some of them get tired. They want to give up. You keep saying, *Press your way. He's almost there.* You know, *Come on. Let Him on in.* It's different little phrases that you could use working with souls." Mother Grayson selected "different little phrases" based on her ability to read a soul spiritually (directing the move from calling for Jesus to thanking Jesus) and to read a seeker physically (encouraging them past moments of fatigue).

Mother Grayson shows us the intricacies of intimate religious labor involved in harvesting souls. She gained insight into the "interpersonal ritual, bodily information, [and] personal vulnerabilities" of individuals, when "some of them get tired [and] want to give up."[47] She relied on endearing and private language (*I know you can do it*) to attend to the spiritual upkeep of those in her care (*Let Him on in*). In addition to love, patience, stamina, and know-how, her intimate religious labor demanded precision because "you have to know *when* . . . to make those shifts." She went on, "[You only know that from] working with people, from experience. You train first and then you get to experience, from doing that." That Mother Grayson knows what to do from "working with people" at the altar suggests on-the-job training.

While saints talked about altar work training and experience in a cyclical fashion, one entry point for the beginning of training can be found in narratives that described the ways in which, as younger converts, they followed the examples set by older saints. Mother England and Mother Grayson "sat under" the first-generation altar workers of Refuge Temple, emulating the practices of the founding mothers and missionaries of COOLJC. These apprenticeships showed how altar workers not only "creat[ed] and sustain[ed] social and emotional ties" individually and communally but also facilitated spiritual ties between themselves, seekers, God, and the church.[48] Mother Grayson was "always interested in souls being saved," a desire born out of "watching the missionaries I came under. You know, I really stuck to them, like glue."

Godmother, Auntie and other women who modeled altar work not only inspired Mother Grayson's generation to take up the labor of love but also passed along specific techniques of intimate engagement needed to "bring souls through." And if, by way of love, patience, stamina, and know-how, the Holy Spirit moves into a soul, the labor of altar workers also enlarges the congregation. In this way, intimate life converges with services that have a market value, as the organization grows. Money donated by members makes institutional expansion possible—locally, regionally, nationally, and internationally. Churches' ability to institute initiatives and increase their real property holdings depends on financial contributions from members brought into the fold by way of the altar. Following scripture, dedicated members contribute weekly (or monthly) tithes, which is 10 percent of gross earnings (see Mal. 3:10). In addition, they donate money spontaneously as "freewill" offerings for special services, projects, and events. On Sunday, before the service begins, the collection plate is passed in Sunday school, and members drop one or two dollars in the plate for the "missionary offering," before the main "offering time" during worship. Throughout a typical week of worship, members give at each service they attend—on Monday, Wednesday, and Friday. Mindful of the connections between loving labor, soul cultivation, and organizational yield, Godmother, Auntie, Mothers Grayson and England, and countless others bonded across generations, passing on intimate skills for the social and spiritual reproduction of COOLJC.

BIRTHING NEW SOULS

Sister Holmes, who labored with Veronica at the altar in this chapter's opening narrative, spent her early years "stuck like glue" to her godmother, Mother England, and the England family. Sister Holmes is a lifelong church member who represents a younger generation of church workers. She came of age as an altar worker in the 1980s, when she was in her late teens. "I started right after I was saved," she recalled, because she, too, "had a love for souls." Sister Holmes is a third-generation Apostolic Pentecostal. In the late nineteenth century, her great-grandmother, a Baptist missionary, traveled from Little Rock, Arkansas, to Monrovia, Liberia, with two young daughters, Cordelia and Pearl (Sister Holmes's grandmother). As Pearl entered adulthood in Liberia, she converted to Apostolic Pentecostalism and soon after met and married an African American Apostolic Pentecostal missionary. She remained in the missionary field for sixty years, after which she returned to New York.[49] Sister Holmes's mother, then, is from Liberia, while her father is from Sierra Leone. Sister Holmes, the youngest of five children, was born and raised in Brooklyn, and at the time of our interviews, she was in her early forties. Married and a mother of three, she holds a master's degree in social work and was working with the New York City Board of Education. Within the local church, Sister Holmes was a member of the Women's Council, the Ministers' and Deacons' Wives Guild (her husband was a deacon), and the Missionary Department, and she directed the choir. At the national level, she was the director of the Auxiliary of Apostolic Teens and the assistant director of the Music Department.

Sister Holmes compared the altar worker to "the midwife during the birthing process," explaining, "It's preparing, pushing out, nurturing, soothing, comforting the mother who is about to give birth to a baby. The altar worker is responsible for that same experience for the person [seeking]." In addition to encapsulating the qualifications expressed by Mother Grayson and other older saints—love, patience, stamina, know-how, and precision—midwifery carries a particular history of intimate religious labor within African American communities.

From the late 1800s into the 1980s, Black midwives asserted religious connotations of their work, reporting that "God called them [to midwifery] through a vision or dream."[50] Midwives and altar workers operated in equivalent spiritual registers. In fact, women crossed over between being spiritual leaders in church and being midwives, so that "the ability to summon the Holy Ghost [was] apparent in many of the midwives' practices."[51] Midwives were known to "maintain communication with spiritual forces, praying, laying on hands, and using oil to consecrate a mother's belly."[52] Both the altar worker and midwife prayed to ready themselves for the job at hand, trusting that a successful outcome was due to the power of God. Midwives, like altar workers, relied on intergenerational training in which mothers, grandmothers, or other elders "encourage[d] particular women to join them," creating women-controlled networks of recruitment and training, which resonates with the experiences of Mother Grayson with her godmother and Sister Holmes with Mother England.[53] These types of intergenerational apprenticeships trained "traditional" or "direct-entry" midwives.

The first half of the twentieth century witnessed a decline in traditional midwifery nationally. Yet the practice did not see a major decline in the South, where most Black people resided, until after the 1950s, just as Black women's primary wage work remained concentrated in domestic services until the 1960s.[54] On the national stage, into the 1930s, physicians denigrated midwives and represented pregnancy and birth as dangerous and complex events that required specialists. Midwives, however, continued to treat childbirth as an everyday, natural occurrence. The campaign against midwives proved successful, but doctors could not service all the women needing birthing care. The shortage of birthing attendants led to institutional midwife training that produced a new category of "nurse-midwife," distinct from the traditional or direct-entry midwife.[55] Soon after the demise of traditional midwifery's last bastion—Black and rural southern communities—America witnessed the rise of the home-birth movement. The convergence of feminist political movements and consumerist culture in the 1960s and 1970s reintroduced direct-entry midwifery as a "natural-birth" choice for middle-class women and their families.[56]

As a result of medical thinking that has labeled women's health care practices unskilled, when compared to male institutional training and licensing, midwives continue to operate on the margins of professional and unprofessional status within mainstream medical systems and public perception.[57] As with the working relationship between nurse-midwives and doctors, altar workers are both closely aligned with, yet distinct from, preachers and pastors. Within COOLJC (and in the wider public), each domain—altar worker and preacher—is gendered and carries distinct meanings of status and professionalization. By and large, the church community recognizes the expertise and importance of altar workers. However, the scholarly focus on structural leadership obscures the ways in which altar workers are critical to the spiritual and economic well-being of the church, as well as ignoring the contours and significance of the labor involved in harvesting souls.

While Sister Holmes would acknowledge the importance of the sermons and prayers of male ministers in "bringing people through," her midwife imagery not only reinforces altar work as women's work but also represents spiritual transformation in gendered terms. As an altar worker, she has the responsibility to "work people out of the intensive contraction when they're thinking about their past lives, and if they're worthy to move into this next phase of their spiritual life, if they're ready to release." She went on, "[Sometimes I think it's like an expectant] mother who's never had a child [thinking], *I'm no longer going to be this person without a baby. Now I'm going to have something else to take care of.* They [may wonder if they're] worthy of this spirit that they're trying to get to come inside of them." She likened the seeker to a first-time mother, facing new responsibilities on the horizon, but one who has some feeling of what's in store. She's preparing for "the next phase of [her] spiritual life." There is concern, but it's a planned pregnancy, if you will. However, that is not always the case. Sister Holmes also described those who come to the altar during their first church visit, "like a teenage mother [who] has no idea what she's about to get herself into.

Some people [have] this amazing, life-altering experience because of what has happened before the altar call," she explained. "The music has moved them, the words of the songs, the preached word. . . . I cannot assume that I know anything about their experience. Whatever that thing is that has led you to where you are now, the altar, you're working through it. . . . It's just a soul who is crying out for something. I don't know if it's help or comfort [or] an expression of joy."

While Sister Holmes steered clear of speculating about the reasons souls came to the altar or exactly what they felt, she presumed that the experience, for many, was confusing.

They're feeling all [kinds of] things, guilt and remorse, regret, joy, peace. They don't know where to put it, how to compartmentalize it, or to explain it to themselves. . . . [W]hen I'm ministering and/or speaking . . . to bring them through it, I'm constantly saying things [to] remind them that this is a safe place and that God loves them. . . . We all seek validation from somewhere, and the ultimate comfort is knowing that the Being that is higher than all of us, God, loves us despite . . . the litany of things that are going on in their heads and in their hearts. I don't want to deal with that. . . . I just want to work with their heart.

Whether someone "just needed to have a good cry," needed a minister to pray for them, or came seeking the Holy Ghost, once they were at the altar Sister Holmes wanted parishioners "to get through it feeling like . . . they can take a breath afterwards, like they got the release they needed, and feel safe enough to come back. And if they want to finish this at any other time, they know that the altar is a safe place 'til they land on their feet, without judgment. . . . I just want you to land safely and feel knowledgeable while you're landing. I just want to be there to support you and be the midwife that moves you through the journey."

CHANGE OVER TIME

Sister Holmes's understanding of her role in the spiritual birthing process highlights changes in how workers at COOLJC view the mandate and job of altar work; notably, some shifts are analogous to those in American midwifery practices. On the one hand, midwife imagery recalls a legacy of intergenerational networks created by powerful Black women to address the reproductive health needs of poor and rural women. On the other hand, the imagery calls to mind a late twentieth-century, primarily White, middle-class women's movement constructed at the intersections of individual choice (as a liberal ideology), consumerism, and feminism.

With regard to the first point, "[traditional] midwives, along with teachers, were the female counterparts to preachers as the most influential people" within Black communities.[58] Highly skilled and valued, midwives were integral in binding "a moral and spiritual set of relationships among God, the midwife, the pregnant woman, the family, and the community."[59] These women served the health needs of communities that were excluded from public health services because of racial and economic discrimination. Without midwives Black women had irregular (or no) prenatal, birthing, and postnatal treatment. In that way, midwifery was a communal imperative revolving around the health and wholeness of women and families.

In a manner similar to traditional midwives, earlier generations of altar workers saw their mission as a spiritual imperative—soul saving that connected God, the altar worker, the seeker, the family, and community. (Recall Mother Grayson's godmother, shepherding the neighborhood children in her care to the altar.) Just as pregnancy demands medical urgency because, "God willing," birth is imminent, the COOLJC theology of the imminent return of Jesus calls for religious urgency because saints are always living in "the last and final days." Only those who are "saved, sanctified, and speaking in tongues" will be "caught up" in the Rapture. Winning souls to Christ is also pressing because "you're fighting against Satan wanting to keep [the unsaved]." Mother Grayson typified the altar worker who carried spiritual urgency forward; with gentle persistence, she advised the unsaved to "get to the altar."

With regard to the second point, Sister Holmes's desire to have petitioners feel "validated" and "safe enough to come back," should they decide to do so, resonates with twenty-first-century midwifery philosophy. Like senior saints, she looked forward to the Rapture and wanted to "bring the seeker through." Yet she promoted an atmosphere in which choice played a larger role, in much the same way that the contemporary home-birthing movement supports opportunities for women to feel safe and validated with alternative birthing methods. When she described the exertion ("pushing" and "intensive contraction") and pointed out the emotional intensity and confusion that is part and parcel of spiritual transitioning, she replaced the language of "fighting spirits" with "working with the heart."

Changes in altar workers' perspectives and practices may on their face appear to fall neatly into generational groupings; however, age did not determine whether a woman adhered to the older stance of spiritual urgency or embraced the newer mind-set that supported choice. Younger women spoke about the urgency of "fighting against Satan" for souls, while some of the older mothers acknowledged that over the years they have relaxed their determination to bring everyone to the altar. Mother England, a self-described "stickler" when it came to doctrine, was confident in (even excited about) the imminent return of Jesus and the Rapture. But she said, "You have to work out your own salvation." And how and when you do is "between you and your God." Mother England said her increasingly lenient attitude was in response to changes in the church and its young people.

The church allowed young people (and all the unsaved) to participate in more activities than when she was coming up. "We couldn't take communion unless we were saved," she said. "Now it's whosoever will. I think [the young people] don't understand the seriousness of being saved. . . . There are so many false prophets—people saying one thing and doing another, [so] young people today have a different desire to be saved. When I was growing up it used to be a spiritual jealousy. If a friend got saved, you wanted to get saved. Nowadays these young people are independent minded." Mother England tolerated the changes because, ultimately, to receive the Holy Ghost you have to "have your mind made up," but over the years she was much less inclined to try and convince the unsaved to make up their mind. Regardless of COOLJC women's different views on the urgency of salvation, they held on to the apprenticeship model of training, passing on intimate techniques for tending souls.

CONFUSION AT THE ALTAR

As in any job, however, tensions can surface when workers question the qualifications of a coworker. Mother Grayson pointed out one of the ways in which workers evaluate each other. "[If] you don't see [someone] in church in so long," she said, "and all of a sudden people [are] at the altar and [that person is] going up there and going to work with 'em. You know, it's like *When did you pray? Where have you been all these weeks?*" In other words, coworkers and others in the religious community needed to see altar workers "put in their hours" in worship and prayer to have confidence in their abilities.

"Hah! Some people *think* they're altar workers," one church mother divulged, with a sarcastic chuckle. She said she could identify an unskilled worker when "there's confusion" at the altar. "And," she declared, "God is not a spirit of confusion!" (see 1 Cor. 14:33). When asked to clarify what she meant by "confusion," she said that workers should not "hop from person to person." She explained the importance of this in a manner similar to Mother Grayson's discussion of patience. A skilled worker would commit the necessary time to someone tarrying for the Holy Ghost. "And another thing," she continued, "you should never move in on another altar worker." More than one saint talking to a seeker was "distracting and confusing." Praying silently or quietly nearby was fine, and "for that matter, you can pray from across the room." As she continued to spell out how she assessed the aptitude of an altar worker, her tone took on a slight annoyance, as if the hypothetical unskilled altar worker I was asking about was someone in particular. "And never, never put your hands on the person. That's a no-no! Because you can disrupt the move of Spirit." I asked her how these types of situations are managed. "If there are problems, your leaders will handle it," she said. "The pastor or the mothers will take care of it."

The solution seems simple enough; however, COOLJC operations are structured to run both horizontally and vertically. On the one hand, going to a leader might be moving along a vertical axis—going to the pastor, the head of the church. On the other hand, the leader of choice might be a mother who operates across horizontal axes of power. Navigating systems of authority that are formal and informal—administrative and spiritual— can be a delicate proposition. Sister Holmes recalled a conflict that engaged spiritual and hierarchical authority. "When Mother [Marsha] Fairfield came to the church [about ten years ago], she added the dynamic [of] touching people, . . . controlling in a way that we had never operated before." Mother Fairfield had joined TDC after marrying a recently widowed deacon, and she brought a practice from her former Pentecostal church, which was "a no-no" within COOLJC. "We don't touch [people who are tarrying]," Sister Holmes reiterated. "[So] she threw this kind of monkey wrench in the equation, the way she was doing things."

Part of the problem, in addition to touching, stemmed from social-religious order protocols. Sister Holmes indicated that she and a coworker, Sister Louise Franklin, had tried to have casual conversations with Mother Fairfield, but it was tricky. Sister Holmes and Sister Franklin were in their early thirties at the time, and Mother Fairfield was about twenty years their senior. They had spiritual seniority as altar workers within COOLJC, yet Mother Fairfield had generational and titled seniority. She rebuffed their overtures, so "Louise and I asked for an altar workers' meeting with Bishop Cook." That was unusual. Before Mother Fairfield had arrived at TDC, altar workers "had never had to have a meeting," but the two younger women finally requested it because Mother Fairfield "was discrediting [them]." Here we can see the intimate labor of altar work converge with the emotion management required in worker-to-worker relationships, in which "worker status shapes the experience of emotion management on the job."[60] The dispute began over the issue of correct practices and developed into a question of spiritual authority between the younger women and the church mother. Sisters Holmes and Franklin felt that Mother Fairfield challenged their expertise, while their attempts to adjust Mother Fairfield's practices amounted to a challenge of her seniority (read: spiritual authority). Resolving the situation took two meetings, in which Bishop Cook skillfully reinforced COOLJC teachings while emphasizing the seniority of church mothers. Because Mother Fairfield had come from another Pentecostal church, she did not come through the same training as those we have seen so far, who were raised, acculturated, and mentored from an early age in the ways of COOLJC. Still, a process does exist to authorize altar work for those who join the church as adults—prayer immersion.

AUTHORIZED BY PRAYER

Mother Lester was married with young children when she converted from her Baptist faith to Apostolic Pentecostalism. In the early 1940s, after hearing Mother Carrie Lawson on a Sunday night radio broadcast from Harlem's Refuge Temple (see chapter 2), she decided, "God was calling me out of [the Baptist church] to a higher calling, . . . to be filled with the Holy Ghost." Once a member, Mother Lester joined the intercessory prayer band (which had ushered her in), those saints praying for people who called on Sunday nights during and after the radio broadcast. Soon she joined the six o'clock morning prayer band. After some years of deep immersion in prayer bands, she began "working with souls."

Mother Lester's progression through prayer bands to altar work illustrates the importance of prayer in training for the position.[61] "You really have to have a [prayer life], a devotional life with the Lord," Mother Grayson stressed, "or you can't work around altars or deal with souls. It's just not fair to them to even try." She explained that, beyond developing the ability to guide souls during the transition into Spirit baptism, prayer provided spiritual armor because "[at the altar] you're fighting against all kinds of spirits. That person came into the church, and you don't know what they be doing all their lives. And you're fighting against Satan, wanting to keep them out there, so you need to be prayerful so you can deal with that."

One church sister confirmed Mother Grayson's perspective. Recalling her struggle at the altar, she said, "It was such a fight! Everybody knows about God. Everybody loves God. But I didn't know there was a Devil. . . . [But] there was something that was trying to destroy me, something that was trying to kill me." The altar worker assisting her "opened up the Bible [to 1 John 1:9], got down on her knees with me, and told me to read."[62] "The fight," according to the sister, was intense; she cried and pleaded, physically "fighting with my vocal cords . . . to gain control" and recite the scripture. In telling of her "transition to freedom," she underscored the intense labor of the altar worker. It went on for "a long time," which she could not quantify, except to say that she and the altar worker were "the last ones" to leave the church. "[Her name was] Sister [Lettie] Williams," she said. "I'll never forget her. . . . She stayed with me, . . . [reciting the verse] with me, . . . over and over, . . . battling with the enemy to set me free."

According to Mother Grayson, attending to seekers at the altar without adequate preparation was a recipe for failure. "If you've been running around all day, and haven't prayed," she said, "for you to go up and deal with souls is a waste of time. You're not in that spiritual state of mind to even deal with them." Acquiring the spiritual skill set needed for working with souls was impossible without immersion in prayer work; one had to be "in touch with the Lord." Another church mother put it this way: "An altar worker is to take direction from the Lord *each and every time* they pray with a soul. Is the Lord telling you in *that* moment to pray with that *particular* soul?" She reiterated that the only way to know is to stay "prayed up," which means "it's not about a few minutes here and there or a few minutes when you get to church."

Devoting numerous hours to prayer means women make adjustments based on family and job demands. Mother Lester remembered regular prayer services when she first joined COOLJC in the 1940s. "[At Refuge back then], we had prayer service at six in the morning, twelve noon, [and] five in the evening, every night." She had flexibility to attend because "my husband didn't let me go to work. I had to stay home . . . with my [four] children." That changed once the children were older. "I went to work after the kids got in junior high [and] high school." Mother Lester wanted to join the workforce since she "didn't have any money," but she saw the interruption of her prayer schedule as an opening for "the Devil" to derail her spiritual training. She explained, "The Devil said, 'Well, you can't belong to the prayer band now because now you're working.' . . . Well, [I say] you put the Devil under your feet!" Her strategy for "stomping the Devil down" was to take advantage of the semiprivacy afforded by a work cubicle, posting the names of people who needed prayer (her "prayer list") on the wall, and praying throughout the day.

A coworker who occupied the cubicle for the next shift saw the list and reported it to the supervisor. The next day, the supervisor asked to see Mother Lester. "I understand that you got a prayer list," she stated. Mother Lester, concerned, replied, "Yes, I do." Her apprehension was eased by the supervisor's next question: "Would you put my mother on your prayer list?" The supervisor's request seems to indicate that she already considered prayer as one viable way to handle her mother's problem. Nonetheless, for Mother Lester, the exchange demonstrated the ways in which participating in the workforce provided opportunities to "win people to Christ." In that way, she connected the specific labor of "harvesting souls" at church to the larger enterprise of "planting seeds." She explained that bringing the prayer list (and prayer) to the job "was a substitute" for six o'clock morning prayer because she was "still on business for the Lord." When she retired, Mother Lester went back to attending prayer services, the morning being her favorite time. She preferred six o'clock because it was "a sacrifice." And sacrifice held the promise of reward. "When you start reading the scriptures," she explained, "[you see that] all of those men of God, whom God used—Abraham, Isaac, and Jacob, the three patriarchs—they got up early in the morning [and] God used [them]." Tying her prayer practice to biblical figures confirmed her authorization from God to work at the altar.

"I wake up anywhere between five and six for my morning prayer and devotion," Mother Grayson revealed. "So even if I can't get to church, there are times I'm still with the Lord." Her participation in church prayer services had fluctuated over the course of her adult life owing to family and job obligations. Before her marriage and up until the birth of her son in the 1960s, Mother Grayson did administrative work with a Manhattan insurance company. She became a stay-at-home mom until her son (an only child) started school, and she then returned to work. Serious health challenges disrupted every aspect of her life—church, family, and job—for ten years. After her retirement, because of her declining health, Mother Grayson didn't go out every day, so she attended prayer services less frequently than she had in earlier years. Nonetheless, she said that in addition to morning prayer, "I meet the Lord from seven to eight in the evening, [and] sometime during the day, like between twelve and two, I have another time with Him." Echoing the sentiment of other altar workers, Mother Lester put it this way, "I know everybody cannot attend the 6:00 a.m. prayer, but if you can, there's a blessing in coming out early in the morning to pray. Now, if you can't get [to church], you can begin the day with the Lord [by] getting on your knees in your own home or apartment or wherever you are."[63]

Sister Holmes had morning prayer in her apartment. She lived forty minutes away from the church, so making it to daily prayer services was not possible. "My alarm is set for five forty-five," she said, describing her morning routine. "I move through[my house alone, quietly in the morning[,] . . . to pray [before my husband and kids get up]. I pray in my car on the way to work . . . and when I'm coming home from work, so I spend a lot of time by myself praying. I try to make sure I read scriptures at my desk in the morning before the day starts, actually on my cell phone or iPad, and sometimes I pull it up on my computer screen and read." Even though weekday attendance was impossible, Sister Holmes regularly attended Monday and Friday evening prayer and worship services, as well as Sunday services. All COOLJC members desired deep communion with God, but labor at the altar required "meeting God" several hours each day. A dedicated prayer life assured altar workers of divine authority to work with souls at the altar.

CONCLUSION

By harvesting souls, altar workers power the mission of the church. In spite of these women's close proximity to preachers in Sunday worship, scholars have overlooked the ways altar workers function in direct relationship to, yet independent of, the preacher and his sermon. Looking at the work involved in harvesting souls, we see how altar workers understand the intimate labor entailed in the tasks at hand and the inextricable link to spiritual, social, and organizational reproduction. The stories of the founding missionaries and mothers, told by the women they mentored, show that the task of social and spiritual reproduction moved beyond the church walls to connect souls, families, and communities.

Once under the care of altar workers, petitioners descend into a realm of physical, emotional, spiritual, and doctrinal intimacy. Altar workers harness intimate techniques—moving in close physical proximity; breathing soft and warm words and sounds of encouragement in the ear; bearing witness to praying, weeping, and wailing—to smooth the way for spiritual transitioning. Without women's intimate labor, the social-spiritual reproduction of the church community is unimaginable. Operating across generations, navigating conflict and change, altar workers (re-)generate horizontal networks for training and spiritual upkeep.

Intimate work in the church falls disproportionately on women, as in most formal and informal economies. In today's global economy, women's intimate labor benefits institutions and "men as a class, who on average carry less of the burden and enjoy more of the benefits of caring work." In many ways, the church is no different.[64] We need to consider, however, "the ways in which the social value of caring labor" shapes and is shaped by "the social location of the giver and receivers."[65] In COOLJC, altar workers talked most readily about their labor benefiting the soul who had come through and the Kingdom. The narratives also revealed reasons why altar workers find satisfaction in this particular form of intimate labor. They have the pleasure of seeing someone through, the pleasure of being needed, the pleasure of creating positive intergenerational social-emotional bonds, and the pleasure of moving into deeper communion with God. Too, these women show a deep understanding of the ways in which spiritual-social reproduction and institutional well-being depend on the intimate labor of harvesting souls for Christ.

As members welcome new souls into the body of Christ, they convey in word and actions another type of religious labor that sits at the heart of Apostolic Pentecostalism—the aesthetic labor that brings together appearance and spiritual power, to live in "the beauty of holiness" (Psalms 96:9).

THE BEAUTY

OF HOLINESS

God has a distinct group recognized
not only by their appearance but by their power.

———

Apostle Gentle Groover

Apostle Groover stressed the connection between personal appearance,
spiritual authority, and collective identity to the thousands assembled in
St. Louis's America's Center for Friday evening service at the Annual International Convocation. "We're thankful to God," he said, "for having chosen
us to represent Him in spite of the proliferation of evil." He warned the followers of "true Apostolicism" that they faced "much pressure . . . living in a
time of compromise. . . . It's important for us not to change course even if
the winds of change blow." Then, encouraging the rapt gathering, he pronounced, "Thank God we're not playing church, [we're] people who are
truly filled and tongue talking! . . . Jesus is real tonight!" Cheers and praise
erupted from the sea of enthusiastic attendees, mostly women, dressed in
their distinctive style. Saints held Apostle Groover in high regard; in addition to overseeing the Florida diocese, he was one of twelve who sat on the
governing Board of Apostles of the Church of Our Lord Jesus Christ of the
Apostolic Faith, Inc. (COOLJC). Beyond his positions, saints spoke of "his

love for God" and "love for people." On this night, he urged saints to hold on to the status of "distinct" and "chosen" by maintaining the standards set by the church. Moreover, Apostle Groover insinuated that the price followers would pay for compromise was a loss of power.

This chapter examines the ways in which COOLJC women perform *aesthetic labor* in interconnected material and immaterial realms to produce, reproduce, and reconfigure the meanings of the beauty of holiness. Regulations on dress, which the church codifies most rigorously on women's bodies, demonstrate the standard of respectable appearance in COOLJC. Examining the aesthetics of presentation and its history, we gain insight into the particular ways in which the saints understand that a woman, by her appearance, exemplifies not only herself as one of the "ambassadors for Christ" but also the institution (see 2 Cor. 5:20). At the same time as she visually sets a standard, she is also a conduit for access to sacred realms, the "power" cited by Apostle Groover. Women perform aesthetic labor in unrestrained liturgical practices—music making and worship—rendering the invisible (spirit) visible (embodied) to model the beauty and power of holiness. In every service congregants work to "usher in" the Holy Ghost; given that women are in the majority and that Spirit infilling is egalitarian, the religious bodies of COOLJC women most often actualize the "anointing." Musical and liturgical work by COOLJC women produces, reproduces, and reconfigures church theology, doctrine, and aesthetics, creating a passageway that provides access to the past-present-future of the "Kingdom in the midst" and "new heaven and new earth" (see Rev. 21:1). By way of unrestrained and restrained bodily practices, women address ideologies of power and respectability that are foundational to understandings of gender in COOLJC. Women's spiritual and material aesthetic work reinforces communal and self-understandings of women as spiritual gatekeepers while keeping church polity intact.

WITHOUT A SPOT OR WRINKLE

The ongoing attention to the presentation of Black women's bodies within COOLJC comes out of the American religious, cultural, and political landscape of the late nineteenth and early twentieth century that gave rise to the wider Holiness-Pentecostal movement. The sociohistorical and religious history render the bodies of Black women "triply damned" through the stigma of enslavement, stereotypes of hypersexuality, and Eve's centrality to the "fall of man." At the same time, within COOLJC, women's bodies become doubly "revered," showing both power, through Spirit infilling by the unbounded Holy Ghost, and also respectability, through modest dress and comportment. In emergent Pentecostalism, notions of Black holy women's self-presentation were inextricably tied to a political and social history rooted in enslavement, a "sexual economy" in which each Black woman's body became the point of production.[1] The ensuing postemancipation shift from Reconstruction to Jim Crow–era America found the majority of Black people precariously situated between the "politics of respectability" and Black folk cultural ways of knowing.[2]

Holiness-Pentecostals adhered to certain markers of respectability, such as strict codes regarding leisure activity and sexual behavior, whereas music, preaching and teaching styles, and other elements of worship remained firmly rooted in African American–Black Atlantic aesthetics.[3] The Holiness-Pentecostal theology of Spirit baptism embraced ecstatic worship, which flew in the face of Black mainstream politics of representation. At the same time, members demonstrated restraint in dress and comportment, rooted in both a politics of representation and also the Bible.[4] Holy Ghost infilling and the imminent return of Jesus for a church without "spot or wrinkle," "holy and without blemish," required each individual to maintain a pure vessel, signified by their outward appearance (see Eph. 5:27).[5] Pentecostal dress and demeanor also countered hypersexualized stereotypes projected onto Black people—stereotypes that always carried the real threat of violence when acted on by the barbaric.

This history and its legacy helped shape COOLJC doctrine, as wider sociopolitical concerns and Christian values internal to the church converged in formulating gendered aesthetics of holiness.[6] The dress code for COOLJC women prohibits sleeveless tops, pants, hemlines at or above the knee, slit skirts that expose the knees, open-toed shoes, bare legs (without stockings or tights), makeup, earrings, and uncovered heads. These regulations apply strictly within the sanctuary, and most COOLJC women carry them into daily life to varying degrees.

Exploring the production of COOLJC women's attire broadens the work sites open to examination of on-the-job aesthetic labor by scholars who consider the "embodied capacities and attributes" that employees bring to a potential job and that employers further exploit for organizational gain.[7] (For example, a boutique owner may look for prospective employees to have a particular cosmopolitan demeanor—in clothing style, speech, and carriage—which the employer will further tailor to appeal to his or her specific product-clientele.) Like workers in public-contact service work, who are "constantly on display," churchwomen by their outer appearance and demeanor reflect the institution—as Apostle Groover made clear.[8] Yet there is a key distinction between COOLJC women and service-sector workers who bring embodied qualities and styles to the job (and further develop these qualities), in that, for a saint, the bulk of the aesthetic labor of presentation begins after she commits to a Jesus-led life. In fact, the community values a radical transformation in dress and comportment from before salvation to after salvation, as a marker of the new self.

Recent analyses of aesthetics in religious communities that engage with the mass media can be applied to the material and spiritual aesthetic labor of presentation as well. Birgit Meyer's work on Ghanaian Pentecostal filmmaking and images in the public sphere makes an important intervention in that she moves away from thinking about representation as an imaginary field. Instead of dividing the material and immaterial, Meyer argues that "the relevance of aesthetics, and the concomitant importance of style," is key in "grasp[ing] the material dimensions of religious modes of forming subjects and communities."[9] The work of presentation done by COOLJC women shows the ways in which dress, as a religious aesthetic, is seen as an embodiment of holiness. Dress presents one of many ways that members live the theology of being "all on one accord," like the disciples on the day of Pentecost (see Acts 1:14 and 2:1). On that day, being "on one accord" facilitated baptism by the Holy Spirit and the beginning of the Christian church. In addition to regulations on dress generally, the women's auxiliaries each have designated colors for their attire. At auxiliary-sponsored services, the Women's Council dons white and purple, the missionaries black and white, and ministers and deacons' wives dark blue and white. Oftentimes, women overseeing services will select a color for clothing. During one Sunday's announcements, Sister Wanda Madison informed congregants, "This Friday's young people service is sponsored by Sister [Georgia] Rogers, and she's asking everyone to wear orange. The color for Friday is orange, so we want to all be together. Amen? Show we're all on one accord. Amen?"

THE LABOR OF STYLE

Physical, spiritual, and psychic exertion that materializes theology in the sanctuary is preceded by the everyday labor required for self-presentation. Keeping up with the dress code can be laborious. Newly converted women may find they need to give up their old clothes and acquire new ones.[10] Women with children take on the added task of keeping church clothes organized for the whole family. I was running Saturday errands with a sister; one stop was the cleaners. She did a monthly drop-off of church clothes for her family of five. I was stunned by the size of the pickup. "You know how we worship," she said, laughing. "We wear something once, and it's soaked [with perspiration]." We made a few trips to get everything to the car. This sister's good nature represents how many women matter-of-factly fold the extra work and expense of keeping clothes prepared for church into the rest of their daily religious labor.

Women, too, carry the burden of conforming to same-color attire for special services and wearing the appropriate "uniform" colors for women's auxiliary services. Some men participate by adding color-coordinated ties or handkerchiefs, but as one church mother said in an exasperated tone, "Oh, they leave the men alone" about uniforms. "I hate uniforms," declared Mother Lucille Grayson, a COOLJC member for over sixty years. "It's so much trouble," she explained, "to have to keep your clothes organized that way. I almost didn't come to that service last week 'cause I wasn't sure if my whites were clean. It's such a hassle! But, thank God, I did have another suit in the closet 'cause I really did want to come." And she would not have attended out of uniform.

POLICING

The parameters of the dress regulations come from the male leadership, and they, along with the senior missionaries, make sure members adhere to the rules. In addition to altar work (as detailed in the last chapter), the spiritual responsibilities of missionaries include overseeing the conduct, duties, and church attire of women and children. The International Missionary Department motto, "'Lifting Up a Standard for the People' (Isaiah 62:10) in Action, Attitude and Appearance," informs a missionary's approach to her labor.[11] Missionaries must embody "the beauty of holiness," thereby "lifting up a standard," to which they hold others. In her study of teaching and learning between Black mothers and daughters, Suzanne Carothers calls attention to the importance of acquiring household work skills within the context of a sense of aesthetics. For example, a task such as baking could be *done*, but only when the daughter had learned "to get [her] biscuits to look pretty" did she consider the task *done well*.[12] In much the same way, the self-presentation of a COOLJC woman is integral to church work itself, and missionaries see to it that church work is done well.

Even as Mother Grayson made clear that missionary women have different attitudes about the "hassle," many women still take the charge of overseeing appearance quite seriously. Mother Esther Pea, the president of the Missionary Department at True Deliverance Church (TDC), was one such woman. She would admonish one-on-one or in front of the congregation if a sleeve or hemline was too short, a garment too tight, or a skirt split too high. She reprimanded according to COOLJC doctrine; however, she also carried a standard of "proper dress" instilled by her Methodist mother.[13] She recalled, "My mother told me if ladies don't wear gloves and put their hat on their head, she ain't dressed. That just stuck with me." Born in 1913, Mother Pea had meticulously maintained her stylish wardrobe for decades—two- and three-piece long skirt suits from the 1930s, 1940s, and 1950s, complete with matching hats and gloves, of course. Her mother made all her clothes when she was coming up, "the ruffles, the lace, the ribbons. . . . I loved what she made for me. That's why you see me with all this lace now because I come up with it."

As Methodists, her parents were fully immersed in the early twentieth-century "politics of respectability." They, too, became caught up in the waves of the Great Migration, moving with their five children from farm life in Anderson, South Carolina, to the promises of industrialized Asheville, North Carolina. Her father secured one of the two "top-leading jobs [for Black men] down there, . . . cleaning engines for the railroad." The other "top-leading job" was at the post office. Both parents stressed education, and her mother insisted that the girls "be ladies." As Mother Pea hit her preteen years and her hips "started to spread," her mother's instructions to dress "nice and neat" expanded, too. "She told me, 'You gotta put on that corset, otherwise you're gonna be out of shape,'" Mother Pea recalled. "Well, I didn't want to be out of shape! And I grew up to be a big girl. You're talking about a six-teen proper shape? I had it! [She howled with laughter.] Ooooh!" Her happy childhood recollections were rife with racialized "gender-laden and class-laden meanings" that permeated the rhetoric of respectability—an ideology that fought against "every black woman regardless of her income, occupation, or education [being perceived as] the embodiment of deviance."[14]

Mother Pea epitomized the convergence of a politics of respectability with the standard of sanctified attire, in which dressing "as becometh holiness" both harks back to early twentieth-century race, gender, and class politics and also signals the indwelling Holy Ghost. The missionaries of COOLJC, like those of the Women's Department in Anthea D. Butler's study of the Church of God in Christ (COGIC), "wish to be pleasing to God," viewing "the body . . . [as] a marker of the self" and their devotion to Christ.[15] Mother Pea, however, came into COOLJC in 1973, at sixty years of age. She had been in New York since 1934, when, with her parents' permission and forewarnings, she journeyed to the city with a girlfriend, found employment, got into nursing school, and "brought myself honor." She remembered a different attire among Holiness women from her youth in the South. "[They] didn't wear clothes like I wear," she explained. "The women in Holiness back in my day wore these long black skirts, white blouses, and an apron. And they wore that bonnet hat on their head. Holiness was different than it is now." Mother Pea found the changes in style between her own and preceding generations acceptable. Notably, she attributed changes in style to "Holiness [being] different than it is now." At the same time, she balked at changing styles in "this modern holiness." Her comments, too, highlight the ways in which women's self-presentation remains the primary marker, as she charged that "young *people* [are] dressing too slack. . . . They should wear their *dresses* a little bit longer" (emphasis added).

Mother Pea joined COOLJC decades after a major postwar shift in holy women's style of dress. She therefore missed the earlier transition that other senior members had experienced, in which older missionaries criticized "these young people [and] their dress." Mother Pearl Norris, a second-generation member of COOLJC for over seventy-five years, explained that the pre–World War II style of plain dress was a combination of a "holdover of the Victorian type of dress" and low income levels. "Back then [in the 1930s and early 1940s] in Harlem most people didn't have a lot," she said, "so they dressed more modestly." She remembered the change as coinciding with her entrance into college. "Around the mid-1940s and 1950s we started to dress more modern," she said. "People had more [money]. It was after the war. . . . We moved to the new temple [in 1945]. We thought we were something! And we *dressed*. Hats [and outfits of] all different colors. We were hot stuff!"[16] Yet dressing "more modern" did not occur without conflict. Other saints who came of age in the same period talked about the displeasure of the older missionaries and the evolution of their own biblical perspectives. Stringent dress conventions "didn't hurt us [when we were young]," one senior missionary recalled, "but a lot of stuff wasn't necessary. When I think about it now and match it up with the Word, [the Bible] really don't have nothin' to do with all that stuff [about dressing] they were telling me."

"YOU DON'T REPRESENT HOLINESS . . ."

Even with a mature understanding of a gap between scripture and doctrine, women rarely contest the "hassle" of dress regulations or openly clash with church leadership. However, one such incident occurred on a sweltering Friday night in August, when a dispute about obedience to the dress code boiled over at the Queens church. Tensions around dress can run high among saints because policing can take place in the public domain, making a saint's relationship to political and spiritual authority visible to the entire church. For some, policing ensures the moral standard will be maintained. For others, policing carries a host of assumptions about one's personal relationship with God.

On this particular night, Sister Patricia Roland had sponsored a service themed "United for Christ: Back to Basics," in which she used a makeup kit to talk about the benefits of "being in Christ," the premise being that unsaved women use makeup to brighten their appearance and uplift their spirits, while COOLJC women use Christ and the Word. As is customary, the end of the service was turned over to Bishop Crosley J. Cook. He opened with, "Sister Roland talked about the woman's face. I thought she was going to go into the women's clothing." He went on, "We have to dress to a standard of holiness. . . . You have to dress for the Lord. . . . The Praise Team sets a tone. You usher in the Spirit. If you don't represent holiness you can hinder the Spirit. . . . You're not dressed representing holiness if your legs are bare and your feet are out." On this ninety-degree Friday night, none of the four singers on the Praise and Worship Team had on stockings; one wore open-toed shoes, and two wore sandals.

Bishop Cook continued his reprimand, asking rhetorically, "How can you help usher in the Spirit if you're a distraction?" Moving forward, he would be dispatching the ministers to meet with all the auxiliaries "to make clear the standards." Emphasizing his role as spiritual father, he explained, "I am trying to get you in readiness. I say this not to chastise you, but because I love you." Finally, to reinforce the connection between "dressing to a standard" and holiness, he summoned the memory and authority of the beloved departed first lady of the church. "Mother [Reva] Cook never let any of her children enter the house of God dressed inappropriately," he reminded them. "Not one ever entered with her legs not covered or her feet out."

Mother Geneva Reeves raised her hand to be recognized and stood. "I'm really glad you brought this out, Bishop. The mothers have a hard time when we uphold the standard. Someone wants to know where it is in the scripture that women must wear stockings." She then answered the anonymous query with a response frequently offered when a direct connection between scripture and doctrine was tenuous. "Well," she said, "when you truly have the Holy Ghost, He deals with you, and . . . you want to dress to a standard. And I'm going to search out the scripture to find it." Bishop Cook encouraged her quest, "Yes, Mother, you search it out and bring it to us."

After the benediction, a member of the Praise and Worship Team, who was sitting next to me, turned and said indignantly, "Well, I guess I'm going to hell." As folks filed out of the sanctuary and into the thick, hot August air, clusters of women formed on the sidewalk to talk about the issue. Some had on the proper attire. Others wore sandals with no stockings under their nearly floor-length skirts. Mother Reeves was in the middle of an excited discussion with some saints. One in particular, Sister Diane Comstock, a contemporary of Mother Reeves, challenged the scriptural basis for requiring stockings and prohibiting open-toed shoes. Mother Reeves was "surprised" that Sister Comstock would question doctrine because she was a lifelong member. "That's my point," Sister Comstock stated emphatically. "I've been in the church since I'm ten years old." Mother Reeves shot back, "Then you should know better!" Not backing down, Sister Comstock said, "I've been dressing like this my whole life. I have on stockings, but I've been wearing sandals every summer my entire life. There's nothing wrong with it." Then, leveling an "out-of-order" accusation at Mother Reeves, she exclaimed, "And you have on diamond earrings!" Acknowledging that her large diamond studs were not "according to the standard," Mother Reeves responded, "I know. I said it was wrong [when I spoke up in the sanctuary]."

Sister Ruth Holmes (open-toed shoes and no stockings) and Mother Jessie England (proper attire) walked out of church together and approached the group. Talking to Mother England but speaking loud enough to be heard by everyone assembled, Sister Holmes held up her large cluster of keys and jangled them. "I'm g-r-o-w-n. Grown! And I'm going to *my* car," she said. About a block down, she joined another group of women already in discussion. One of them, Mother Regina Highland, who was in her sixties and highly respected by young and old alike, noted that she was not wearing stockings. One would have had to look closely to tell because underneath her floor-length dress, her slip-on shoes exposed only small portions of the top of her feet. Laughing, she said, "Well, I guess I'm not going to make it [to heaven]."

"Well, I want to go where you go!" Sister Holmes responded.

Mother Highland continued, "I believe He looks at your heart. There are times where, if you have to go home and change, you might not come to church. It's better to come."

Sister Holmes then shifted to confront the notion of women's "improper" dress "distract[ing]" worshippers. She charged, "If my ashy feet get you excited, you have a *big* problem! It's not *my* problem."

Sister Eileen Hansen, a youthful middle-age grandmother who always dressed according to the standard, picked up from Sister Holmes. "The women are always responsible for how men act," she noted. "Why do we have to be responsible or more responsible?"

Sister Holmes retorted, "Well, we know that men wrote the rules. It's all about control." Control indeed. Notably, no men were present as the women grappled with the pastor's public reprimand. Although "men wrote the rules," heated, open debate about implementation fell to women. Inside the church, only saints who agreed with Bishop Cook spoke up; those who disagreed sat in silence. Although the actions that constituted not adhering to the dress code were open disagreement, verbally disagreeing with the pastor in front of the church would have been highly irregular. All concerned adhered to protocol, keeping church polity intact. Dress standards have become codified, too, because "church mothers emulated, articulated, and embraced sanctification ideas and images in [and on] their person."[17]

Yet not all agree about the level of importance. Mother Grayson, who hated the "hassle" but complied, asserted that too much focus on women's garb caused the church to "major in the minors." She agreed with Mother Highland that "[God] looks at your heart."

On that August night, there was a fundamental disagreement about representation and *the thing* being represented. Bishop Cook and his supporters contended that the Spirit responded to the outer embodiment of holiness, while the others maintained that the Spirit responded to a person's internal being—the cultivated relationship with God. They were indignant about the ways in which women's dress can overshadow the full extent of the aesthetic labor devoted to servicing the family of faith.

The women on the Praise and Worship Team who sparked the pastor's reprimand were second- and third-generation saints between the ages of twenty-five and forty-five—committed members who had accepted the job of preparing the sanctuary for worship by bringing the congregation into communion with the Spirit through song. For every service, Praise and Worship Team members come in time to be "on their post" at the front of the sanctuary as congregants arrive.[18] On one Monday evening, as folks assembled, Sister Rogers and the team moved to the front of the sanctuary. She removed the microphone from its stand, placed the stand behind her, and, in her robust alto, launched into the buoyant "This Is the Day the Lord Has Made": "This is the day / This is the day / That the Lord has made / That the Lord has made. I will rejoice / I will rejoice / And be glad in it / And be glad in it . . ."[19] Like most songs presented during this portion of service, "This Is the Day" is lyrically sparse and repetitive to encourage participation.[20] The rest of the Praise Team and some congregants joined in, singing and clapping. Near the end of the song, a woman stood and was recognized by Sister Rogers, the Praise Team leader. The woman began with a standard opening, "Praise the Lord, saints. Giving honor to the spirit of Christ, the head of my life, to my pastor, to the ministers, mothers, deacons, and all to whom honor is due." She was "glad on today" because her son had received good news about his civil service exam.

In response, Mother Eula Fulton rose from her pew, singing, "It's another day's journey, and I'm so glad . . ." An octogenarian whose stature and appearance belied her years, her singing was thin, yet spirited. Responding to intent more than quality, Sister Rogers and the team pushed the song with powerful gospel harmonies. Energized by the thrust, other saints jumped into the up-tempo song. The organist and drummer had not yet arrived, so infectious call-and-response layers of tambourines, hand clapping, and foot stomping accompanied Mother Fulton's sung praise. As the song ended, she began her spoken testimony: "I thank God for my family . . ." As she continued, "*Halleluuujah!*" was sprinkled throughout her declarations; she raised her hands; moved by the Spirit, her body bent quickly to the right at the waist; she straightened up and thanked God for her health. The saints recognized Mother Fulton's anointing. Proclaiming, "Thank you, Jesus!" and "Glory to God!" they impelled her, each other, and the Holy Ghost into deeper spiritual union. Ending, Mother Fulton asserted, "It's a privilege to get up everyday and come to the house of prayer. Pray for me in Jesus's name." Right away, Mother Bettina Evans sprang up from her pew and in her rich, raspy, booming voice sang the up-tempo spiritual "I Got Joy, Joy."

A beat after the ending of "I Got Joy, Joy," a sister stood, proclaiming, "I thank God for being saved, sanctified, and filled with the Holy Ghost. Speaking in tongues as the Spirit of God gave utterance. . . . I thank God for waking me up this morning!" Sister Rogers and the Praise and Worship Team exuberantly intoned the song "Lord, I Just Want to Thank You." Leading praise and worship requires the team leader to have songs ready to impel the church "higher," whether moving from song to song, or from personal testimony to song. At all services, the team works to "usher in the Spirit," while the team leader carries responsibility for the overall arc, transitioning the congregation from praise to worship. Effective Praise and Worship Team leaders need to have "a true anointing" and an encyclopedic knowledge of the church's musical literature, which includes Psalms, scriptures, traditional praise songs, gospel songs, and folk spirituals. After the extended and rousing version of "Lord, I Just Want to Thank You," Sister Roland stood, declaring, "I thank God for the women of God and the love of God that sustains me as a single mother raising my daughters." The Praise and Worship Team leader launched into "The Jesus in Me Loves the Jesus in You." Everyone joyously joined in, and Sister Rogers and the Praise and Worship Team, seguing from tune to tune, led folks through another fifteen minutes of impassioned singing.

FILL "ALL THE HOUSE" WITH SOUND

Music dominates COOLJC worship services from beginning to end— devotional (praise and worship), the processional of the choir, the prayer hymn, the Lord's Prayer, the morning hymn, selections by the children's and young adult choirs, a solo meditation, a standing congregational song, the message song bearing up the sermon, and altar call invitational hymns.[21] Saints transmit and reinforce the theological underpinnings of faith through song. Music's predominance in worship as an aesthetic sensibility connects to the biblical foundation of COOLJC doctrine, Acts 2:2–4, which states, "And suddenly there came a sound from heaven as of a rushing mighty wind, and it filled all the house where they were sitting. And there appeared unto them cloven tongues like as of fire, and it sat upon each of them. And they were all filled with the Holy Ghost, and began to speak with other tongues, as the Spirit gave them utterance." The first indication of divine activity on the day of Pentecost was sound completely filling the space, so the musical soundscape of service (re-)produces Bible time at each gathering. Services can move in dynamic sonic waves, from quietly meditative to extremely loud, pushing the sound system to distortion. In these moments, singing, preaching, praying, hand clapping, foot stomping, and instrument playing are deliberate and forceful.

The next signal of the Holy Ghost's presence in sacred history and the present is the tongue being split into new language. Here, internal biblical logic joins a culturally specific approach to song making in Black gospel music, as saints fill "all the house" with sound, in terms of both quantity and quality. Horace Boyer, a gospel music scholar, explains, "Perhaps the most unusual characteristic of gospel singing is its text interpolation, the adding of extra words to the original text."[22] Sister Celeste Brooks was a powerhouse vocalist in COOLJC, and one of her renditions of "The Lord Strong and Mighty" epitomized this aesthetic approach.[23] With organ and drums in accompaniment, she set up the high-energy offering in a fairly straightforward fashion for the choir entrance. "The Lord our God is strong and mighty / The Lord our God is mighty in battle / Sound the alarm on the holy mountain / He's wonderful and powerful and mighty in His power." The choir repeated the full chorus, as Sister Brooks had set out, and she began to weave in and out, rhythmically splitting and adding text: "The Lord our God, *oh yes He is*, strong and mighty, *he's mighty* / The Lord our God, *our God, mighty, mighty* in battle . . ." Skilled gospel singers "create emotional climaxes by bombarding listeners with perpetual sound" by overlapping phrases, employing internal call-and-response patterns, and elongating notes to "bridge almost all rests and phrases."[24]

When scripture is fulfilled in song, the entire body is filled with divine power that overflows into divine utterances, which can be realized in sound quality. After a few times around, when Sister Brooks hit "*sound* the alarm," she shifted her rich-textured voice into a full-throated raspy tone and used a similar, but slightly intensified, grain on "wonderful and *powerful*." Like other accomplished COOLJC singers, she knew how to "flip a switch"—that is, generate tones that pierce the air and set the church alight. Singers may do this to bring the Spirit down; as well, shifts in tone can indicate she is under the anointing. Those familiar with the singer and the aesthetic practices will understand the meaning of "innumerable variations of vocal color . . . and nuances in vocal contour."[25] Folks at the service—standing, shouting, and praising God—felt Sister Brooks's "variations of vocal color" and intensity.

These "aesthetics of self-presentation" in music demonstrate a communal "sense of value and appropriateness" as well as a "politics of personal value."[26] It's important to note that within COOLJC men and boys are gifted singers, too. So, for our purposes, the democratized realm of singing needs to be understood within the overall context of women's aesthetic church work. Whether with the Praise and Worship Team or a choir, or as a soloist, the work that women do to usher in the Spirit through song (re-)produces agreed-on aesthetic values for the church, as well as reinforcing their value to the community of faith, and the work is always situated within COOLJC's gendered ideologies of power and respectability. Still, as histories of COOLJC women's dress and the August night conflict over proper attire show, aesthetic values are not fixed. The aesthetic labor of COOLJC women becomes a site where values of holiness can be reinforced, disputed, or altered, all the while reinforcing the importance of women as spiritual gatekeepers.[27]

SPIRITUAL GATEKEEPERS

At the same gathering that witnessed Sister Brooks's commanding rendition of "Strong and Mighty," Mother Viola Gilbert, the speaker for the evening, issued a clarion call: "Women were last at the cross and first at the tomb and will remain! Stand and be counted!" She encouraged those gathered to "develop [the] spiritual sensitivity and spiritual power absolutely necessary" to withstand "warfare," thus reiterating the topic of her fiery "lesson" (not sermon), "Women's Spiritual Warfare."[28] The spiritual fortitude of Mary Magdalene and Mother Mary during the crucifixion, death, and resurrection of Jesus epitomized having "the power to go through and give your testimony for that other sister." Placing the church-family relationship of "sister" onto the women at the cross, Mother Gilbert brought all of them together into shared spaces of faith, endurance, and possibility, as "faith must ever claim its promised rights." Centering the lives of Jesus and the faithful women around him bolsters churchwomen as they press through the challenges of contemporary life.

The women of COOLJC, like many Pentecostal women, look to the lives of specific biblical women to model their walk with God. Yet oneness and the founding theology of Bishop Robert C. Lawson, which placed the blood of "colored women" in Christ, sets these women apart from the mainstream of Pentecostalism.[29] Numerous weekly services, too, afford women ample opportunity to develop their own biblical understandings and to bring those interpretations into conversation within the wider church community. Members gather for Bible study and worship services on Monday, Wednesday, Friday, and Sunday, as well as for daily prayer services at six o'clock in the morning and at noon. Women usually program the weeknight services, integrating religious instruction and group discussions under the rubric of worship. Special regional and national assemblies, such as the Annual Women's Day, the International Women's Convention, and women's auxiliary gatherings, offer additional spaces for sharing biblical interpretations.[30] On the night Mother Gilbert spoke they had gathered for a quarterly Tridistrict missionary service, which brought representatives from a few local churches into fellowship.[31]

Pulling women, who were "last at the cross and first at the tomb," into the current moment, Mother Gilbert evoked holy women as spiritual gatekeepers over time, who "will remain!" Connecting the past actions of holy women to current and future strategies and successes in "women's spiritual warfare," she also tapped into the "already and not yet" theological foundation of the church. Generally understood in Christianity as the present and forthcoming Kingdom, within COOLJC theology and practice "already and not yet" sheds light on the particular paradoxes and ambiguities that women navigate as they move between the material and spiritual realms.[32] In what follows, we will see women as spiritual gatekeepers performing aesthetic labor to keep the present Kingdom (the church) aligned with the directives of God, so that the future Kingdom will be realized in "the end times." They do this by materializing a whole, coherent "already and not yet" in the present.

RUNNING FOR JESUS

One February evening, guest singers came from a sister church in Brooklyn to fellowship with the Queens TDC congregation. Oftentimes, when a soloist, choir, or minister visits a sister church, members of their congregation come along. Too, when guest singers or speakers are known to be adept at setting the church alight, members will invite friends and family, saved and unsaved, to come and have "a good time in the Lord." So the transition from corporate prayer into worship service on this evening saw folks moving, not only throughout the church, but also coming from outside. During the buzz of folks hanging up coats and greeting each other in the anteroom, the Praise and Worship Team worked in the sanctuary to "usher in the Spirit" through song.

While the congregation was settling, two visiting musicians positioned themselves at the organ and drums, which were tucked in the front right corner of the sanctuary below the elevated choir pews. They were both "highly anointed" and excellent musicians, and their interplay with the skilled women of the Praise and Worship Team quickly raised the sonic and spiritual temperature to "higher heights."[33] It was a Sunday evening service, so saints were offering testimonials—a word or song about "God's wonder-working power." It wasn't until the young drummer came out from behind the drum kit and hobbled to the front of the sanctuary to testify that it became clear that he did not have the use of his left side. "I wasn't going to testify tonight," he said, "but I have to talk about the goodness of Jesus." A serious car accident had left him in critical condition and in need of major surgery. He survived the surgery only to suffer a paralyzing stroke during recovery. A husband and the father of a toddler, he described the anxiety of coping with the impact on his young family and the emotional devastation of ending his musical career. Once out of the hospital, he threw himself back into the church and "playing to the glory of God." Throughout his testimony, saints praised God: "Hallelujah!" "Thank you, Jesus!"

"God gave me back my drumming," the young man declared. "God has been faithful. The only thing I can't do is run. I still can't run. I need three people to run around this church for me!" Immediately one woman jumped up and began to run counterclockwise around the sanctuary. Before she had gotten halfway up the outer aisle, a second woman, then a third, and then a young boy, about ten years old, joined them. As they whipped around the sanctuary, two of the women were crying, and all were calling out to God. The congregants began to stand, shout, clap, praise God, and speak in tongues as the anointing fell on many. The organist joined in, underscoring the sound of bodies with percussive chord hits. The physical acts of running, crying, and shouting praises brought the Spirit down instantly. Merging the material, spatial, and temporal realms, women's religious bodies materialized "already and not yet."[34] The runners physically incorporated themselves into the testimony of the young drummer, making God's promise of a future healing a present reality. Harnessing spiritual power and (en-)circling the congregation, the proxy runners carried the entire church into the restorative present-future while actualizing the drummer as one member of a whole, healthy body in Christ.

Here, Catherine Bell's work on ritualization is useful. Ritualization occurs when practical activities are carried out in strategic ways in particular social circumstances.[35] First, these types of practices are context specific. A practical activity, like running, became distinct in the sanctuary and held new meaning. Second, running was "strategic and economic," that is, effective and basic.[36] The runners carried out a deliberate activity that got right to the heart of the matter. Third, the action was particularly effective because of "a fundamental 'misrecognition' of what it [was] doing, . . . of its limits and constraints."[37] In running to realize healing for the drummer, women performed aesthetic labor that recovered and reinforced an understanding of the "end of times." Fourth, the action raises the question, why did they run? In what ways did they produce, reproduce, and reconfigure relations of power? Bell identifies this as "its vision of redemptive hegemony."[38] The women runners demonstrated a "vision of empowerment rooted in [their] perceptions and experiences of the organization of power" within COOLJC.[39]

Reproducing the church's idea of the link between appearance and power, each runner at that February service was dressed "according to a standard." The first runner, a small-framed woman who appeared to be in her mid-thirties, wore an A-line shirtwaist dress, falling to midcalf. The cardigan sweater she wore on top could have been indicative of a sleeveless garment underneath or an extra layer to move the shape of her outfit outward. Her pumps with their inch-and-a-half heel produced a soft and insistent thumping on the burgundy-carpeted floor, while her lace doily-style head covering strained against the bobby pin that kept it attached to the crown of her head. The other two women were adorned in straight-line, midcalf-length skirt suits with appliqué-lapelled jackets that fell below the hips, a style commonly seen on Sundays. Both wore modest hats, one a wide-brimmed cloche and the other a beret. Women's style presented an outward marker of distinction for a self-described "chosen generation, a royal priesthood, an holy nation, a peculiar people" (1 Pet. 2:9).[40] This liturgical work reiterated biblical teachings and did so within the bounds of COOLJC's gendered expectations of the female body and its appearance.

The runners performed aesthetic labor by reinforcing appropriate COOLJC values in worship, self-presentation, and community relations. They demonstrated "the beauty of holiness" in appearance and in action as spiritual gatekeepers. In this way, members experienced, in real time, the paradoxical proclamation of Jesus that the Kingdom is both present and forthcoming— "already and not yet."

Operating within the COOLJC aesthetic-religious environment, the three women runners—the first responders—unleashed their spiritual power to bind the congregation, to "believe God for a healing," and to democratize "already and not yet." Here we see Bell's idea of misrecognition at play. On its face, running responded to the need for physical healing. Running, however, demonstrated an active amalgamation of materiality and spirituality and presented an "already and not yet" infused with particular raced and gendered meanings. When women catalyze congregational anointing, their actions stand in relief to the male-headed church polity, as they pull "the true power of the living God" into the space from their position below the dais. Sprinting counterclockwise around the whole of the sanctuary, each woman called attention to and displaced the top-down hierarchy. She produced the "already and not yet" of "neither male nor female" in Jesus Christ, just as her enslaved pre-Pentecostal forebears, moving counterclockwise in ring shouts, activated "neither bond nor free" (Gal. 3:28). She reiterated the materiality-physicality of self-making and community making while operating in a spiritual register. Cleaving the tension between boundless spirit and gendered delineations of respectability, she yanked the democratized "not yet" of the Kingdom into "the already" of the earthly church. Running to heal the drummer, too, acted to realize healing of the church body and restore it to the fullness of "already and not yet."

The runners' ability to push material boundaries sits in stark contrast to doctrinal regulation, so rigorously regulated on women's bodies. Liturgical work of this sort produces, reproduces, and reconfigures the meanings of the sounding bodies of women that are both spontaneous and regulated. Worship places women's bodies at the heart of religious life, as "the body mediates that 'more' and makes visible what cannot be seen."[41] Holy Ghost anointing, singing, shouting, crying, speaking in tongues, and running collaborate, making women's bodies and the sounds they create definitive markers of community aesthetics, that which is deemed correct and valuable. The church relies on women's spiritual power, exhibited in particular agreed-on ways, to set the church on fire and display the beauty of holiness.

CONCLUSION

On the day Louise Franklin passed away, women gathered to handle material and spiritual tasks, to prepare themselves, the house, and soon the community of faith for the hours, days, and months ahead. At first glance, it might be easy to view the sweeping, scrubbing, polishing, washing, and folding as solely caring labor, the sometimes paid, sometimes unpaid work that so many women do all the time. But on closer examination we understand that the good women performed intimate, emotional, and aesthetic religious labor as well. When Mother Geneva Reeves sang, her emotional labor attended to everyone present, as she worked to rub a sonic salve into the open wounds.[1] Concocting the salve required aesthetic labor, pulling and weaving healing tones valued by the community. And as saints came and went throughout the day, the intimacy of holding, comforting, and praying was ever present.

The homegoing service for Louise was the first of quite a few I would attend over the course of this work. Of the saints you have met, Bishop Crosley J. Cook, Mother Esther Pea, Mother Jessie England, Mother Lucille Grayson, and Bishop William J. Bonner have all gone on "from labor to reward." The women of the Church of Our Lord Jesus Christ of the Apostolic Faith, Inc. (COOLJC) have managed the tasks associated with death innumerable times, and will continue to do so. During times of loss, the labor is intense and all-consuming, yet as we've seen, the faithful expend tremendous amounts of spiritual, physical, and mental energy on a regular basis. One sister who held a part-time job said, "On Mondays, as soon as my husband and kids are out, I turn off my phone and lay down. I'm exhausted after Sunday services!" She, like many, would start the day in Sunday school and stay through evening services. She rotated on the Kitchen Committee and sang in the choir. Known in the community as "truly anointed," she sang, played the tambourine, prayed, and worshipped with spiritual and physical intensity. The same could be said for many of the women on these pages. And they also carry responsibility for all manner of church operations, as well as families and paid jobs, most full-time.

Since COOLJC began in 1919, women have been pivotal in defining the ways the church knows itself. Carrie F. Lawson took the spiritual power she had shared within the church and gathered new members through the sound of her anointed voice as "the Praying Mother of the Air." Robert C. Lawson, as the public face and official head of the church, crafted a compelling theology that centered Black women in the atonement. At the same time, he advanced a doctrine that prohibited women from official permanent decision-making positions. The collocation of Spirit power and male headship has shaped the ways women carry out their divine mandates. It has determined the church's understanding of women's work and has governed the ways women operate to assure a "politics of incomplete male domination."[2]

From early on, organizing into horizontal networks allowed women to function in multiple roles throughout the church community. In this way, they kept a functional overview of everything needed to grow the body of Christ, while passing on to younger generations the strategies for getting things done. As Dr. Ruby Littleton relayed, when she was growing up, "the missionaries ran everything. . . . I didn't know the word then, but they were multitasking. . . . I lived that. I learned to do that." Missionaries taught her how to work and stay "in the Word," through Bible study and teaching services. Immersed in Bible time and committed to the community of faith, these oneness women strove to align themselves in thought, word, and deed with the indwelling Jesus.

An unmediated relationship with Jesus remains at the heart of women's awareness and practices of spiritual and organizational authority. Even as professional opportunities expand in the twenty-first century and COOLJC women move into official decision-making positions in the world, in the church, and at home, they adhere to having "men on the top." To stay in accordance with doctrine, they develop strategies and create negotiated spaces, ultimately formulating a politics of righteousness. Thus, they are able to (re-)produce women-driven patriarchies, emboldened by the knowledge that, like Jesus, they "have the power to submit." The ways in which women have organized and the mechanisms they employ to carry out work show that a vital part of their power lies in keeping the church polity intact. Navigating the chain of command in the institution of the "church family" while demanding a meritocracy in the paid labor force means women acquire a range of emotion management skills. Bishop Cook called on the women to bring those skills to bear and "teach men that they can have leadership." When male leaders call on women to exercise their unique skills to help men, it means more work that only women can (and have to) do, while reinforcing women's complicated authority.

Whereas emotion management across spheres of religious labor strengthens the influence of women, intimate labor at the altar and aesthetic labor in worship solidify women as the nucleus of the church. Through intergenerational apprenticeship networks, women carry out the work of spiritual, social, and institutional reproduction by bringing new souls to Christ and new members into the body of the church. Even with changes or conflicts in the ways altar workers conceptualize the job, it persists as a primary location of women's spiritual authority. Too, the aesthetics of embodied theology buttresses spiritual power. Women numerically dominate, and therefore the presence of the Holy Ghost is most often revealed through women. In this way, the church comes to know itself. The sounds, motions, and presence of women are instrumental in catalyzing worship. And, as we have seen, spiritual power allows women to address essential theological concerns. Altar work and the aesthetic labor in worship of COOLJC women "uncover the kinds of power African-American women derive from the most intimate of religious experiences—the direct encounter with the divine."[3] Saints understand themselves to be a "chosen generation, a royal priesthood, an holy nation, a peculiar people" (1 Peter 2:9). The women of COOLJC gear their religious labor toward personally growing in Christ and growing the church—both the institution and the Kingdom. They perform religious labor with "the goal of becoming an authentic religious subject."[4] Navigating webs of spiritual, social, and organizational relationships calls for women to acquire and hone a wide range of skills across material and immaterial boundaries, to carry out the demanding labor of faith.

NOTES

INTRODUCTION

1   *Mother* is an official title granted to older churchwomen who have exhibited years of consistent spiritual and organizational leadership. According to C. Eric Lincoln and Lawrence H. Mamiya, "the phenomenon of the 'church mother' has no parallel in white churches; it is derived from the kinship network found within black churches and black communities." *Black Church*, 275. Cheryl Townsend Gilkes gives a detailed analysis of the role of church mothers across Black denominations, particularly Black Holiness, Pentecostal, and Apostolic churches. *"If It Wasn't,"* 103–4. For a denominationally specific study, see Butler, *Women*, 43–48.

2   I use the King James Version for all scriptural references, as do the members of the Church of Our Lord Jesus Christ of the Apostolic Faith, Inc.

3   Cox, *Fire from Heaven*; Murphy, *Working the Spirit*; Hurston, *Sanctified Church*; Paris, *Black Pentecostalism*; and Raboteau, *Slave Religion*.

4   The church's theological roots go back to John Nelson Darby's late nineteenth-century Bible conferences and to Keswick movement revivalists Dwight L. Moody and Cyrus I. Scofield. James I. Clark Jr. argues that the *Scofield Reference Bible* significantly shaped African American Apostolic Pentecostal theology. Published in 1909, "it was the only Bible for my tradition and most, if not all, African-American Apostolic Pentecostalists from 1919 to the last decade of the 1950s." "Christian Religious Education," 85. During the late twentieth century, alternate versions, most often the *Thompson Chain Reference Bible*, came into use.

5   See also 1 Thess. 4:16–17: "For the Lord himself shall descend from heaven with a shout, with the voice of the archangel, and with the trump of God: and the dead in Christ shall rise first: Then we which are alive and remain shall be caught up together with them in the clouds, to meet the Lord in the air: and so shall we ever be with the Lord."

6   "The absolute deity of Jesus" is one of the church's core principles of faith and is printed in weekly church bulletins. The principles are detailed in chapter 1. For doctrinal distinctions between Charismatics, Classical and Neo-Pentecostals,

Holiness-Pentecostals, and Apostolics, see Synan, *Holiness-Pentecostal Tradition*; and Anderson, *Introduction to Pentecostalism*.

7 John 10:30: "I and my Father are one." John 12:44–45: "Jesus cried and said, He that believeth on me, believeth not on me, but on him that sent me. And he that seeth me seeth him that sent me."

8 Notable exceptions include Du Bois, *Souls of Black Folk*; Fauset, *Black Gods*; and Hurston, *Sanctified Church*.

9 See Schechter, *Ida B. Wells-Barnett*; Lee, *For Freedom's Sake*; Jones, *Labor of Love*; Hudson-Weems, "Resurrecting Emmett Till"; and Gilmore, *Gender and Jim Crow*.

10 Weisenfeld, "We Have Been Believers," 1.

11 Higginbotham, *Righteous Discontent*, 121.

12 See Weisenfeld, *African American Women*.

13 See E. Brown, "Negotiating and Transforming," for an examination of the period of transition in late nineteenth-century Virginia, as the center of civic and political life shifted away from the church.

14 Frederick, *Between Sundays*, 14.

15 Frederick, *Between Sundays*, 138.

16 See Crumbley, *Saved and Sanctified*.

17 Crumbley, *Saved and Sanctified*, x.

18 African American women report the highest level of religious commitment of any U.S. demographic, with 84 percent "saying religion is very important to them" and 59 percent attending weekly services. A Pew Research Center report notes, "No group of men or women from any other racial or ethnic background exhibits comparably high levels of religious observance." See "A Religious Portrait of African-Americans," *Pew Research Center: Religious and Public Life*, January 30, 2009, http://www.pewforum.org/2009/01/30/a-religious-portrait-of-african-americans/. Joel Robbins notes that women compose 75 percent of Pentecostal/Charismatic churches worldwide. See Robbins, "Globalization," 132. In American Christianity generally, women's majority status has been well documented. Women dominate in nearly every Christian group. Specifically, "members of Protestant churches are eight percentage points more likely to be women than men (54% to 46%); a similar gap is seen among Catholics. Among historically black Protestant churches and Jehovah's Witnesses, however, women constitute a somewhat higher percentage (60%)." See "U.S. Religious Landscape Survey: Religious Affiliation and Demographic Groups," *The Pew Forum on Religion and Public Life*, February 2008, http://www.pewforum.org/2008/02/01/chapter-3-religious-affiliation-and-demographic-groups/. While I have no data to support my supposition, I suggest a gap exists between the numbers of men who report being a member and those who are active participants. Within the COOLJC no organization-wide survey has been conducted; however, my data from New York churches are consistent with Robbins's global data, with women constituting closer to 80 percent of active members.

19 Frederick, *Between Sundays*, 213.

20 Weisenfeld, "We Have Been Believers," 3.

21 E. Brown, "Womanist Consciousness," 622; emphasis added.

22 "The question of 'who exercises power?' can[not] be resolved unless [we ask] the question of '*how does it happen?*'" Foucault, *Politics, Philosophy, Culture*, 103.

23 See Hochschild, *Managed Heart*. See Folbre, *Invisible Heart*, for a brilliant analysis of fundamental conceptual errors made by economists who adhere to the dichotomy between public-productive-male and private-unproductive-female.

24 See Grandey, Deindorff, and Rupp, *Emotional Labor*; Mirchandani, "Challenging Racial Silences"; and DeVault, "Comfort and Struggle." For "boundary-spanning" labor, see Wharton and Erickson, "Managing Emotions on the Job and at Home."

25 Boris and Parreñas, "Introduction," 7.

26 Warhurst and Nickson, "'Who's Got the Look?,'" 386.

27 Harley, "Introduction," 1.

28 See Baron, "Gender and Labor History."

29 The official leadership pathway for men is from brother, through deacon, minister, (officially ordained) elder, and bishop, to apostle. If they attend church faithfully, men are expected to advance to deacon within a relatively short period of time. There is no institutionalized time frame, so a man's promotion from brother to deacon can occur at any time. During my fieldwork, two men joined the church and advanced to deacon within two years.

30 Gilkes, "*If It Wasn't*," 6.

31 Gilkes, "*If It Wasn't*," 6.

32 Gilkes, "*If It Wasn't*," 6.

33 I did teach one course each semester at Barnard College during 2004–2005.

34 Gilkes, "*If It Wasn't*," 108.

35 For an overview of literature across disciplines in the field of Pentecostal studies, see Corten, "Growth of the Literature." For a study of the religious movement's history, with particular focus on its late twentieth-century development in Africa, see Kalu, *African Pentecostalism*.

1. THE INSTRUMENTS OF FAITH

1 Apostolic Pentecostals use the term *sleep* for death. The scriptural basis is found in 1 Thessalonians 4:13–18, which describes the Rapture. Upon the return of Jesus, those who "sleep in Jesus, will God bring with him." Jesus, too, uses *sleep* when talking about the death of Lazarus.

2 Converted members throughout Holiness-Pentecostalism refer to themselves and each other as "saints." This is also of biblical origin: "Saints—'holy ones' who consecrate themselves for God's Service" (Barton, *Life Application*, 2427).

3 See Psalms 29:2 and 96:9.

4 Csordas, "Charismatic Persuasion and Healing," 132.

5 Mahmood, *Politics of Piety*, 135, 157. Mahmood references *habitus* in the Aristotelian sense, which addresses ethical formations as resulting from specific practices, such that moral practice becomes part of one's disposition. She notes that this is distinct from the class-based, unconscious habitus of Pierre Bourdieu. *Politics of Piety*, 134–39.

6 While COOLJC women acknowledge the work it takes to maintain a sanctified existence, many claim that Spirit baptism "convicted" them immediately in certain areas of their lives. Becoming Spirit filled can take away old "worldly" desires and instantaneously instill new sanctified ones. Testimonies by saints about an instant change in outlook offer a challenge to Mahmood's argument and create a space between conduct that is driven by desire and practice that shapes desire. There is nevertheless an affinity in processes of spiritual maturation between the women in Mahmood's study and the saints of COOLJC.

7 J. Smith, "Bare Facts of Ritual," 116–17.

8 Bell, *Ritual Theory, Ritual Practice*, 107.

9 Bell, *Ritual Theory, Ritual Practice*, 107.

10 See Cox, *Fire from Heaven*, 139–57; Ward, "Filled with the Spirit," 103–10; and Levine *Black Culture*, 174–89.

11 Hoyt, "Testimony," 96.

12 See 2 Tim. 4:2: "Preach the word; be instant in season, out of season; reprove, rebuke, exhort with all long suffering and doctrine."

13 Hoyt, "Testimony," 94.

14 G. Davis, *I Got the Word*, 27–30.

15 The attitudes of COOLJC toward medical science resonate with those of other evangelical organizations. In *God's Daughters*, a study of the Women's Aglow Fellowship, a predominantly White American evangelical prayer organization, R. Marie Griffith observes, "Doctors, hospitals, and the techniques of modern scientific medicine . . . are more often readily accepted as complementary instruments in the total healing process. Miracles are believed not to be limited to instantaneous and inexplicable events but to encompass a whole range of more gradual movements toward health as well" (91).

16 Gracing the cover of the fall 2004 issue of *Contender for the Faith Magazine*, the organizational publication, are "some of the Inspiring Prominent, Productive Pentecostal Achievers in the COOLJC." Along with bank and business executives, attorneys, university professors, and a dean are the chief of anesthesia of Baptist Medical Center in Jacksonville, Florida; the director of inpatient services for a South Carolina medical center; the director of team leaders at Pfizer Inc.; and a doctoral candidate conducting cancer and hematology research.

17 Anderson, *Introduction to Pentecostalism*, 212.

18 See Curtis, *Great Physician*.

19 Curtis, *Great Physician*, 18.

20 See Luhrmann, *When God Talks Back*. She notes a "general model" for effective prayer: "God wants to be your friend; you develop that relationship through prayer; prayer is hard work and requires effort and training; and when you develop that relationship, God will answer back, through thoughts and mental images he places in your mind, and through sensations he causes in your body" (41).

21 Luhrmann, *When God Talks Back*, 41.

22 Luhrmann, *When God Talks Back*, 41.

23 Giddings, *Ida*, 230.

24 Sister Allen and Mother Reeves represent the last wave of African Americans in the Great Migration, leaving the South in the 1960s and 1970s. See Wilkerson, *Warmth of Other Suns*.

25 This is in keeping with the biblical mandate found in Matthew 6:1, which states, "Take heed that ye do not your alms before men, to be seen of them: otherwise ye have no reward of your Father which is in heaven."

26 In 1998 TDC built a one-million-dollar Christian school facility, around the corner from the church, for preschool through eighth-grade students.

27 Louise gave the church a check for $2,000. In 2005 TDC purchased the property, increasing the total net worth of the church to over $5 million.

28 Louise's confession of healing can be likened to the "positive confessions" of Swedish charismatics, whereby "inspired words gain . . . efficacy . . . manifested in the material world." Coleman, "Materializing the Self," 168.

29 *Adult Student Handbook (Summer)*, 24–25.

30 *Adult Student Handbook (Summer)*, 25.

31 Hezekiah's story of being "sick unto death" is told in 2 Kings 16:20–20:21, 2 Chronicles 28:27–32:33, and Isaiah 36:1–39:8.

32 I asked Sister Holmes to explain the place of mourning. "[Bishop Cook] is an older and tougher cookie," she said. "I think he knows people will grieve. You can mourn, but don't *be* mournful."

33 Bell, *Ritual Theory, Ritual Practice*, 107.

34 Similar rhetorical practices can be seen in Swedish charismatic and Tanzanian Pentecostal communities. See Coleman, "Materializing the Self"; and Lindhardt, "'If You Are Saved.'" "Rather than an outward, sincere or insincere, expression of an internal state," Martin Lindhardt observes, ". . . the utterance became a way of capturing a divinely ordained state and appropriating it into the self" (258). Unlike Word of Life (Swedish) and New Life in Christ (Tanzanian) adherents, however, COOLJC members do not grant power solely to "the force of the word" (258).

2. CHURCH BUILDING

Epigraph: Spellman and Thomas, *Life, Legend and Legacy*, 66.

1 See Banks, "Interview," for details about the river baptisms of the early church.

2 For studies that highlight women church builders, see Best, *Passionately Human*; Fauset, *Black Gods*; and Hurston, *Sanctified Church*.

3 Gilkes, *"If It Wasn't,"* 5.

4 For an in-depth analysis and critiques, see Collins, *Black Feminist Thought*; and Hull, Scott, and Smith, *All the Women*.

5 French, "Early Oneness Pentecostalism," 198.

6 Norwood, Mother Miriam, "The Unique Woman of Worth,"cooljc *Constituent: The Official Newsletter of the International Convention Committee*, vol. 2, no. 2 (March 2011), p. 1.

7 A passport application filed by Lawson in 1923 gives his birth year as 1888, while a draft registration card from 1917 has 1887. The passport application also indicates that he was a second-generation New Iberian; it was his father's birthplace as well. U.S. passport application no. 343224, September 29, 1923.

8 Spellman and Thomas, *Life, Legend and Legacy*, 41.

9 Synan, *Holiness-Pentecostal Tradition*, 172; and Wacker, *Heaven Below*, 153.

10 For a superb analytical history of Methodism, see Hempton, *Methodism*.

11 Jacobsen, *Thinking in the Spirit*, 57.

12 "Weird Babel of Tongues: New Sect of Fanatics Is Breaking Loose; Wild Scene Last Night on Azusa Street; Gurgle of Wordless Talk by a Sister," *Los Angeles Times*, April 18, 1906, I11, ProQuest Historical Newspapers.

13 See MacRobert, *Black Roots*, 46–47.

14 *Apostolic Faith*, September 1906, p. 1, col. 4.

15 See DuPree, *Holiness Pentecostal Movement*, xxxvi.

16 Bartleman, *Azusa Street*, 61.

17 "Bluk Feet, Little, and Big, Scrubbed," *Indianapolis Star*, June 16, 1907, p. 10, Indianapolis Star Online Archive (1907–1922).

18 For a fascinating study of the women's division of the Ku Klux Klan in Indiana, see Blee, "Ku Klux Klan Movement."

19 French, "Early Oneness Pentecostalism," 118.

20 French, "Early Oneness Pentecostalism," 124–26; and Jacobsen, *Reader in Pentecostal Theology*, 174.

21 The racial and ethnic landscape of early American Pentecostalism showed more complexity than a black-white binary. See Espinosa, *Latino Pentecostals in America*. For a study of contemporary Latino Pentecostal identity within Assemblies of God congregations, see Sanchez-Walsh, *Latino Pentecostal Identity*.

22 See Alexander, *Black Fire*, 177; and Synan, *Holiness-Pentecostal Tradition*, 71, 126.

23 See DuPree, *Holiness Pentecostal Movement*, 395.

24 See Butler, *Women*, 30; Jacobsen, *Thinking in the Spirit*, 261; and Synan, *Holiness-Pentecostal Tradition*, 153–56. For a treatment of the history of theology and racism in the Assemblies of God through 1994, see Newman, *Race*.

25 See Alexander, *Black Fire*, 211; and Gerloff, "Black Oneness (Apostolic) Theology," 88.

26 See Alexander, *Black Fire*, 215; Jacobsen, *Reader in Pentecostal Theology*; Tyson, *The Early Pentecostal Revival*; and Clark, "Christian Religious Education."

27 See Alexander, *Black Fire*, 216; and French, "Early Oneness Pentecostalism," 181.

28 See Alexander, *Black Fire*, 222–23.

29 Jacobsen, *Thinking in the Spirit*, 12.

30 Jacobsen, *Thinking in the Spirit*, 10.

31 Jacobsen, *Thinking in the Spirit*, 264.

32 Jacobsen, *Thinking in the Spirit*, 263.

33 See Corbould, *Becoming African Americans*; Dray, *At the Hands*; and Tuttle, *Chicago*.

34 See Baker, *From Savage to Negro*, 93.

35 See Clarke, "Marcus Garvey," 14–15, 17–19.

36 Spellman and Thomas, *Life, Legend and Legacy*, 13.

37 Lawson would go on to receive a doctorate in divinity from Virginia Union Theological Seminary in 1944.

38 See Jacobsen, *Thinking in the Spirit*, 263–86.

39 See Lawson, *Anthropology of Jesus*, preface (n.p.).

40 Lawson, *Anthropology of Jesus*, preface.

41 Lawson, *Anthropology of Jesus*, 13.

42 Lawson, *Anthropology of Jesus*, 13.

43 Lawson, *Anthropology of Jesus*, 270. For a discussion of the infusion of an African past into Harlem public discourse from 1919 to 1939, see Corbould, *Becoming African Americans*, 57–87. Corbould overlooks the significance of churches in constructing relevant notions of Africa for the Harlem public.

44 Corbould, *Becoming African Americans*, 86.

45 See Lawson, *Anthropology of Jesus*, 5, 23.

46 Lawson, *Anthropology of Jesus*, 1.

47 Lawson, *Anthropology of Jesus*, i–ii, 28, 42.

48 Lawson, *Anthropology of Jesus*, 26.

49 Lawson, *Anthropology of Jesus*, 24–26, 30.

50 Lawson, *Anthropology of Jesus*, 23.

51 In 1949 Lawson printed an open letter in the organization-wide journal, *Contender for the Faith*, summarizing his theology. "Is it a surprise to you to know," he began, "that a 'Colored' woman was the first mother of the Tribe of Judah?" His reiteration of this two decades after the original publication ensured that new generations of Apostolics understood fundamental elements of church theology. Over fifty years later and thirty-four years after Lawson's passing, the church leadership issued yet another reprint. The fall 2000 issue of *The Contender for the Faith Magazine* carried Lawson's letter from 1949 in an article entitled, "Remembering Words from Our Founder, Bishop R. C. Lawson: Women of Color in the Ancestry of Jesus Christ" (32).

52 "Bishop; R. C. Lawson; Church; Refuge; Christ; Brooklyn; Harlem; Sundays," *Negro Star*, February 3, 1939, 1. Also see "Refuge Church of Christ Prospering: Bishop R. C. Lawson's Organization Also Runs Grocery, Industrial Department," *New York Amsterdam News*, March 25, 1939, 16, ProQuest Historical Newspapers.

53 In *Thinking in the Spirit*, Jacobsen argues that "pentecostal [sic] theology embraces a holistic style of spirituality that places equal value on the affective, moral, and doctrinal dimensions . . . a full gospel of feeling, action, and belief" (362). Lawson was one of the earliest theologians to bring all three aspects together in one church.

54 See "Refuge Church of Christ Prospering."

55 See Spellman and Thomas, *Life, Legend and Legacy*, 17; "On the Air," *Plaindealer* (Kansas City, KS), April 20, 1934, 6; and "This Is New York," *Plaindealer*, April 26, 1935, 3.

56 Spellman and Thomas, *Life, Legend and Legacy*, 65.

57 Spellman and Thomas, *Life, Legend and Legacy*, 66.

58 Kansas City, Kansas Population Census 1895, 9. Ancestry.com, http://sharing .ancestry.com/1966327?h=efcccf. The closeness in age between her mother, Anna (twenty-one), and her brothers, Joe (eleven) and George (eight), suggests the boys may have been extended family, possibly siblings of one of the parents.

59 See French, "Early Oneness Pentecostalism," 211; and Alexander C. Stewart, "The Centennial Oneness Jesus Name Apostolic Movement," *Contender for the Faith*, Fall 2013, 17.

60 Spellman and Thomas, *Life, Legend and Legacy*, 66.

61 Spellman and Thomas, *Life, Legend and Legacy*, 66.

62 Spellman and Thomas, *Life, Legend and Legacy*, 66.

63 Conrad Clark, "12,000 Attend Mother Lawson Funeral Rites: Thousands View Body of Church Worker," *New York Amsterdam News*, August 14, 1948, 21.

64 Clark, "12,000 Attend."

65 Clark, "12,000 Attend."

66 Lawson, "Short Sketch," 2.

67 See Butler, *Women*, 99–109; and Higginbotham, *Righteous Discontent*, 211–21.

68 Lawson, "Short Sketch," 2.

69 "On the Air"; "Aids Poor," *Chicago Defender*, national edition, February 4, 1939, 5, ProQuest Historical Newspapers; and "Bishop R. C. Lawson Backs Dahoga Club," *New York Amsterdam News*, March 18, 1939, 17, ProQuest Historical Newspapers.

70 "Bishop Flays 2 Elders in Unfrocking: Bigamy, Refusal to Live with Wife Given as Reasons," *Chicago Defender*, national edition, September 5, 1936, 1.

71 Spellman and Thomas, *Life, Legend and Legacy*, 21.

72 See DuPree, *Holiness Pentecostal Movement*. Unclassified Federal Bureau of Investigation reports show "a persistent monitoring of Pentecostal and Spiritualist groups suspected of expressing Black Nationalist ideology, anti-war sentiments during World Wars I and II, and communist sympathies during the 1950s" (395).

73 DuPree, *Holiness Pentecostal Movement*, 31.

74 Rob Ryser, "Lawsonville Remembered," *Journal News* (White Plains, NY), February 21, 2006, B1.

75 Malcolm Nash, "Orderly Crowd," *New York Amsterdam News*, May 25, 1957,
    ProQuest Historical Newspapers; and Sara Slack, "All Kinds of Groups Rode
    Freedom Train," *New York Amsterdam News*, May 25, 1957, 1, ProQuest Histori-
    cal Newspapers.

76 A. Philip Randolph, Martin Luther King, Jr., and Roy Wilkens, "Call to a
    Prayer Pilgrimage for Freedom," dated April 5, 1957, accession no. 001608–
    024–0703, 0704–0706, A. Philip Randolph Papers, Bowdoin College, Bruns-
    wick, ME.

77 "Prayer Pilgrimage Program," accession no. 001608–024–0711, 0711 [3], A. Philip
    Randolph Papers, Bowdoin College, Brunswick, ME.

78 "Bishop Lawson Relates Colorful Story of His Trip around World: In Memory
    of Gandhi," *New York Amsterdam News*, April 22, 1950, 16, ProQuest Historical
    Newspapers.

79 "Lawson Gets Endowment to Teach Amharic," *Chicago Defender*, March 31,
    1951, 3, ProQuest Historical Newspapers.

80 "Selassie's 'Closed Car' Visit Angers Harlemites," *New York Amsterdam News*,
    June 12, 1954, 1, ProQuest Historical Newspapers.

81 "Eisenhower to Speak in Harlem Tomorrow; Motorcade through the Area
    Will Precede Talk," *New York Times*, October 24, 1952, 18, ProQuest Historical
    Newspapers.

82 DuPree, *Holiness Pentecostal Movement*, 444.

83 See Alexander, *Black Fire*, 224–26; DuPree, *Holiness Pentecostal Movement*,
    256; and "Bishop S. C. Johnson, Founder and Former Pastor (1933–1961),
    Church of the Lord Jesus Christ of the Apostolic Faith, *Official Website for
    Church of the Lord Jesus Christ of the Apostolic Faith*, 2016. http://www.tcljc
    .com/NewSite/BSCJ.html.

84 See Alexander, *Black Fire*, 226–27; and DuPree, *Holiness Pentecostal Movement*,
    268.

85 See Alexander, *Black Fire*, 227–28; and DuPree, *Holiness Pentecostal Movement*,
    425.

86 "The Founder and Church History," *The Official Website Bible Way Church
    World Wide, Inc.*, 1999. http://www.biblewaychurch.org/about-us/the-founder
    -church-history.

87 Spellman and Thomas, *Life, Legend and Legacy*, 34.

88 Spellman and Thomas, *Life, Legend and Legacy*, 96.

89 Women who have not risen to the title of "mother" before their husband pas-
    tors a congregation are referred to as the first lady of the church.

90 "Two of Bishop R.C. Lawson's Most Blessed Sons in the Gospel: A History
    Lesson for Aspiring Preachers," *Contender for the Faith Magazine*, August/
    September, 1988, 34.

91 I gleaned most of the information in this section from the authorized biography
    of Bishop Bonner, written by the W. L. Bonner Literary Committee, which
    was assembled at his behest and led by June Bonner, his sister-in-law. See
    Bonner and Bonner, . . . *And the High Places*. I was able to verify key dates and

appointments through the Spellman and Thomas, *Life, Legend and Legacy*, and cooljc journals.

92 Bonner and Bonner, . . . *And the High Places*, 12.

93 Bonner and Bonner, . . . *And the High Places*, 15.

94 Bonner and Bonner, . . . *And the High Places*, 25–26.

95 "A Picture Tribute to the Late Lady Ethel Mae Bonner—'Queen Bonner,'" *Contender for the Faith Magazine*, Fall 2000, 65; emphasis added.

96 "A Picture Tribute," 66; and Spellman and Thomas, *Life, Legend and Legacy*, 107–8.

97 See Spellman and Thomas, *Life, Legend and Legacy*, 100.

98 Spellman and Thomas, *Life, Legend and Legacy*, 100.

99 "Bishop Bonner Speaks on Plight of Black Men," *New York Amsterdam News*, August 30, 1969, 31; and "Refuge Temple to Launch Its Drug Program," *New York Amsterdam News*, February 28, 1970, 42.

100 "We Must Never Compromise this Apostolic Doctrine: Dedicatorial Sermon Delivered at the Memphis Refuge Church Of Our Lord Jesus Christ, Sermon by Bishop W.L. Bonner, Presiding Apostle, Church Of Our Lord Jesus Christ," *Contender for the Faith Magazine*, Fall 1988, 27.

101 Gilkes, *"If It Wasn't,"* 56.

102 Gilkes, *"If It Wasn't,"* 82.

103 "About Us," *The Church of Our Lord Jesus Christ of the Apostolic Faith, Inc.*, 2013, http://www.cooljc.org/about-us-2/.

104 Spellman and Thomas, *Life, Legend and Legacy*, 118.

105 "50th Anniversary at Apostolic Church," *New York Amsterdam News*, September 27, 1969, 35, ProQuest Historical Newspapers.

106 Minute books in author's possession.

107 See Alexander, *Black Fire*, 246; and DuPree, *Holiness Pentecostal Movement*, 253. Alexander reports 45,000 cooljc members, while DuPree reports 65,000. I have averaged it out to 55,000. All membership numbers of denominations and churches are based on self-reporting. Neither the U.S. Bureau of the Census nor the Pew Research Center gathers data on Black Pentecostal church membership by denomination.

108 See Alexander, *Black Fire*, 246; DuPree, *Holiness Pentecostal Movement*, 263; and Burgess, *New International Dictionary*, 382.

109 The current Bible Way World Wide and International Bible Way came about as the result of a split in 1983 within the larger Bible Way Church founded by Williams in 1957. See Alexander, *Black Fire*, 228–29.

110 See Alexander, *Black Fire*, 246–48.

111 See Burgess, *New International Dictionary*, 286.

112 Burgess, *New International Dictionary*, 286.

113 In 2005 Bishop Cook relayed this version of the founding story to the congregation during an anniversary service. In our interview, Bishop Cook told me that the Florida trip was a vacation and Mother Cook had seen a home she

wanted them to purchase but he "felt the need to return to New York." Within Apostolic narratives of God's work, some details are less important than others. The point was not why they were going but why they returned.

114 Field notes of TDC business meeting, August 26, 2006.

115 In oral TDC history, members credit Mother Cook with having a vision to build the academy. *The Contender for the Faith Magazine* states the True Deliverance Christian Academy "is the fulfillment of a vision given to Mother Reva Cook and her husband, Bishop Crosley Cook" (2000, 52). Yet the dedication plaque on the building reads, "The vision of DISTRICT ELDER CROSLEY COOK founder and builder of the TRUE DELIVERANCE CHRISTIAN SCHOOL."

3. CHURCH SUSTAINING

1 Mother England became president of the MDWG while her husband, Elder England, was alive. She retained the position after his death in 1998.

2 Quarterly meetings are regional diocese conventions. In this case, TDC belongs to New York's Tri-diocese, which includes churches in Queens and part of Brooklyn. Up until recently, it included churches in the Bronx as well, hence the name.

3 Apostle Robert L. Sanders, Sr. "Greetings from the Apostle to the Women's Auxiliaries." *The Beacon*, 2005, Fall/Winter, 5.

4 Church of Our Lord Jesus Christ, *Discipline Book*, 70.

5 Church of Our Lord Jesus Christ, *Discipline Book*, 70.

6 Waid, *Blessed Life*, 5.

7 Church of Our Lord Jesus Christ, *Outstanding Women*, 17.

8 Church of Our Lord Jesus Christ, *Discipline Book*, 70.

9 Church of Our Lord Jesus Christ, *Discipline Book*, 70–71. For "fruit of the spirit" see Gal. 5:22–23.

10 Church of Our Lord Jesus Christ, *Discipline Book*, 70.

11 Church of Our Lord Jesus Christ, *Discipline Book*, 70. For the work of missionaries at the altar, see chapter 5, "Harvesting Souls for Christ."

12 See Church of Our Lord Jesus Christ, *Outstanding Women*, 26–29. For church-planting activities by Church of God in Christ women in the early twentieth century, see Butler, *Women*, 50–51. For church planting by women in Brooklyn, New York, see Taylor, *Black Churches of Brooklyn*, 172.

13 Church of Our Lord Jesus Christ, *Outstanding Women*, 87.

14 Church of Our Lord Jesus Christ, *Discipline Book*, 70.

15 Gilkes, "*If It Wasn't*," 4.

16 Sid Bell, "Meet 'Mother Ada' Washington: Religion-Key to Life's Ups," *Contender for the Faith Magazine*, 2013, Fall 31. (Reprinted from *Welch Daily News*, West Virginia n.d.)

17 Butler, *Women*, 72.

18 Carothers, "Catching Sense," 237.

19   Carothers, "Catching Sense," 240.

20   Carothers, "Catching Sense," 235.

21   See 2 Tim. 2:15: "Study to shew thyself approved unto God, a workman that needeth not to be ashamed, rightly dividing the word of truth."

22   The international organization allows flexibility for each church to set the specifics of its auxiliaries' agendas and goals, as long as they are in keeping with the presiding apostle's goals. At TDC Bishop Cook does not allow the Missionary Department to sponsor any fund-raising or entertainment events. He sees missionary work as strictly spiritual—home, hospital, nursing home, and prison visitation.

23   See "New Expansion Church Purchased in Milwaukee, Wisconsin," *Contender for the Faith*, 1988, Summer/Fall, 58. The missionaries donated $12,000, the Women's Council $13,000, and the local congregation $5,000 toward the $55,000 purchase.

24   Church of Our Lord Jesus Christ, *Holy Council*, 10–11. The COOLJC historical records are unclear about the exact date. *The Holy Council: Guides for the International Women's Council* reports Mother Perry having "the vision" sometime before 1952 and revealing it to the State Mothers' Council on June 1, 1952. They, in turn, presented a written resolution to the COOLJC National Convocation in August 1952. Spellman and Thomas, *Life, Legend and Legacy*, mark the Women's Council's as being founded in 1951, 70 and 77.

25   The proposed constitution of the IWC of the COOLJC is printed in Church of Our Lord Jesus Christ, *Holy Council*, 53–61. The constitution was compiled and presented by Mother Mabel Thomas in 1990. Once accepted by a majority vote, it was submitted to the Executive Board of COOLJC for final approval. As of this printing, *The Holy Council* is under revision, to be resubmitted for ratification. It is not clear from the documentation whether the proposed constitution has been ratified. *The Discipline Book* has been out of print since 2005. I am working from the sixth edition, published in 1991.

26   Church of Our Lord Jesus Christ, *Holy Council*, 14.

27   Church of Our Lord Jesus Christ, *Holy Council*, 34.

28   See Butler, *Women*; Gilkes, *"If It Wasn't"*; Taylor, *Black Churches of Brooklyn*; and Higginbotham, *Righteous Discontent*.

29   Gilkes, *"If It Wasn't,"* 114.

30   Church of Our Lord Jesus Christ, *Holy Council*, 6.

31   Beckford, "Black Suits Matter," 145.

32   Church of Our Lord Jesus Christ, *Holy Council*, 7.

33   Church of Our Lord Jesus Christ, *Holy Council*, 7.

34   "Praise Is What I Do," words and music by William Murphy III, Lilly Mack Music, Inglewood, California 90302.

35   Church of Our Lord Jesus Christ, *Holy Council*, 2.

36   See Robert A. Emmons and Charles M. Shelton "Gratitude and the Science of Positive Psychology," Snyder and Lopez, *Handbook of Positive Psychology*, 459–471.

37 Church of Our Lord Jesus Christ, *Holy Council*, 17.

38 Gilkes, *"If It Wasn't,"* 115.

39 See the introduction to this book, note 17.

40 "MDWG History" COOLJC website 2013, accessed September 4, 2013, http://www.cooljc.org/?page_id=56.

41 Church of Our Lord Jesus Christ, *Discipline Book*, 75.

42 Talises D. Moorer, "Beloved Mother and First Lady Ethel Mae Bonner Laid to Rest," *New York Amsterdam News*, January 13–19, 2000, 39.

43 Church of Our Lord Jesus Christ, *Discipline Book*, 75. Emphasis added.

44 Church of Our Lord Jesus Christ, *Discipline Book*, 75; bold in original.

45 Church of Our Lord Jesus Christ, *Discipline Book*, 75.

46 Pastors of the COOLJC can be called on to preach away from their home churches, but people are respectful of a pastor's responsibilities at his home congregation.

47 Church of Our Lord Jesus Christ, *Discipline Book*, 76.

48 Church of Our Lord Jesus Christ, *Discipline Book*, 75.

4. WOMEN'S WORK

1 Gilkes, *"If It Wasn't,"* 58.

2 Eph. 6:14: "Stand therefore, having your loins girt about with truth, and having on the breastplate of righteousness." Also see Isa. 59:17.

3 Mahmood, *Politics of Piety*, 29.

4 Mahmood, *Politics of Piety*, 29.

5 Mahmood, *Politics of Piety*, 29.

6 Mahmood, *Politics of Piety*, 29.

7 Hochschild, *Managed Heart*, ix. Hochschild's groundbreaking study keeps the dichotomy of public and private intact, defining *emotional labor* as paid-public and *emotion work* as unpaid-private. Four decades of scholarship in social science and business fields has since called attention to overlapping lived experiences that upend either-or models. See Grandey, Deindorff, and Rupp, *Emotional Labor*. Hochschild also introduced *emotion management*, which has since become an umbrella term encompassing *emotional labor* and *emotion work*. Rebecca J. Erickson and Clare L. Stacey recently coined *emotional practice* to cover perceived gaps between the management of emotions and "the embodied emotional experience (not just its management) [that] is a fundamental part of the processes under consideration in both the human and commercial sectors." "Attending," 188. I consider the push to have social scientists, economists, and organizational scholars incorporate embodied experience a critical intervention. Nonetheless, for the purposes of this study, I hold on to emotional *labor*, emotion *work*, and emotion *management*, and I use them interchangeably to highlight the breadth of effort and exertion by churchwomen as they self-manage and manage the feelings of others across the sacred and secular realms.

8　See Pierce, *Gender Trial*; and Leidner, *Fast Food, Fast Talk*.

9　See Barker, "Beyond Women and Economics"; DeVault, "Comfort and Struggle"; and Wharton and Erickson, "Managing Emotions."

10　Wharton and Erickson, "Managing Emotions," 464–66.

11　Mirchandani, "Challenging Racial Silences," 722.

12　See Woodhead, "Feminism," 77. Linda Woodhead points to the centrality of feminist theory in theoretical shifts to "relational religion" in the sociology of religion. Feminist theory argued against the public-private paradigm in social (and religious) theory and called attention to women's "'situated' and already relational self . . . in a network of connection."

13　Gilkes, "*If It Wasn't,*" 108.

14　See Butler, *Women*, 48–50.

15　Stack, *All Our Kin*, 93–94, 122–23. Suzanne Bergeron also inspired my thinking about church organization outside of nuclear family structures. See Bergeron, "Interpretive Analytics."

16　With the passing of Bishop Cook, TDC installed a new pastor and first lady (who was not a mother), in a congregation with a number of older church mothers who had been members for decades. Further complicating the nuclear family model, the new pastor (father) and his wife were raised in the church and are a spiritual son and daughter to many of the church mothers.

17　Collins, *Black Feminist Thought*, 192.

18　The church requires, too, that men submit to the authority of higher-ranked men. The important distinction for women, however, is that the church precludes women from ever reaching a titled rank equivalent to or higher than that of any titled man.

19　I coined the phrase *leading from the background* before the Obama administration's Libyan strategy, which became known as "leading from behind." See Ryan Lizza, "Leading from Behind," *New Yorker*, April 27, 2011, http://www.newyorker.com/online/blogs/newsdesk/2011/04/leading-from-behind-obama-clinton.html.

　　I use *background* in concert with the women of this study and would suggest an important distinction between *background* and *behind*. *Behind* suggests linear relationships, whereas *background* implies cross-cutting, expansive spheres of influence. Women's background leadership permeates the church world; it is "a condition of living, a creative strategy, and a place of righteousness." Alexandra Vazquez, "Background Noise: Critical Interferences from the Fly Girls to Back-Up Singers and Beyond," panel abstract, Experience Music Project Conference, Seattle, Washington, April 17, 2009.

20　Hochschild, *Managed Heart*, 165. See Ashforth and Humphrey, "Emotional Labor," for a discussion of genuine expression as a "means of accomplishing emotional labor" (94).

21　Field notes and COOLJC Conspectus, 85th Holy Convocation, August 6–12, 2004, St. Louis, Missouri.

22 See Gill, "'Like a Veil'"; and Hallum, "Taking Stock."

23 Mahmood, *Politics of Piety*, 29.

24 Sunday school class delineations follow age groupings: children (prekindergarten through second grades), juniors (third through sixth grades), junior high (seventh through ninth grades), senior high (tenth through twelfth grades), advanced youth (age eighteen through early twenties), young adults (midtwenties through early thirties), and adults. The New Converts class welcomes adults of all ages who are new to the church.

25 Mahmood, *Politics of Piety*, 29.

26 Gilkes, *"If It Wasn't,"* 109.

27 See A. Brown, "Afro-Baptist Women's Roles," 173; and Williams, *Community*, 31.

28 Women in COOLJC, like most Black women, work out of economic necessity. Their "desire[s]" manifest in educational and career aspirations.

29 Williams, *Community*, 60.

30 Wharton and Erickson, "Managing Emotions," 471.

31 2 Cor. 6:14: "Be ye not unequally yoked together with unbelievers: for what fellowship hath righteousness with unrighteousness?"

32 Eph. 5:22–29: "Wives, submit yourselves unto your own husbands, as unto the Lord. For the husband is the head of the wife, even as Christ is the head of the church: . . . Husbands, love your wives, even as Christ also loved the church, and gave himself for it; . . . So ought men to love their wives as their own bodies. He that loveth his wife loveth himself. For no man ever yet hated his own flesh; but nourisheth and cherisheth it, even as the Lord the church."

33 The Pew study *Spirit and Power: A 10-Country Study of Pentecostals* reports the education and income of U.S. Pentecostals as being below the levels for the overall Christian population, with 56 percent of all Christians having some college or higher degrees compared to 35 percent of Pentecostals (2006, 37). The study reports that 33 percent of Pentecostals have middle or upper incomes compared to 44 percent of all Christians in the same bracket. Recent studies of specifically African American Pentecostalism note an upward shift in the socioeconomic status of congregants. See Synan, *Holiness-Pentecostal Tradition*; and Cox, *Fire from Heaven*. In *African American Religion*, Baer and Singer question, inconclusively, whether the change in social composition is due to adherence to the Protestant work ethic, overall post–civil rights socioeconomic improvements, or new middle-class membership. Sanders, *Saints in Exile*; Gilkes, *"If It Wasn't"*; and McRoberts, "'New' Black Pentecostal Activism," maintain that the upward class mobility of lower-class congregants and new members from the middle class are both factors. Also see Butler, *Women*, for discussion of the professionalization of COGIC women from the 1940s to the 1960s.

34 Gilkes, *"If It Wasn't,"* 108–9.

35 Mirchandani, "Challenging Racial Silences," 721.

36 I appreciate Jennifer Scanlon for pushing me to think through a distinction between acceptable disobedience and acceptable resistance.

37 Gilkes, "If It Wasn't," 108–9.

38 Wingfield, "Are Some Emotions?," 258.

39 This exchange is representative of others I experienced in which a knowing look might accompany a statement. My position as a Black woman meant that members would often assume that I shared a common racial and gendered understanding.

40 See Moreton, *To Serve God*. This compelling study of Wal-Mart charts the ways in which "workers and customers alike brought rural, Protestant family ideals into the workplace, changing the face of postindustrial America" (51). Also see Marshall, "Power in the Name," in which "non-believers" and potential employers in Lagos, Nigeria, comment on the "trustworthiness and reliability" of Pentecostals (29).

41 Folbre, *Invisible Heart*, 11.

42 Gilkes, "If It Wasn't," 109.

43 See Frahm-Arp, *Professional Women*. Pentecostal women moving into the corporate world in postapartheid South Africa, too, described attitudes of superiority shown by White male bosses, coworkers, and subordinates as the women moved up the corporate ladder. In South Africa in the early 2000s and in New York in the 1980s, the presence of Black women in upper management levels was new. Yet a striking difference surfaces in that "very little of the actual work [South African women] did [in the business world] was spoken of in religious terms or 'handed over to God' " (183). In her study Frahm-Arp expands the definition of *professional* to suit the ways women in her study used the term; it includes those women who are educated beyond secondary school, have authority over coworkers, and have expectations of career advancement (15).

44 Wingfield, "Are Some Emotions?," 259.

45 Also see Luke 17:1–2.

46 Wharton and Erickson, "Managing Emotions," 467.

47 Wharton and Erickson, "Managing Emotions," 480.

48 Dunbar, "We Were the Mask," 615.

49 Mirchandani, "Challenging Racial Silences," 722. Kiran Mirchandani argues that managing one's own feelings (not always masking them) is one of three interrelated types of on-the-job emotion work that many workers perform. Emotion work also involves managing the feelings of others and working to make the job meaningful to oneself.

50 "Prominent Pentecostal Achievers in COOLJC," *Contender for the Faith Magazine*, Fall 2004, 44–50.

51 See White, *Too Heavy a Load*.

52 These intergender tensions are reminiscent of the ways in which late nineteenth- and early twentieth-century Bible bands exacerbated disputes between men and women regarding women's education, authority, and roles in church polity. Anthea D. Butler maintains, "Compounding the problem was the role Bible bands played in promoting women's literacy, which offended some

illiterate male pastors. Threatened by their lack of education, pastors sought to silence women who were literate in both reading ability and scriptural knowledge." *Women*, 26. Also see Higginbotham, *Righteous Discontent*, 73. Bernice Martin writes, "The implicit deal seems to be that a substantive shift toward greater gender equality can be tolerated as long as women are not seen to be publicly exercising formal authority over men." "Pentecostal Gender Paradox," 54.

5. HARVESTING SOULS FOR CHRIST

1 *Devotional* is participatory singing that opens the Sunday morning service. Led by the Praise and Worship Team, a small group of singers at the front of the sanctuary, devotional begins at eleven o'clock to "usher in the Spirit" and set the tone for worship. During this time congregants gather in the sanctuary preparing for the service. Many who do not attend Sunday school arrive just before and during devotional. Songs are congregational style and part of a body of literature that is well known to the saints. The Praise Team leader will most often raise (begin) the songs and determine how long each one is sung, based on her ability to spiritually discern the needs of the congregation.

2 The Bible contains numerous references to harvesting—adding to the followers of Christ. See Matt. 9:37–38: "Then saith he unto his disciples, The harvest truly is plenteous, but the labourers are few; Pray ye therefore the Lord of the harvest, that he will send forth labourers into his harvest." The leadership of the Church of Our Lord Jesus Christ of the Apostolic Faith, Inc. (COOLJC), designated "It's Harvest Time" as the theme for 2011 and 2012, to focus on expanding church membership. Within COOLJC, "harvesting souls" may refer to evangelizing in general, as well as the many types of labor that go into evangelizing. Altar work is one example of that labor.

3 Members of COOLJC do not use the terms *converted* or *born again*. To identify their new state of being, they say, "I'm saved, sanctified, and filled with the Holy Ghost—speaking in tongues as the Spirit of God gave utterance."

4 Boris and Parreñas, "Introduction," 7.

5 Boris and Parreñas, "Introduction," 4–5.

6 Zelizer, "Caring Everywhere," 268; original was in italics.

7 Zelizer, "Caring Everywhere," 268.

8 Zelizer, "Caring Everywhere," 268.

9 Boris and Parreñas, "Introduction," 5.

10 Zelizer, "Caring Everywhere," 269.

11 See de la Luz Ibarra, "My Reward," 124–27.

12 For an overview of scholarship on caring labor, see Barker and Feiner, "Affect, Race, and Class." For the conceptual conflict between care and labor, see Folbre, " 'Holding Hands at Midnight.' "

13 Members find financial compensation for church work acceptable for preachers and guest speakers (male and female), collected on the spot as a "goodwill

offering." Many pastors maintain outside employment beyond the ministry and receive compensation in church through special collections by the Pastor's Aid Auxiliary and special services, such as Pastor Appreciation Day.

14 See Gilkes, *"If It Wasn't,"* 53–54.

15 See Zelizer, "Caring Everywhere," 269. She identifies four spheres of intimate labor: "unpaid care in intimate settings, unpaid care in economic organizations, paid care in intimate settings, and paid care in economic organizations."

16 See Robbins, "Globalization."

17 For an overview of the literature across disciplines in the field of Pentecostal studies, see Corten, "Growth of the Literature." See Kalu, *African Pentecostalism,* for a study of the religious movement's history, with particular focus on its late twentieth-century development in Africa.

18 Butler, *Women,* 68.

19 Butler, *Women,* 68.

20 Most saints experienced Spirit baptism at the altar, but for some the event took place in a prayer service at church, during a singing program, during choir practice, at a large convocation, or at home alone.

21 Frahm-Arp, *Professional Women,* 81.

22 Frahm-Arp, *Professional Women,* 81.

23 Goldsmith, *When I Rise,* 119.

24 Goldsmith, *When I Rise,* 119.

25 Goldsmith, *When I Rise,* 119.

26 Goldsmith, *When I Rise,* 210.

27 Goldsmith, *When I Rise,* 119.

28 Smitherman, *Talkin and Testifyin,* 104.

29 Smitherman, *Talkin and Testifyin,* 108.

30 G. Davis, *I Got the Word,* 30.

31 Austin-Broos, *Jamaica Genesis,* 129.

32 Church of Our Lord Jesus Christ, *Discipline Book,* 70.

33 Mother England's experience, of bringing her parents into the church, did not appear to be unusual within COOLJC. I spoke to a number of congregants who had similar experiences. Scholarly interest in family members' influence on each other's religious participation focuses, for the most part, on spouse-to-spouse and parent-to-child influences. Mary P. Ryan's "A Women's Awakening: Evangelical Religion and the Families of Utica, New York, 1800–1840," a study of the "Burned-Over District" in western New York during the nineteenth century, uncovers the critical role of women in bringing spouses and other male relatives into the evangelical movement, as "the first family member to enter the church was twice as likely to be female as male" (604). Nicole Rodriquez Toulis, in *Believing Identity,* describes how one of her interlocutors sent her children to church but stayed away because of the weekly demands of job and home. She eventually acquiesced to the prodding of her son and joined the church. According to Barbara M. Cooper's *Evangelical Christians*

in the Muslim Sahel, mission records would seem to indicate that young men were the first to attend mission schools and convert. Cooper notes, however, "Indeed, when men tell the story of the growth of the church it is almost impossible to detect the role of women at all, despite the fact that some of the central male figures in the church I interviewed remarked that 'apart from [their] mother,' they were the first Christian in the family" (172–73). Outside of a religious community, but within an African American context, Carol Stack's *Call to Home* reveals how children led the way in Black American return migration to the South in the mid-twentieth century.

34   As detailed in chapter 2, "Old Refuge" housed the congregation before 1945, when it moved to its current location on 7th Avenue (Adam Clayton Powell Blvd.) at 124th Street and became the Greater Refuge Temple.

35   See Amott and Matthaei, *Race, Gender and Work*, 158.

36   Shaw, *What a Woman Ought*, 114.

37   Mattingly, "Home and the World," 371.

38   Glenn, "Caring and Inequality," 48.

39   See Roberts, "Spiritual and Menial Housework"; and Barker and Feiner, "Affect, Race, and Class."

40   For the recent turn against the dichotomies of private-public and unproductive-productive, see Folbre, *Invisible Heart*.

41   For an analysis of Black women's centrality to churches in late nineteenth-century Richmond, Virginia, as members reassessed their positions within the Black community and wider politics, see E. Brown, "Negotiating and Transforming."

42   See Folbre, *Invisible Heart*; and Barker and Feiner, "Affect, Race, and Class."

43   For a notable exception, see Wallace, *Black Women*.

44   See Mattingly, "Home and the World," 372.

45   1 Thess. 4:16–17: "For the Lord himself shall descend from heaven with a shout, with the voice of the archangel, and with the trump of God: and the dead in Christ shall rise first: Then we which are alive and remain shall be caught up together with them in the clouds, to meet the Lord in the air: and so shall we ever be with the Lord."

46   See Prov. 2:23 and Joel 2:28. Also see Alexander C. Stewart, "Trinitarian verses Oneness," *Contender for the Faith Magazine*, Fall 2012, 21–22.

47   Boris and Parreñas, "Introduction," 5.

48   Boris and Parreñas, "Introduction," 5.

49   Copies of the personal diaries of Pearl Stevens Holmes are in the author's possession. Also see Wallace, "Aaron and Pearl Holmes." Sherry Sherrod DuPree, in *African-American Holiness Pentecostal Movement*, shows Aaron and Pearl Holmes as Pentecostal Assemblies of the World missionaries deployed to Liberia sometime between 1916 and 1922 (xxxviiii). This is most likely the years of Aaron Holmes's departure to Liberia. Pearl Holmes's personal diaries detail her trip with her mother in 1896.

50   S. Smith, *Sick and Tired*, 120. Also see Weisenfeld, "We Have Been Believers," 10.

51 Holmes, "African American Midwives," 277.
52 Holmes, "African American Midwives," 276.
53 Smith, *Sick and Tired*, 120. Also see Dougherty, "Southern Midwifery."
54 See Smith, *Sick and Tired*, 119.
55 See Foley, "Midwives, Marginality," 190.
56 See Fraser, "Modern Bodies, Modern Minds," 54, 55.
57 See Davis-Floyd, Pigg, and Cosminsky, "Introduction"; Foley, "Midwives, Marginality"; and Foley, "How I Became."
58 Smith, *Sick and Tired*, 119.
59 Fraser, "Modern Bodies, Modern Minds," 48.
60 Erickson and Stacey, "Attending," 189. Also see chapter 4 for emotional labor.
61 In the early 1970s, Bishop William L. Bonner, the chief apostle of COOLJC, published a tract entitled "Rules and Responsibilities of Altar Workers" that included a thirteen-point section "Rules That Must Be Followed by Those Who Tarry with Souls." A church expansion program had prompted Bonner to issue the document; he was sending junior bishops into "barren territories" to open new churches. Missionaries from established churches were dispatched to train new missionaries in tarrying and other duties. The document was meant to reinforce the women's teachings and provide the new churches with written guidelines. It codified the intergenerational apprenticeship training that altar workers detail in this chapter (Dr. Littleton, personal communication, July 8, 2013). It's important to point out that of the twelve altar workers I interviewed, only one was aware of the document.
62 See 1 John 1:9: "If we confess our sins, he is faithful and just to forgive us our sins, and to cleanse us from all unrighteousness."
63 Many COOLJC members have a six o'clock morning prayer routine, but, without exception, each altar worker interviewed identified morning prayer as essential to the work.
64 Glenn, "Caring and Inequality," 58.
65 Barker and Feiner, "Affect, Race, and Class," 47.

6. THE BEAUTY OF HOLINESS

1 See A. Davis, " 'Don't Let Nobody.' "
2 See Higginbotham, *Righteous Discontent*, for analysis of the "politics of respectability" as it relates to the Black Baptist women's movement in the late nineteenth and early twentieth centuries. Higginbotham identifies the ideology and practices as politically resistant yet socially and culturally as-similationist. Black Baptists believed adhering to dominant societal norms of decorum and aesthetics would lead to inclusion in the body politic, countering segregation. From the beginning, Holiness-Pentecostalism's relation to Black mainline denominations was conflicted, at odds over cultural and orga-nizational models. Ecstatic practices of embodiment in Holiness-Pentecostal worship were at the heart of cultural conflicts, which carried religious, social,

and political implications as well. African Methodist Episcopal, African Methodist Episcopal Zion, and Baptist churches, working to develop religious and social profiles based, in large part, on a "politics of respectability," renounced Black folk culture, fueling the religious schism with Holiness-Pentecostals. Also see Collier-Thomas, *Jesus, Jobs, and Justice*, 116–19; and Hunter, *To 'Joy My Freedom*, 137–44, 177–79. Many Holiness-Pentecostals rejected the large centralized organizational framework of mainline denominations, opting for locally controlled congregations. See Best, *Passionately Human*; and Taylor, *Black Churches of Brooklyn*.

3 See Maultsby, "Africanisms in African-American Music"; Boyer, "Contemporary Gospel Music"; Levine, *Black Culture*; and Williams-Jones, "Afro-American Gospel Music."

4 See Butler, *Women*, 64–70, 77–86; and Crumbley, *Saved and Sanctified*, 144–46.

5 Notable affinities exist with nineteenth-century Afro-Catholic women in New Orleans who donned habits and twentieth-century African American Muslim women who don hijab. See Fessenden, "Sisters of the Holy Family"; and Rouse, *Engaged Surrender*. Twenty-first-century COOLJC women, too, "use dress as a marker of the true soul beneath the fabric." Klassen, "Robes of Womanhood," 41.

6 See Casselberry, "Politics of Righteousness."

7 Warhurst et al., "Aesthetic Labor," 4. Also see Parreñas, *Illicit Flirtations*, 98–99.

8 Warhurst et al., "Aesthetic Labor," 5.

9 Meyer, "Introduction," 10.

10 I had to go shopping for enough appropriate attire to fit in with COOLJC style and be "in uniform" for the numerous specially designated services. It was exhausting.

11 The International Missionary Department's motto is based on Isaiah 62:10, which reads, "Go through, go through the gates; prepare ye the way of the people; cast up, cast up the highways; gather out the stones; lift up a standard for the people."

12 Carothers, "Catching Sense," 238.

13 Mother Pea's mother was born in the latter half of the nineteenth century and, by Mother Pea's description, adhered to Victorian ideals of femininity. For more on Black women and the "cult of true womanhood," see Collins, *Black Feminist Thought*; and Giddings, *When and Where*.

14 Higginbotham, *Righteous Discontent*, 204, 190.

15 Butler, *Women*, 77, 84.

16 Butler documents a similar shift in the attire of COGIC women in the 1950s. She observes, "Early [plain] dress codes created a distinctive style that remained in place until the 1950s. (In the 1950s and afterward, COGIC women began to abandon their plain dress and to distinguish themselves instead by elaborate trendy clothing)." *Women*, 80.

17 Butler, *Women*, 86.

18　During weeknight and Sunday evening services, this opening portion includes sung and spoken testimonies from parishioners. Sunday morning services employ the skills of the team for "devotional," which opens the worship service and draws on some of the same music but without congregational testimony.

19　"This Is the Day," words and music by Alen VonShea Norman, Fred Hammond, and Pamkenyon M. Donald, Bridge Building Music, Inc., 2005. C/o Capital CMG Publishing, Brentwood, TN.

20　See Neely, "Belief, Ritual, and Performance." Although the COGIC and COOLJC operate under different theological mandates, they have similar approaches to music in worship.

21　This represents the order of the Sunday morning service at TDC. Other COOLJC churches I visited had a similar order of service and musical elements.

22　Boyer, "Contemporary Gospel Music," 27. For a comprehensive overview of gospel and regional developments and distinctions, see Boyer, *How Sweet the Sound*.

23　"The Lord Strong and Mighty," words and music by Kurt Carr, Lilly Mack Music, Ingelwood, CA, 1997.

24　Boyer, "Contemporary Gospel Music," 29.

25　Williams-Jones, "Afro-American Gospel Music," 381.

26　Herzfeld, *Anthropology*, 285, 289.

27　For nonstatic aesthetic values, see Herzfeld, *Anthropology*, 292.

28　Preaching remains the province of men. Women's orations, regardless of their expertise in biblical exegesis and style of delivery, are understood as teaching, not preaching—lessons, not sermons. See Butler, *Women*, 34–40, for details of COGIC women's teaching and preaching activities. Also, Gilkes explores power dynamics in the teaching sites and practices of sanctified women. *"If It Wasn't,"* 50–52, 105–6.

29　See chapter 2 for Bishop Lawson's theology.

30　See chapter 3 for a detailed description of Annual Women's Day services.

31　See chapter 3, note 2.

32　The present Kingdom is referenced in Luke 17:20–21: "And when he was demanded of the Pharisees, when the kingdom of God should come, he answered them and said, . . . for, behold, the kingdom of God is within you." For references to the forthcoming Kingdom, see Luke 21:28–31: "And when these things begin to come to pass, then look up, and lift up your heads; . . . know ye that the kingdom of God is nigh at hand."

33　Church members refer to those who exhibit spiritual maturity or highly developed spiritual gifts as being "highly anointed." In this particular instance, a church mother leaned over to me during praise and worship (as I was taking notes) to inform me that the musicians were "highly anointed."

34　For analysis of "already" and "not yet" centered on COOLJC, see Clark, "Christian Religious Education." James I. Clark Jr. applies an "already" and "not yet" analysis to the Sermon on the Mount and its lesson for today's church. ("Blessed *are* the poor in spirit: for theirs is the kingdom of heaven"; Matt. 5:3.)

He argues that the present tense indicates "a reality that can be experienced in the here and now. . . . This present reality is a form of realized eschatology in the sense that there is a future to the benefits it affords the believer" (125). The call to occupy a conflicted time-space realm is directed to a community already committed to Christ (and the Christian project), "those . . . having already accepted 'salvation' and understanding 'the requirements of eschatological revelation' " (127). He contends that COOLJC, in the eschatological tension of "already" and "not yet," has abdicated its responsibilities for social justice, alluded to in Matthew, in favor of focusing on the heavenly Kingdom. Clark analytically separates "already" and "not yet" while holding them in tension. I argue, however, that "already and not yet" is a unified conceptual model within the aesthetic practices and labor of women.

In "From Proclamation to Narrative," Paul Ricoeur examines "already" and "not yet" in the transition of the Gospels from oral (preached) to written (scripture). He draws on the proclamation of Jesus, "The Kingdom of God is within you" (Luke 17:21), to argue that "the proximity of the Kingdom lies entirely in the anticipating capacity linked to Jesus' proclamation and in the crisis it opens" (505). He sees "already" and "not yet" as dialectical, in that Jesus's preaching of the future Kingdom is "the sign of the already aspect of this expectation" (507). For an argument against dialectical analysis through Pauline text, see Hae-Kyung Chang's "Christian Life." Chang contends that Paul's text does not exhibit a tension between "already" and "not yet"; in Romans, Paul privileges "already" in chapters 6 and 8, which frame chapter 7.

For a study that takes this eschatological tension into the civic realm, see Rosemary P. Carbine's "Ekklesial Work." Carbine engages "already" and "not yet" as a means to construct an ideal political vision—a feminist public theology. Building on Elisabeth Schüssler Fiorenza's *ekklesia* of wo/men, Carbine proposes *ekklesia* in the context of Christian eschatology, but operating within a human-political reality that suggests the inability to actualize the ideal. By this reading, the "not yet" is unattainable, which undermines the proleptic and paradoxical characteristic of "already and not yet."

35   Bell, *Ritual Theory, Ritual Practice*, 74.
36   Bell, *Ritual Theory, Ritual Practice*, 82.
37   Bell, *Ritual Theory, Ritual Practice*, 82.
38   Bell, *Ritual Theory, Ritual Practice*, 83.
39   Bell, *Ritual Theory, Ritual Practice*, 84.
40   In *Subculture*, Dick Hebdige argues, "The 'point' behind the style of all spectacular subcultures . . . [is] the communication of a significant difference" (102). He further maintains, "Subcultures can be more or less 'conservative' or 'progressive,' integrated into the community, continuous with the values of that community, or extrapolated from it, defining themselves against the parent culture" (127). Too, the status of "saint" is one of being set apart, "in the world, but not of the world." In this way, style does communicate "a significant difference." The members of COOLJC, however, disrupt the either-or model

that Hebdige puts forth. On the one hand, saints regenerate and uphold many mainstream societal mores regarding gender ideals, marriage, family structure, and responsible citizenship. On the other hand, they reject (and redefine) conventional notions of power and respectability through doctrinal beliefs and ways of worship. They are both integrated into and segregated from dominant society ("the parent culture").

41 Copeland, *Enfleshing Freedom*, 7.

CONCLUSION

1 In the words of Ronnie J. Steinberg and Deborah M. Figart, the emotion work of Mother Reeves attended to "both the emotions of the [one] performing the labor and the emotions of others to whom these emotions are addressed." "Emotional Labor," 10.

2 Gilkes, *"If It Wasn't,"* 58.

3 Weisenfeld, "We Have Been Believers," 4.

4 Avishai, " 'Doing Religion,' " 413.

BIBLIOGRAPHY

Adult Student Handbook (Summer). Hazelwood. MO: Pentecostal Publishing House, Word Aflame, 2005.

Alexander, Estrelda Y. *Black Fire: One Hundred Years of African American Pentecostalism*. Downers Grove, IL: InterVarsity, 2011.

Amott, Theresa, and Julie Matthaei. *Race, Gender and Work: A Multi-cultural Economic History of Women in the United States*. Boston: South End, 1996.

Anderson, Allan. *An Introduction to Pentecostalism: Global Charismatic Christianity*. Cambridge: Cambridge University Press, 2004.

Ashforth, Blake E., and Ronald H. Humphrey. "Emotional Labor in Service Roles: The Influence of Identity." *Academy of Management Review* 18, no. 1 (1993): 88–115.

Austin-Broos, Diane J. *Jamaica Genesis: Religion and the Politics of Moral Orders*. Chicago: University of Chicago Press, 1997.

Avishai, Orit. "'Doing Religion' in a Secular World: Women in Conservative Religions and the Question of Agency." *Gender and Society* 22, no. 4 (2008): 409–33.

Baer, Hans, and Merrill Singer. *African American Religion: Varieties of Protest and Accommodation*. Knoxville: University of Tennessee Press, 2002.

Baker, Lee D. *From Savage to Negro: Anthropology and the Construction of Race, 1896–1954*. Berkeley: University of California Press, 1998.

Banks, Mother Hattie. "Interview with Mother Hattie Banks, March 12, 1991 by Alexander C. Stewart, transcription by Mrs. Elaine McQueen." In *The Silent Spokesman: Bishop Robert Clarence Lawson, Founder of the Church of Our Lord Jesus Christ of the Apostolic Faith, Inc., New York City*, edited by Alexander C. Stewart and Sherry S. DuPree. Gainesville, FL: Displays for Schools, 1994.

Barker, Drucilla K. "Beyond Women and Economics: Rereading 'Women's Work.'" *Signs* 30, no. 4 (2005): 2189–209.

Barker, Drucilla K., and Susan F. Feiner. "Affect, Race, and Class: An Interpretive Reading of Caring Labor." *Frontiers: A Journal of Women Studies* 301 (2009): 41–54.

Baron, Ava. "Gender and Labor History: Learning from the Past, Looking to the Future." In *Work Engendered: Toward a New History of American Labor*, edited by Ava Baron, 1–46. Ithaca, NY: Cornell University Press, 1991.

Bartleman, Frank. *Azusa Street: An Eyewitness Account, the Centennial Edition, 1906–2006.* Gainesville, FL: Bridge-Logos, 2006.

Barton, Bruce E., general editor. *Life Application Study Bible.* Wheaton, IL: Tyndale House, 1989.

Beckford, Robert. "Black Suits Matter: Faith, Politics and Representation in the Religious Documentary." In *Black Religion and Aesthetics: Religious Thought and Life in Africa and the African Diaspora,* edited by Anthony B. Pinn, 135–51. New York: Palgrave Macmillan, 2009.

Bell, Catherine. *Ritual Theory, Ritual Practice.* New York: Oxford University Press, 1992.

Bergeron, Suzanne. "An Interpretive Analytics to Move Caring Labor off the Straight Path." *Frontiers: A Journal of Women Studies* 30, no. 1 (2009): 55–64.

Best, Wallace. *Passionately Human, No Less Divine: Religion and Culture in Black Chicago, 1915–1952.* Princeton, NJ: Princeton University Press, 2005.

Blee, Kathleen M. "Women in the 1920s' Ku Klux Klan Movement." *Feminist Studies* 17, no. 1 (1991): 57–77.

Bonner, June, and William L. Bonner. . . . *And the High Places I'll Bring Down: Bishop William L. Bonner, the Man and His God.* New York: W. L. Bonner Literary Committee, 1999.

Boris, Eileen. "From Gender to Racialized Gender: Laboring Bodies That Matter." *International Labor and Working-Class History* 63 (2003): 9–13.

Boris, Eileen, and Rhacel Salazar Parreñas. "Introduction." In *Intimate Labors: Cultures, Technologies, and the Politics of Care,* edited by Eileen Boris and Rhacel Salazar Parreñas, 1–12. Stanford, CA: Stanford Social Sciences, 2010.

Boyer, Horace Clarence. "Contemporary Gospel Music." *The Black Perspective in Music* 7, no. 1 (1979): 5–58.

———. *How Sweet the Sound: The Golden Age of Gospel.* Washington, DC: Elliot and Clark, 1995.

Brown, Audrey Lawson. "Afro-Baptist Women's Church and Family Roles: Transmitting Afrocentric Cultural Values." *Anthropological Quarterly* 67, no. 4 (1994): 173–86.

Brown, Elsa Barkley. "Negotiating and Transforming the Public Sphere: Africa American Political Life in the Transition from Slavery to Freedom." In *Jumpin' Jim Crow: Southern Politics from Civil War to Civil Rights,* edited by Jane Dailey, Glenda E. Gilmore, and Bryant Simon, 28–66. Princeton, NJ: Princeton University Press, 2000.

———. "Womanist Consciousness: Maggie Lena Walker and the Independent Order of Saint Luke." *Signs* 14, no. 3 (1989): 610–33.

Burgess, Stanley M., editor, and Eduard M. Van Der Mass, associate editor. *The New International Dictionary of Pentecostal and Charismatic Movements.* Grand Rapids, MI: Zondervan, 2003.

Butler, Anthea D. *Women in the Church of God in Christ: Making a Sanctified World.* Chapel Hill: University of North Carolina Press, 2007.

Carbine, Rosemary P. "Ekklesial Work: Toward a Feminist Public Theology." *Harvard Theological Review* 99, no. 4 (2006): 433–55.

Carothers, Suzanne. "Catching Sense: Learning from Our Mothers to Be Black and Female." In *Uncertain Terms: Negotiating Gender in American Culture*, edited by Faye Ginsburg and Anna Lowenhaupt Tsing, 232–47. Boston: Beacon, 1990.

Casselberry, Judith. "The Politics of Righteousness: Race and Gender in Apostolic Pentecostalism." *Transforming Anthropology* 21, no. 1 (2013): 72–86.

Chang, Hae-Kyung. "The Christian Life in a Dialectical Tension? Romans 7:7–25 Reconsidered." *Novum Testamentum* 49, no. 3 (2007): 257–80.

Church of Our Lord Jesus Christ. *The Discipline Book.* 6th ed. New York: Church of Our Lord Jesus Christ of the Apostolic Faith, 1991.

———. *The Holy Council: Guides for the International Women's Council of the Church of Our Lord Jesus Christ of the Apostolic Faith, Inc.* Compiled by Mother Susie Nelson McCoy. New York: Church of Our Lord Jesus Christ of the Apostolic Faith, 2001.

———. *Outstanding Women and Their Contributions to the Church of Our Lord Jesus Christ of the Apostolic Faith, Inc.* Vol. 3. New York: International Missionary Department, 2011.

Clark, James I., Jr. "The Role of Christian Religious Education in Transforming the African-American Apostolic Pentecostal Church's World View and Mission." PhD diss., Columbia University, 2001.

Clarke, John Henrik. "Marcus Garvey: The Harlem Years." *Transition* 46 (1974): 14–19.

Coleman, Simon. "Materializing the Self: Words and Gifts in the Construction of Evangelical Identity." In *The Anthropology of Christianity*, edited by Fenella Cannell, 163–84. Durham, NC: Duke University Press, 2006.

Collier-Thomas, Bettye. *Jesus, Jobs, and Justice: African American Women and Religion.* New York: Alfred A. Knopf, 2010.

Collins, Patricia Hill. *Black Feminist Thought: Knowledge, Consciousness, and the Politics of Empowerment.* New York: Routledge Classics, 2009.

Cooper, Barbara M. *Evangelical Christians in the Muslim Sahel.* Bloomington: Indiana University Press, 2006.

Copeland, M. Shawn. *Enfleshing Freedom: Body, Race, and Being.* Minneapolis: Fortress, 2009.

Corbould, Clare. *Becoming African Americans: Black Public Culture in Harlem, 1919–1939.* Cambridge, MA: Harvard University Press, 2009.

Corten, André. "The Growth of the Literature on Afro-American, Latin American and African Pentecostalism." *Journal of Contemporary Religion* 12, no. 3 (1997): 311–34.

Cox, Harvey. *Fire from Heaven: The Rise of Pentecostal Spirituality and the Reshaping of Religion in the Twenty-First Century.* Boston: Da Capo, 2001.

Crumbley, Deidre Helen. *Saved and Sanctified: The Rise of a Storefront Church in Great Migration Philadelphia.* Gainesville: University Press of Florida, 2012.

Csordas, Thomas J. "Elements of Charismatic Persuasion and Healing." *Medical Anthropology Quarterly* 2, no. 2 (1988): 121–42.

Curtis, Beth. *Faith in the Great Physician: Suffering and Divine Healing in American Culture, 1860–1900*. Baltimore: Johns Hopkins University Press, 2007.

Davis, Adrienne. "'Don't Let Nobody Bother Yo' Principle': The Sexual Economy of Slavery." In *Sister Circle: Black Women and Work*, edited by Sharon Harley, 103–27. New Brunswick, NJ: Rutgers University Press, 2002.

Davis, Gerald L. *I Got the Word in Me and I Can Sing It, You Know: A Study of the Performed African-American Sermon*. Philadelphia: University of Pennsylvania Press, 1985.

Davis-Floyd, Robbie, Leigh Pigg, and Sheila Cosminsky. "Introduction. Daughters of Time: The Shifting Identities of Contemporary Midwives." *Medical Anthropology: Cross-Cultural Studies in Health and Illness* 20, nos. 2–3 (2001): 105–39.

de la Luz Ibarra, María. "My Reward Is Not Money: Deep Alliances and End-of-Life Care among Mexicana Workers and Their Wards." In *Intimate Labors: Cultures, Technologies, and the Politics of Care*, edited by Eileen Boris and Rhacel Salazar Parreñas, 117–31. Stanford, CA: Stanford Social Sciences, 2010.

DeVault, Marjorie L. "Comfort and Struggle: Emotion Work in Family Life." *Annals of the American Academy of Political and Social Science* 561 (1999): 52–63.

Dougherty, Molly C. "Southern Midwifery and Organized Health Care: Systems in Conflict." *Medical Anthropology: Cross-Cultural Studies in Health and Illness* 6, no. 1 (1982): 113–26.

Dray, Philip. *At the Hands of Persons Unknown: The Lynching of Black America*. New York: Random House, 2002.

Du Bois, W. E. B. *The Souls of Black Folk*. Edited by Henry Louis Gates Jr. and Terri Hume Oliver. New York: W. W. Norton, 1999.

Dunbar, Paul Laurence. "We Wear the Mask." In *Call and Response: The Riverside Anthology of the African American Literary Tradition*, edited by Patricia Liggins Hill, 615. Boston: Houghton Mifflin, 1998.

DuPree, Sherry Sherrod. *African-American Holiness Pentecostal Movement: An Annotated Bibliography*. New York: Garland, 1996.

Erickson, Rebecca J., and Clare L. Stacey. "Attending to Mind and Body: Engaging the Complexity of Emotion Practice among Caring Professionals." In *Emotional Labor in the 21st Century: Diverse Perspectives on Emotion Regulation at Work*, edited by Alicia A. Grandey, James M. Deindorff, and Deborah E. Rupp, 175–96. New York: Routledge, 2013.

Espinosa, Gaston. *Latino Pentecostals in America: Faith and Politics in Action*. Cambridge, MA: Harvard University Press, 2014.

Fauset, Arthur Huff. *Black Gods of the Metropolis: Negro Religious Cults of the Urban North*. 1944. Philadelphia: University of Pennsylvania Press, 2002.

Fessenden, Tracy. "The Sisters of the Holy Family and the Veil of Race." *Religion and American Culture: A Journal of Interpretation* 10, no. 2 (2000): 187–224.

Folbre, Nancy. "'Holding Hands at Midnight': The Paradox of Caring Labor." *Feminist Economics* 1, no. 1 (1995): 73–92.

———. *The Invisible Heart: Economics and Family Values*. New York: New Press, 2001.

Foley, Lara. "How I Became a Midwife: Identity, Biographical Work, and Legitimation in Midwives' Work Narratives." *Gender Perspectives on Reproduction and Sexuality Advances in Gender Research* 8 (2004): 87–128.

———. "Midwives, Marginality, and Public Identity Work." *Symbolic Interaction* 28, no. 2 (2005): 183–203.

Foucault, Michel. *Politics, Philosophy, Culture: Interviews and Other Writings 1977–1984*. New York: Routledge, 1988.

Frahm-Arp, Maria. *Professional Women in South African Pentecostal Charismatic Churches*. Leiden: Brill, 2010.

Fraser, Gertrude J. "Modern Bodies, Modern Minds: Midwifery and Reproductive Change in an African American Community." In *Conceiving the New World Order: The Global Politics of Reproduction*, edited by Faye D. Ginsburg and Rayna Rapp, 42–58. Berkeley: University of California Press, 1995.

Frederick, Marla F. *Between Sundays: Black Women and Everyday Struggles of Faith*. Berkeley: University of California Press, 2003.

French, Talmadge Leon. "Early Oneness Pentecostalism, Garfield Thomas Haywood, and the Interracial Pentecostal Assemblies of the World (1906–1931)." PhD diss., University of Birmingham, 2011.

Gerloff, Roswith I. H. "Blackness and Oneness (Apostolic) Theology: Cross-cultural Aspects of a Movement." Paper presented to the First Occasional Symposium on Aspects of the Oneness Pentecostal Movement. Harvard Divinity School: Cambridge, MA, 1984.

Giddings, Paula. *Ida: A Sword among Lions: Ida B. Wells and the Campaign against Lynching*. New York: HarperCollins, 2008.

———. *When and Where I Enter: The Impact of Black Women on Race and Sex in America*. New York: William Morrow, 1996.

Gilkes, Cheryl Townsend. *"If It Wasn't for the Women . . .": Black Women's Experience and Womanist Culture in Church and Community*. Maryknoll, NY: Orbis Books, 2001.

Gill, Lesley. "'Like a Veil to Cover Them': Women and the Pentecostal Movement in La Paz." *American Ethnologist* 17, no. 4 (1990): 708–21.

Gilmore, Glenda Elizabeth. *Gender and Jim Crow: Women and the Politics of White Supremacy in North Carolina, 1896–1920*. Chapel Hill: University of North Carolina Press, 1996.

Glenn, Evelyn Nakano. "Caring and Inequality." In *Women's Labor in the Global Economy: Speaking in Multiple Voices*, edited by Sharon Harley, 46–61. New Brunswick, NJ: Rutgers University Press, 2007.

Goldsmith, Peter D. *When I Rise Cryin' Holy: African-American Denominationalism on the Georgia Coast*. New York: AMS Press, 1989.

Grandey, Alicia A., James M. Deindorff, and Deborah E. Rupp, eds. *Emotional Labor in the 21st Century: Diverse Perspectives on Emotion Regulation at Work*. New York: Routledge, 2013.

Griffith, R. Marie. *God's Daughters: Evangelical Women and the Power of Submission*. Berkeley: University of California Press, 1997.

Hallum, Anne Motley. "Taking Stock and Building Bridges: Feminism, Women's Movements, and Pentecostalism in Latin America." *Latin American Research Review* 38, no. 1 (2003): 169–86.

Harley, Sharon. "Introduction." In *Women's Labor in the Global Economy: Speaking in Multiple Voices*, edited by Sharon Harley, 1–6. New Brunswick, NJ: Rutgers University Press, 2007.

Hebdige, Dick. *Subculture: The Meaning of Style*. New York: Routledge, 1979.

Hempton, David. *Methodism: Empire of the Spirit*. New Haven, CT: Yale University Press, 2005.

Herzfeld, Michael. *Anthropology: Theoretical Practice in Culture and Society*. Malden, MA: Blackwell, 2001.

Higginbotham, Evelyn Brooks. *Righteous Discontent: The Women's Movement in the Black Baptist Church, 1880–1920*. Cambridge, MA: Harvard University Press, 1993.

Hochschild, Arlie Russell. *The Managed Heart: Commercialization of Human Feeling*. Berkeley: University of California Press, 1983.

Holmes, Linda Janet. "African American Midwives in the South." In *The American Way of Birth*, edited by Pamela S. Eakins, 273–91. Philadelphia: Temple University Press, 1986.

Hoyt, Thomas, Jr. "Testimony." In *Practicing Our Faith: A Way of Life for a Searching People*, edited by Dorothy C. Bass, 89–101. San Francisco: Jossey-Bass, 2010.

Hudson-Weems, Renita. "Resurrecting Emmett Till: The Catalyst of the Modern Civil Rights Movement." *Journal of Black Studies* 29, no. 2 (1998): 179–88.

Hull, Gloria T., Patricia Bell Scott, and Barbara Smith, eds. *All the Women Are White, All the Blacks Are Men, but Some of Us Are Brave: Black Women's Studies*. New York: Feminist Press at City University of New York, 1982.

Hunter, Tera W. *To 'Joy My Freedom: Southern Black Women's Lives and Labor after the Civil War*. Cambridge, MA: Harvard University Press, 1997.

Hurston, Zora Neale. *The Sanctified Church*. New York: Marlowe, 1981.

Jacobsen, Douglas, ed. *A Reader in Pentecostal Theology: Voices from the First Generation*. Bloomington: Indiana University Press, 2006.

———. *Thinking in the Spirit: Theologies of the Early Pentecostal Movement*. Bloomington: Indiana University Press, 2003.

Jones, Jacqueline. *Labor of Love, Labor of Sorrow: Black Women, Work, and the Family, from Slavery to the Present*. New York: Basic Books, 2010.

Kalu, Ogbu. *African Pentecostalism: An Introduction*. Oxford: Oxford University Press, 2008.

Klassen, Pamela E. "The Robes of Womanhood: Dress and Authenticity among African American Methodist Women in the Nineteenth Century." *Religion and American Culture: A Journal of Interpretation* 14, no. 1 (2004): 39–82.

Lawson, Robert C. *The Anthropology of Jesus Our Kinsman (Dedicated to the Glory of God and to the Help of Solving the Race Problem)*. 1925. New York: Church of Our Lord Jesus Christ of the Apostolic Faith, 1969.

———. "A Short Sketch of the Industrial Union of America, West Indies and Canada Its Objects, Etc." 1932. Alexander and Shirlene Stewart Pentecostal Collection,

1925–1993, Box 1, Folder 2. Schomburg Center for Research in Black Culture, New York Public Library, New York.

Lee, Chana Kai. *For Freedom's Sake: The Life of Fannie Lou Hamer.* Urbana: University of Illinois Press, 1999.

Leidner, Robin. *Fast Food, Fast Talk: Service Work and the Routinization of Everyday Life.* Berkeley: University of California Press, 1993.

Levine, Lawrence W. *Black Culture and Black Consciousness: Afro-American Folk Thought from Slavery to Freedom.* Oxford: Oxford University Press, 1977.

Lincoln, C. Eric, and Lawrence H. Mamiya. *The Black Church in the African American Experience.* Durham, NC: Duke University Press, 1990.

Lindhardt, Martin. "'If You Are Saved You Cannot Forget Your Parents': Agency, Power, and Social Repositioning in Tanzanian Born-Again Christianity." *Journal of Religion in Africa* 40, no. 3 (2010): 240–72.

Luhrmann, Tanya. *When God Talks Back: Understanding the American Evangelical Relationship with God.* New York: Vintage Books, 2012.

MacRobert, Iain. *The Black Roots and White Racism of Early Pentecostalism in the USA.* Eugene, OR: Wipf and Stock, 1988.

Mahmood, Saba. *Politics of Piety: The Islamic Revival and the Feminist Subject.* Princeton, NJ: Princeton University Press, 2005.

Marshall, Ruth. "Power in the Name of Jesus." *Review of African Political Economy* 52 (1991): 21–37.

Martin, Bernice. "The Pentecostal Gender Paradox: A Cautionary Tale for Sociology of Religion. In *The Blackwell Companion to Sociology of Religion.* Malden, MA: Blackwell, 2003.

Mattingly, Doreen J. "The Home and the World: Domestic Service and International Networks of Caring Labor." *Annals of the Association of American Geographers* 91, no. 2 (2001): 370–86.

Maultsby, Portia K. "Africanisms in African-American Music." In *Africanisms in American Culture*, edited by Joseph E. Holloway, 185–210. Bloomington: Indiana University Press, 1990.

McRoberts, Omar M. "Understanding the 'New' Black Pentecostal Activism: Lessons from Ecumenical Urban Ministries in Boston." *Sociology of Religion* 60 (1999): 47–70.

Meyer, Birgit. "Introduction: From Imagined Communities to Aesthetic Formations: Religion Meditations, Sensational Forms, and Styles of Binding." In *Aesthetic Formations: Media, Religion, and the Senses*, edited by Birgit Meyer, 1-28. New York: Palgrave Macmillan.

———"Powerful Pictures: Popular Christian Aesthetics in Southern Ghana." *Journal of the American Academy of Religion* 76, no. 1 (2008): 82–110.

Mirchandani, Kiran. "Challenging Racial Silences in Studies of Emotion Work: Contributions from Anti-racist Feminist Theory." *Organization Studies* 24 (2003): 721–42.

Moreton, Bethany. *To Serve God and Wal-Mart: The Making of Christian Free Enterprise.* Cambridge, MA: Harvard University Press, 2009.

Murphy, Joseph M. *Working the Spirit: Ceremonies of the African Diaspora*. Boston: Beacon, 1994.

Neely, Thomasina. "Belief, Ritual, and Performance in a Black Pentecostal Church: The Musical Heritage of the Church of God in Christ." PhD diss., Indiana University, 1993.

Newman, Joe. *Race and the Assemblies of God Church: The Journey from Azusa Street to the Miracle of Memphis*. Amherst, NY: Cambria, 2007.

Paris, Arthur E. *Black Pentecostalism: Southern Religion in an Urban World*. Amherst: University of Massachusetts Press, 1982.

Parreñas, Rhacel Salazar. *Illicit Flirtations: Labor, Migration, and Sex Trafficking in Tokyo*. Stanford, CA: Stanford University Press, 2011.

Pierce, Jennifer L. *Gender Trial: Emotional Lives in Contemporary Law Firms*. Berkeley: University of California Press, 1995.

Raboteau, Albert J. *Slave Religion: The "Invisible Institution" in the Antebellum South*. New York: Oxford University Press, 1978.

Ricoeur, Paul. "From Proclamation to Narrative." *Journal of Religion* 64, no. 4 (1984): 501–12.

Robbins, Joel. "The Globalization of Pentecostal and Charismatic Christianity." *Annual Review of Anthropology* 33 (2004): 117–43.

Roberts, Dorothy E. "Spiritual and Menial Housework." *Yale Journal of Law and Feminism* 9, no. 1 (1997): 51–80.

Rouse, Carolyn Moxley. *Engaged Surrender: African American Women and Islam*. Berkeley: University of California Press, 2004.

Ryan, Mary P. "A Women's Awakening: Evangelical Religion and the Families of Utica, New York, 1800–1840." *American Quarterly* 30, no. 5 (1978): 602–23.

Sanchez-Walsh, Arlene. *Latino Pentecostal Identity: Evangelical Faith, Self, and Society*. New York: Columbia University Press, 2012.

Sanders, Cheryl J. *Saints in Exile: The Holiness-Pentecostal Experience in African American Religion and Culture*. New York: Oxford University Press, 1996.

Schechter, Patricia A. *Ida B. Wells-Barnett and American Reform, 1880–1930*. Chapel Hill: University of North Carolina Press, 2001.

Shaw, Stephanie J. *What a Woman Ought to Be and to Do: Black Professional Women Workers during the Jim Crow Era*. Chicago: University of Chicago Press, 1996.

Smith, Jonathan. "The Bare Facts of Ritual." *History of Religions* 20, nos. 1–2 (1980): 112–27.

Smith, Susan L. 1995. *Sick and Tired of Being Sick and Tired: Black Women's Health Activism in America, 1890–1950*. Philadelphia: University of Pennsylvania Press, 1995.

Smitherman, Geneva. *Talkin and Testifyin: The Language of Black America*. Detroit: Wayne State University Press, 1986.

Snyder, C. R., and Shane J. Lopez, eds. *Handbook of Positive Psychology*. Oxford: Oxford University Press, 2002.

Spellman, Robert, and Mabel Thomas. *The Life, Legend and Legacy of Bishop R. C. Lawson*. Scotch Plains, NJ: Dr. Robert C. Spellman, 1983.

Stack, Carol. *All Our Kin*. New York: Basic Books, 1997.

———. *Call to Home: African Americans Reclaim the Rural South*. New York: Basic Books, 1996.

Steinberg, Ronnie J., and Deborah M. Figart. "Emotional Labor since *The Managed Heart*." *Annals of the American Academy of Political and Social Science* 561 (1999): 8–26.

Synan, Vincent. *The Holiness-Pentecostal Tradition: Charismatic Movements in the Twentieth Century*. Grand Rapids, MI: William B. Eerdmans, 1997.

Taylor, Clarence. *The Black Churches of Brooklyn*. New York: Columbia University Press, 1994.

Toulis, Nicole Rodriquez. *Believing Identity: Pentecostalism and the Mediation of Jamaican Ethnicity and Gender in England*. London: Bloomsbury Academic, 1997.

Tuttle, William, Jr. *Chicago in the Red Summer of 1919*. New York: Atheneum, 1970.

Tyson, James L. *The Early Pentecostal Revival: History of Twentieth Century Pentecostals and the Pentecostal Assemblies of the World, 1901–1930*. Hazelwood, MO: Word Aflame, 1992.

Wacker, Grant. *Heaven Below: Early Pentecostals and American Culture*. Cambridge, MA: Harvard University Press, 2001.

Waid, Ora. *A Blessed Life in the Making: The Life of Bishop R. C. Lawson, Th.B., D.D., L.L.D.* New York: Church of Our Lord Jesus Christ of the Apostolic Faith, 1936. Republished by the International Women's Council, New York: Church of Our Lord Jesus Christ of the Apostolic Faith, 1994.

Wallace, Mary. "Aaron and Pearl Holmes." In *Profiles of Pentecostal Missionaries*, edited by Mary Wallace. Hazelwood, MO: Word Aflame, 1986.

Wallace, Phyllis with Linda Datcher and Julianne Malveaux. *Black Women in the Labor Force*. Cambridge, MA: MIT Press, 1980.

Ward, Larry. "Filled with the Spirit: The Musical Life of an Apostolic Pentecostal Church in Champaign-Urbana, Illinois." PhD diss., University of Illinois at Urbana-Champaign, 1997.

Warhurst, Chris, and Dennis Nickson. " 'Who's Got the Look?' Emotional, Aesthetic and Sexualized Labour in Interactive Services." *Gender, Work and Organization* 16, no. 3 (2009): 385–404.

Warhurst, Chris, Dennis Nickson, Anne Witz, and Anne Marie Cullen. "Aesthetic Labor in Interactive Service Work: Some Case Study Evidence from the 'New' Glasgow." *Service Industries Journal* 20, no. 3 (2000): 1–18.

Weisenfeld, Judith. *African American Women and Christian Activism: New York's Black YWCA, 1905–1945*. Cambridge, MA: Harvard University Press, 1997.

———. "We Have Been Believers." In *This Far by Faith: Readings in African American Women's Religious Biography*, edited by Judith Weisenfeld and Richard Newman, 1–18. New York: Routledge, 1996.

Wharton, Amy S., and Rebecca J. Erickson. "Managing Emotions on the Job and at Home: Understanding the Consequences of Multiple Emotional Roles." *Academy of Management Review* 18, no. 3 (1993): 457–86.

White, Deborah Gray. *Too Heavy a Load: Black Women in Defense of Themselves, 1894–1994.* New York: W. W. Norton, 1998.

Wilkerson, Isabel. *The Warmth of Other Suns: The Epic Story of America's Great Migration.* New York: Vintage Books, 2011.

Williams, Melvin D. *Community in a Black Pentecostal Church: An Anthropological Study.* Pittsburgh: University of Pittsburgh Press, 1974.

Williams-Jones, Pearl. "Afro-American Gospel Music: A Crystallization of the Black Aesthetic." *Ethnomusicology* 19, no. 3 (1975): 373–85.

Wingfield, Adia Harvey. "Are Some Emotions Marked 'Whites Only'? Racialized Feeling Rules in Professional Workplaces." *Social Problems* 57, no. 2 (2010): 251–68.

Woodhead, Linda. "Feminism and the Sociology of Religion: From Gender-Blindness to Gendered Difference." In *The Blackwell Companion to Sociology of Religion*, edited by Richard K. Fenn, 67–84. Malden, MA: Blackwell, 2001.

Zelizer, Vivian. "Caring Everywhere." In *Intimate Labors: Cultures, Technologies, and the Politics of Care*, edited by Eileen Boris and Rhacel Salazar Parreñas, 267–79. Stanford, CA: Stanford Social Sciences, 2010.

INDEX

8, 14, 21, 105–6, 107, 118–20, 122–23, 147, 188n49, 196n1
emotion management/work. *See* emotional labor
England, Jessie (pseud.), 26, 81, 111–12, 125–26, 133–34, 145, 170
ethical pedagogy, 23
eugenics movement, 54

faith, 2–6; challenges to, 22; healing through, 26–27; tools for, 24–25
Farrow, Lucy, 49–50
feminized labor, 8
Fields, Carrie. *See* Lawson, Carrie F.
Flaubert, Gustave, x
Frahm-Arp, Maria, 131
Franklin, Louise (pseud.), 17, 19–20, 32–36
Frederick, Marla F., 4, 5
Freeman, The (newspaper), 51
fund-raising campaigns, 35–36, 54, 75, 86, 88–89, 96, 101–2

Gandhi, Mahatma, 62
Garvey, Marcus, 54, 56
Gaye, Marvin, x
gender: blackness and, 46–47; in church work, 1–2, 8–9, 57; in hierarchical authority, 8–10, 14, 77, 80, 105, 106, 109–11, 146; in preaching, 6, 62–63; 118; roles, 63–64, 114, 123–24, 172; success and, 123
genealogy, church, 29–30
Gilkes, Cheryl Townsend, 9, 85
Glenn, Evelyn Nakano, 136
global capitalism, 8
Global Missions Initiative, 83
glory, goal of, 89
Goldsmith, Peter D., 131
gospel singing, 164. *See also* church music
Grayson, Lucille (pseud.), 125, 130, 134–36, 138–40, 141, 144–50, 156–57, 161, 170
Greater Refuge Temple (COOLJC), 61
Griffith, R. Marie, 176n15
Groover, Gentle, 152–53

Hamitic lineage, 56–57
Harlem Renaissance, 54–58
Harley, Sharon, 8

harvesting souls, 15, 127, 129, 139, 142, 149, 150–51
Haywood, Garfield T., 48, 51–53
Haywood, Ida, 51
healing: Catholic charismatic, 22; divine, 13, 19, 21, 23, 25–27, 36, 43; faith, 26–27; services for, 24; testimonies, 27–28
Hebdige, Dick, 195–96n40
helpmeets, 14, 46, 72, 96–97, 113–18
Herodotus, 55
hierarchical authority. *See* authority
Higginbotham, Evelyn Brooks, 4, 192n2
Hill, Grace, 89, 97
Hochschild, Arlie Russell, 7, 107
holiness, living in, 21–24, 103, 120, 156, 159–61, 169
Holiness-Pentecostal Movement, x–xi; clothing styles, 155–56, 158; COOLJC and, 2, 44, 130, 138; Holy Spirit manifestation, 4, 154; preaching in, 118; respectability in, 154; rise of, 153; speaking in tongues, 3, 51, 86. *See also* Azusa Street Revival
Holmes, Aaron, xi, 60
Holmes, Pearl, xi, 60
Holmes, Ruth (pseud.), 17, 34–35, 41, 160; acceptable disobedience of, 112–13; altar work, 125–27, 130, 133, 140–44, 150; background, 140–41; church activity of, 42, 140; on death, 41; on dress code, 160–61; efficacy of prayer and, 36–37; on God's will, 40, 41, 42; on leadership transparency, 113; on mourning, 177n32; on prayer, 150; on spiritual/hierarchical authority, 146–47; training, 130
holy personhood, 5, 9–10, 14, 79–80, 81–82
Holy Spirit: after crucifixion of Christ, 2–3; anointing, 8; baptism, 3, 21, 48, 49, 59, 126, 129, 130, 136, 138, 154; indwelling, 44, 138; as leader, 22, 23; manifestation, 4, 154; power of, 9–10; revealed through women, 172; tarrying for, 30, 32, 59, 126, 129, 130, 138, 146, 192n61; temporality of, xii; ushering in, 162–63, 166
horizontal networks, 9, 14, 78, 80, 103, 146, 151, 171
Hoyt, Thomas, Jr., 25
Hutchins, Julia, 49–50

IMD. *See* International Missionary Department
Indianapolis Pentecostalism, 48, 50–53

Index · 209

Industrial Union Institute and Training School (COOLJC), 60. *See also* R. C. Lawson Institute

International Bible Way Churches of Our Lord Jesus Christ, 71–72, 182n109

International Convention of the Negro Peoples of the World, 54

International Missionary Department (IMD), 14, 79, 82–89, 133, 156

International Women's Convention, 166

International Women's Council (IWC), 14, 79, 89–95

intimate labor, 7–8, 44, 127–31, 150–51, 170. *See also* caring labor

IWC. *See* International Women's Council

Jacobsen, Douglas, 53

Japhetic lineage, 56

Jesus Christ: absolute deity of, 26, 174n6; Hamitic lineage, 56–57; Jesus-centered theology, 52, 81–82; Pentecost and, 2–3; running for, 168, 169; Second Coming, 3, 26, 138, 144, 145; submission/obedience of, 108; women's relationship with, 171

Johnson, Frederica C., 60

Johnson, Margaret Giles, 68

Johnson, James Weldon, 56

Johnson, Roswell H., 54

Johnson, Sherrod C., 64

Jones, Loïs Mailou, 56

Judah (biblical tribe), 56

Keith, Addie, 83

kin-structured networks, 107–8

Ku Klux Klan, 51, 54

labor of love. *See* altar workers

labor studies, 137

Lawson, Carrie F., 1; background, 58–59; death, 13–14, 59–60, 61, 78; founding of COOLJC, 13, 29, 45–46, 53; influence of, 45, 58–60; as missionary president, 82; as Praying Mother of the Air, 13, 47, 61, 77, 147, 171; as preacher, 47, 53, 62–63

Lawson, Evelyn K., 62–63, 66, 95–96

Lawson, Robert Clarence, 1, 10, 50, 171; background, 47–48; Bonner and, 67; characteristics, 57–58; death, 13–14; founding of COOLJC, 13, 29, 45–46, 53–55;

Gospel Tent, 54–55; on men in church leadership, 57; on "Negro" women's blood in Jesus, 56–57; ordination of, 52; progressive agenda, 47; on racial history, 55–57; on uniting the race, 60, 61–62; on women's ordination, 53

leading from the background, 111–12

Lee, Adele (pseud.), 24, 34–35, 110, 114–15, 117

Lee, Edwin (pseud.), 24–25, 111

Life, Legend and Legacy of Bishop R. C. Lawson, The (Spellman), 58

Littleton, Ruby (pseud.), 84–85, 86–87, 103, 133, 171

Locke, Alain, 56

Los Angeles Times, 49

Luhrmann, Tanya, 29

lynching, 54

Mahmood, Saba, 23, 106

Martin, Mamie, 83

Mary (biblical figure), 35, 56, 165

Mary Magdalene (biblical figure), 165

Mason, Charles H., 52

Mattingly, Doreen J., 135

MDWG. *See* Ministers' and Deacons' Wives Guild

mercy, 37, 38, 134

Meyer, Birgit, 155

Michael, Charles, 60

midwifery, 130, 141–42, 143–44

ministerial service, women in, 97–98

Ministers' and Deacons' Wives Guild (MDWG), 14, 79, 95–103

Mirchandani, Kiran, 188n49

missionary work, xi, 56, 62, 63, 79, 82–84, 88–89, 133, 171, 184n22. *See also* International Missionary Department

mothers, use of term, 9, 173n1

Moultrie, DyAnne, 83

Moultrie, H. A., II, 83

music. *See* church music

Negro Star (newspaper), 61

neo-Pentecostalism, 29–30, 44

New York Amsterdam News (newspaper), 61

Nickson, Dennis, 8

nuclear family model, 107–8

obedience, 112–13, 117

oneness theology, 52, 71, 72. *See also* Church of Our Lord Jesus Christ of the Apostolic Faith, Inc.

oppression, 120–22

oral tradition, 70–71

Parham, Charles, 49

pastors' wives, 99–103

patriarchy, 14, 105–6, 124, 171. *See also* authority, hierarchical

Paul (apostle), 39, 83, 92–93

PAW. *See* Pentecostal Assemblies of the World

Pea, Esther, 27–28, 106, 117, 157–58, 170

Pentecost, day of, 2–3, 35

Pentecostal Assemblies of the World (PAW), 47, 48, 51, 53, 71

Pentecostalism, 29, 45, 49–50; education/income levels, 187n33; in Indianapolis, 48, 50–53; integrated, 50–51; Jamaican, 132; membership, 72; music in, 24; origin of, 2–3; racial division in, 53; segregated, 51–52. *See also* Apostolic Pentecostalism; Holiness-Pentecostal Movement; specific churches

Perry, Delphia, 89–90

Plain Dealer (newspaper), 61

Plessy v. Ferguson, 48

Popenoe, Paul, 54

Powell, Adam Clayton, Jr., 62

praise, practice of, 3, 24–25, 27–28, 43, 92–93, 127, 163, 167

Praise and Worship Team, xii, 24, 36, 162, 163, 166, 167, 189n1

prayer: church genealogy and, 29–30; corporate, 30, 37; for divine healing, 36–37, 43; immersion, 147–50; as spiritual armor, 148

Prayer Pilgrimage, 61–62

Praying Mother of the Air. *See* Lawson, Carrie F.

preaching: gender and, 62–63, 88, 118, 194n28; styles, 154

predestination, 39–41, 97

Prentiss, Henry, 48, 51

Price, Willette, 68

productive labor, women's, 137

race: consciousness, 46–47, 60, 61–62, 68; equality/inequality, 9, 50–51, 55; gender and, 9; riots, 54

Rahab (biblical figure), 56

Randolph, A. Philip, 62

Rapture, 3, 26, 138, 144–45

R. C. Lawson Institute, 60, 90

Reagon, Bernice Johnson, x

Reagon, Toshi, x

Reeves, Geneva (pseud.), 18, 32–34, 177n24; church activity, 41–42; on death, 37–38, 41, 42; on dress code, 160; efficacy of prayer and, 36–37; emotional labor of, 21, 105, 119, 120, 170, 196n1; on God's will, 39–40, 41; labor force experiences, 105–6, 118–19, 120–22; on marriage, 114; on praise, 43; on predestination, 39, 40; ritualization work, 23; song work of, 21–22, 24, 42, 43–44, 170; on supporting husband, 98–99

Refuge Church of Christ, 55, 60, 77

religious labor, ix, 5–8, 170–72; after death, 17–21, 44; case history, 32–36; church genealogy and, 29–30; work ethics, 1–2, 86

reproductive labor, 15, 137

righteousness, 14, 105, 106, 171

ritual, 23, 63, 128, 139

Ross, Essie, 83

Rustin, Bayard, 62

saints, use of term, 175n2

Saints Industrial School (COGIC), 60

sanctification, 4, 48

Satan, 29, 38, 144–45, 148

saved/unsaved people, xii, 30, 116

Schooler, Alexander R., 53

Scriptures: Acts 1:14, 35, 155; Acts 2:1, 155; Acts 2:2, 3; Acts 2:2–4, 163; Acts 2:4, 3, 25, 127; Acts 2:38, 3, 25; Acts 4:12, 26; Acts 9:32–34, 26; Acts 16:25, 92; Acts 21:7–17, 39; 1 Chronicles 16:29, 22; Colossians 2:9, 26, 138; Colossians 3:16, 25; 1 Corinthians 11:26, 26; 1 Corinthians 14:33, 146; 2 Corinthians 5:8, 42; 2 Corinthians 5:20, 153; 2 Corinthians 6:14, 187n31; Deuteronomy 28:13, 121; Ephesians 4:1–16, 35–36; Ephesians 5:22–29, 116, 187n32; Ephesians 5:27, 154; Galatians 3:28, 169; Galatians 5:22–23,